St Valery
The Impossible Odds

EDITED BY BILL INNES

Birlinn

First published in Great Britain in 2004 Birlinn Limited
West Newington House
10 Newington Road
Edinburgh
EH9 1QS

www.birlinn.co.uk

Reprinted 2006

By agreement with the families concerned, the royalties
from this book will be donated to Erskine Hospital

British Library Cataloguing-in-Publication Data
A catalogue record for this book is
available from the British Library

ISBN 10: 1 84341 019 2
ISBN 13: 978 8431 019 5

Typeset by Hewer Text UK Ltd, Edinburgh
Printed and bound by Antony Rowe, Chippenham

Contents .

List of Maps

Acknowledgements

The heroic campaign of the 51st Highland Division in 1940 was a theme of my childhood – especially after the war when so many of the young men of my home island returned from imprisonment. My interest was reawakened in 1988 when I had the privilege of interviewing some of the survivors for a Gaelic TV current affairs programme.

Sadly, their number is ever-diminishing but my thanks in particular to Archie MacVicar, Donald Alan Maclean, Donald Bowie and the late Murdo Maccuish.

None of the major contributors to this book is alive today but my debt to Donald John MacDonald is immeasurable – his poetry has been an inspiration to me for most of my adult life.

Archie Macphee was eighty-nine when I first met him, but still such an impressive figure that it is little wonder the Germans found him a handful!

I never had the opportunity to meet Angus Campbell or Gregor MacDonald but I am grateful to Donald John Campbell for his help with translation of his father's work and for providing background information, and to Janette MacDonald for permission to use such a large section of her father's book and other published material. Douglas Ledingham also gave permission to quote from his private memoir. Other important details came courtesy of Jo MacDonald of the BBC, Ronnie Black and Peter Bowie. Thanks also to Cailean Maclean for sight of copies of *The Camp* newspaper brought back from Stalag IXc by Kenny Mackenzie.

The families have all been most helpful with information and photographs and all readily agreed that royalties from this book should go to the Erskine Hospital.

But the greatest thanks of all must go to the veterans of the 51st Highland Division. It has been a privilege to meet so many of them. May this book remind us how much their generation suffered for the rest of us.

Bill Innes 2004

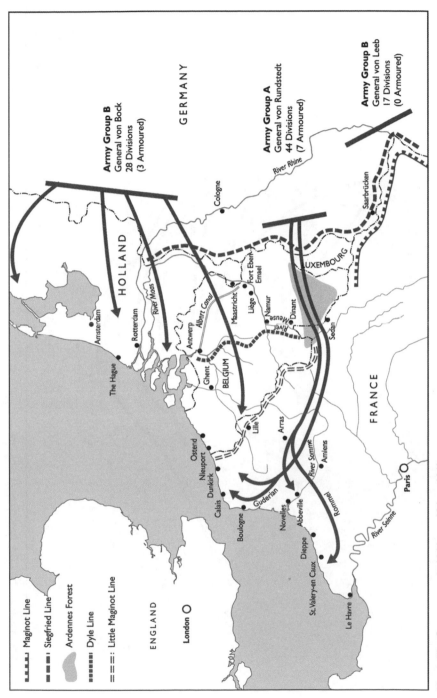

Map I: The German assault, 10 May to 12 June 1940

Maginot Line

Siegfried Line

Ardennes Forest

Dyle Line

Little Maginot Line

GERMANY

Army Group B
General von Bock
28 Divisions
(3 Armoured)

Army Group A
General von Rundstedt
44 Divisions
(7 Armoured)

Army Group B
General von Leeb
17 Divisions
(0 Armoured)

River Rhine

Cologne

Saarbrücken

HOLLAND

Amsterdam

Rotterdam

The Hague

River Maas

LUXEMBOURG

Albert Canal

Fort Eben
Emael

Maastricht

Liège

Namur

River Meuse

Dinant

Sedan

Antwerp

Ghent

BELGIUM

Lille

Arras

Amiens

River Somme

FRANCE

Ostend

Nieuport

Dunkirk

Calais

Boulogne

Guderian

Novelles

Abbeville

Rommel

Dieppe

St Valery-en-Caux

Le Havre

River Seine

Paris

ENGLAND

London

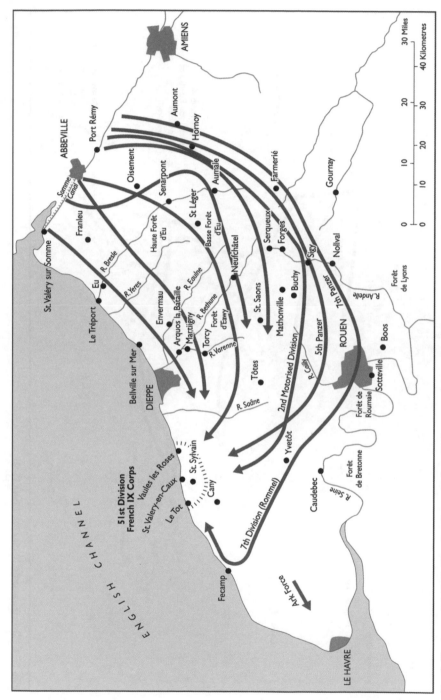

Map 2: The Impossible Odds. The situation on 11 June 1940

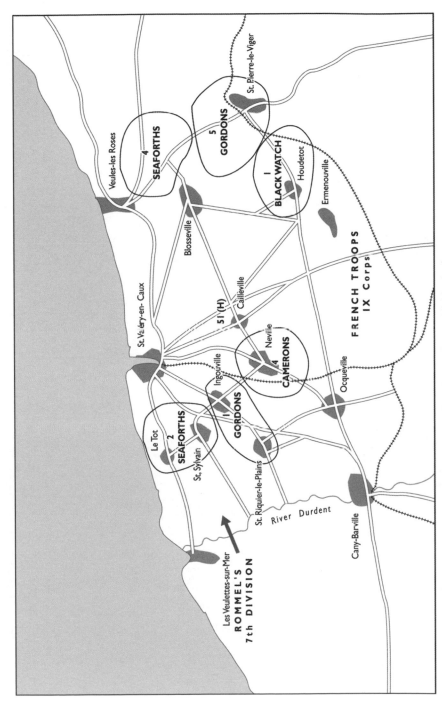

Map 3: Positions around St Valery (based on a sketch by 2nd Lt 'Ran' Ogilvie, Gordon Highlanders)

Introduction

The gallant rearguard action in 1940 which led to the capture of most of the 51st Highland Division at St Valery-en-Caux may have burned itself into the consciousness of the older generation of Scots but it has never been given the wider recognition it deserves. Even in Scotland it has been forgotten that the men of the 51st were still fighting in France ten days after the evacuation of the main British Expeditionary Force from Dunkirk had been completed.

Many of the countless books about the war deal with the first eight months of the 'Phoney War' and the subsequent evacuation from Dunkirk, but very few mention St Valery other than in passing. Yet the defiant rearguard action of the Highland Division against overwhelming odds won the admiration of their final enemy Rommel as well as Allies such as de Gaulle who fought alongside them.

Lack of recognition even in the homeland of the Highland Division has allowed some myths to flourish in the intervening decades. Most persistent is the belief that Churchill deliberately sacrificed the Division as part of his grand scheme to keep the French in the war. The introductory chapters on military background attempt to clarify the chaotic sequence of events leading up to the fateful 12 June 1940 so that some of the legends may be reassessed.

However, the main purpose of this book is to put flesh on the bones of history by bringing together the recollections of four of the men in their own words. Relatively few accounts of the war were written by ordinary soldiers. The fact that two of these contributors were highly respected Gaelic poets adds further value to their assessment of the experience.

The word 'hero' has been devalued in our materialistic times and is now most likely to be applied to a sportsman who earns more in a month than some of these men earned in their lifetimes. In today's compensation culture fewer of us are prepared to take responsibility for our own actions, far less put ourselves in mortal danger for the sake of comrades and country.

The ordinary soldiers who tell their stories in this book would not regard themselves as heroes – but it is a sobering challenge for us all to consider how we might have coped in the situations they endured.

We must not forget how much we owe them.

The Military Background

When war broke out at the beginning of September 1939 it found both Britain and France pitifully unprepared for confrontation with Germany. Memories of the horrors of the First World War were still vivid and during the intervening twenty years there had been few in either government willing to consider the possibility that there could ever be another such.

In 1914 the British Army had been a volunteer force and the cream of the country's young men were eager to join the rush for glory in the war that was to be over by Christmas. As a result, many of the potential leaders of the future had died, revolver in hand, in the muddy quagmires of no-man's-land, while leading their men against German machine-guns. It is difficult not to see some correlation between this futile waste and the subsequent decline of Britain as a world power.

Eventually that 'war to end wars' had cost Britain 700,000 men. But French losses numbered nearly twice as many at 1,322,000 – with nearly 4 million registered as disabled. The death rate among their servicemen was 16 per cent overall but among the officer class it was 19 per cent. Small wonder that many in France had little appetite for war. There were many right-wing thinkers who had considerable empathy with the doctrines of Hitler, perceiving him as a bulwark against Bolshevism. On the other hand, the French Communist Party, which had vociferously denounced Hitler, was thrown into some disarray by his non-aggression pact with Stalin in August 1939.

Like the British, the French had a policy of appeasement, culminating in the infamous 1938 Munich agreement which they signed together with Chamberlain. However, when Hitler occupied Prague in March 1939, Britain and France entered an entente to intervene if Germany attacked Poland. When this agreement forced France into the war in September there was some resentment that the few divisions of the British Expeditionary Force made such a minor contribution to the Allied armies.

There were many reasons for this. In Britain the usual low priority given to defence spending in peace time and the depression of the 1930s had ensured that much military equipment was obsolete. The need to defend and rule a far-flung empire meant that Britain's military forces had to be thinly spread. By April 1938 the government had decided that, in the event of war with Germany, Britain's navy and air force should make the main contribution.

Clearly the navy's role was crucial and so it was given priority for capital expenditure. The late 1930s also saw considerable expansion of the RAF, centred on a general belief that the role of the bomber in destroying civilian morale would be the most important factor in another European war. The mantra of the time, 'the bomber will always get through', overlooked a basic flaw. New bombers such as the Blenheim might be faster than the biplane fighters still used by most RAF squadrons, but they were considerably slower than new monoplanes such as the Hurricane. They were to prove easy prey for the Messerschmitt 109s of the Luftwaffe.

The regular army was the Cinderella of the services. Trained to police the Empire, it was totally unprepared and ill-equipped to fight a European war. The hurried introduction of conscription in the spring of 1939 actually compromised the readiness of the regular battalions, as experienced men had to be detached to train the mixture of reservists and raw recruits. There was a massive shortfall of modern weapons, ammunition and equipment. War Office thinking was that it might take two years to bring the army to a state of readiness to take on Germany.

In the inter-war period, military thinkers such as Captain Basil Liddell Hart and Major General Fuller had attempted to convince the top brass of the importance of the tank in any future conflict. But their theories had been rejected by a blinkered establishment firmly wedded to the role of the cavalry. Liddell Hart in particular was later to be regarded as one of the foremost military thinkers of his time. By 1924 he was already advocating a change from the disastrous static trench tactics of the Great War to what he called an 'expanding torrent' method of attack using concentrated armoured forces. In response, Field Marshal Earl Haig admitted that aeroplanes and tanks might have their uses – but only as accessories to man and horse. He dismissed any suggestion that modern vehicles might supplant the cavalry in war. In 1934 Brigadier Percy Hobart successfully demonstrated the technique in an exercise on Salisbury Plain, but the establishment response was that such a method could not possibly work in a real war.

Though Liddell Hart's writings found little favour within his own military establishment, they were translated into German and became a basic text for the German General Staff. In 1937, as personal adviser to Hore Belisha, the Secretary of State for War, Liddell Hart advocated a major expansion of armoured and anti-aircraft divisions. Even though German rearmament must have been obvious by then, these ideas fell on stony ground. Progress was made on another of his suggestions: that the infantry should be mechanised. In roles in which both Germany and France still used horses, the British Expeditionary Force had trucks. However, by September 1939 only half of the necessary lorries had been delivered so the shortfall had to be made good with hastily-requisitioned vehicles of questionable serviceability.

The French army was still heavily dependent on horse-drawn transport and cavalry. Their failure to mechanise the infantry was to prove a significant factor in the St Valery disaster. German divisions also used a large number of horses to transport men and to pull artillery pieces. In the latter role, however, they rapidly realised that slow transit-speed, aggravated by the cumbersome business of unharnessing and caring for horses before guns could be deployed, made it impossible to match the high-speed advance of forward units. Furthermore, the demands of feed-supply created enormous logistical problems in a dynamic situation. Unlike vehicles, horses require fuel whether or not they are being used.

Ironically, the punitive conditions imposed on Germany by the Treaty of Versailles in the wake of the First World War meant that rearmament there started from scratch, unhampered by a backlog of obsolete equipment. The Germans not only modernised ships, aircraft and weapons but developed Liddell Hart's ideas into a new philosophy of the strategy and tactics of war which was to become notorious as *Blitzkrieg* (lightning war). One of the main architects of this new strategy was General Heinz Guderian, who gave a German perspective on the war in his book *Panzer Leader*.

> It was principally the books and articles of the Englishmen, Fuller, Liddell Hart and Martel that . . . gave me food for thought. These far-sighted soldiers were even then trying to make of the tank something more than just an infantry support weapon . . . it was Liddell Hart who emphasised the use of armoured forces for long range strokes, operations against the opposing army's communications and also proposed a type of armoured division combining panzer and panzer-infantry units . . .*

* Apparently this handsome acknowledgement did not appear in the German original but perhaps that is not too surprising.

Rather than digging in to static entrenchments as in 1914–18, Guderian advocated direct attack concentrated on enemy lines at the weakest point so as to break through the rear. Whereas old-fashioned military operations had been bedevilled by inter-service rivalries and mutual suspicion, he envisaged cooperation on a hitherto undreamt-of scale. Paratroopers, dive-bombers, artillery and modern fast Panzers would work together to pulverise the opposition without necessarily waiting for the support of conventional troops. The essential coordination was to be achieved through the use of radio – which would also permit staff officers to abandon the conventions of the previous war and move with their front line troops.

Lest it be thought that Britain and France had a monopoly on blinkered thinking, it must be recorded that Guderian's revolu-tionary theories encountered considerable resistance among the German old guard. In 1931 General Otto von Stulpnagel told him: 'You are too impetuous. Believe me, neither of us will see German tanks in operation in our lifetimes!' The concept of generals leading from the front also found little favour with the General Staff.

But Guderian's ideas captured the imagination of Hitler himself. The speed and ferocity of the philosophy was to take the rest of Europe completely by surprise. Even when some parts of the theory were put to the test in Poland in September 1939 – so successfully that the country was taken over in eighteen days – Britain and France failed to learn the lessons.

The Germans were surprised and relieved that France did not launch an attack while the bulk of the Wehrmacht was com-mitted in the east but Allied military thinking was still rooted in the static tactics of 1914–18. French strategy was centred on defence against invasion rather than offence. In the interwar years they were lulled into a sense of false security by the construction at vast expense of the Maginot line of mammoth fortifications, which ran the length of their common boundary with Germany. A plan to extend the line to the Channel coast along the border with Belgium had foundered on Belgian government protests that this might endanger Germany's pledges to respect Belgian neutrality in any future war with France. The fatal French assumption that their border with southern Belgium was sufficiently protected by the natural barrier of the Ardennes hills engendered further complacency.

When the British Expeditionary Force (BEF) moved to France they were dismayed at the poor quality of defences along the so-called 'Little' Maginot Line north of the Ardennes on the Belgian border. Staff officers considered themselves fortunate that the relative inactivity of the winter of 1939–40 gave them a breathing space to bring the divisions and defences up to battle readiness. These were the months of the so-called Phoney War and the First World War static mindset caused them to be spent in the construction of elaborate lines of trenches, pillboxes, anti-tank revetments, communication networks and even rail supply lines along the Franco-Belgian border.

The commander of the BEF, Lord Gort, had been a most distinguished and highly decorated officer with the Grenadier Guards in the First World War. In this new war he soon acquired a reputation as one who was more concerned with the detail of planning rather than with overall strategy. The BEF was under French command and the French plan in the event of a German invasion of Holland and Belgium was to move forward to the river Dyle, linking with the Belgian army to prevent a takeover of the whole of Belgium.

From the British point of view this had the advantage of denying the Luftwaffe air bases dangerously close to Britain. But, in order to protect their neutrality, the Belgians refused the Allies permission for any preparatory work on defences at the so-called Dyle Line. So when the Germans eventually flooded into the Low Countries on 10 May 1940 the Allied divisions abandoned their meticulously constructed positions for ill-prepared ones at the Dyle.

In Germany Guderian's revolutionary ideas had gained ground. The principal advocate of a concentrated tank assault through the lightly defended Ardennes sector was General Erich von Manstein, later regarded by many as one of the most able of the German military thinkers. Such a move, in coordination with an attack on the Low Countries, would cut the French forces in half and form a classic pincer movement to trap Allied divisions in Belgium. Like original thinkers elsewhere, however, his ideas were initially rejected by the High Command and in January 1940 he was moved sideways to command an infantry corps on the grounds that he lacked the experience for a tank corps. This manoeuvre to get rid of an original thinker regarded as too pushy backfired for it led to him having a meeting with Hitler himself. The Führer was so impressed by Manstein's plan that he soon began to think of it as his own.

The German High Command did indeed have every intention of repeating First World War tactics and attacking only through Belgium and Holland – the so-called Schlieffen plan. Hitler's intention to implement it in November 1939 was frustrated by atrocious winter weather so it had to be postponed several times, until January 1940. However, on the 10th of that month an officer carrying its details took an unauthorised flight and his aircraft was forced by bad weather to land in Belgium. The knowledge that the plan might now be known to the Allies gave rise to a hurried reappraisal of Manstein's ideas. It is ironic that when the plan was finally implemented he himself was allowed no part in it. But Germany was fortunate that Guderian shared Manstein's views; so did the man who was to become one of the most famous generals of the war – Erwin Rommel. Although he had no experience of tanks before being given command of 7th Panzer Division in February 1940, his inspired leadership from the front was to be a key factor in its success.

However, it was Guderian who took the Manstein plan a stage further. Although the German High Command eventually agreed that the Panzer divisions should make the initial assault through the Ardennes to cross the Meuse, conventional wisdom decreed that they should then wait about ten days for infantry divisions to catch up and consolidate before resuming the advance. Such were the views expressed when the generals of Rundstedt's Army Group A met Hitler to discuss the plan in early March.

Guderian argued that the Supreme Command should decide whether his objective was to be Amiens or Paris. Once across the Meuse, his own view was that he should immediately continue his drive past Amiens to the English Channel. The infantry generals doubted whether he would even get across the river but Hitler was impressed.

> I never received any further orders as to what I was to do once the bridgehead over the Meuse was captured. All my decisions, until I reached the Atlantic seaboard at Abbeville, were taken by me and me alone. The Supreme Command's influence on my actions was merely restrictive throughout.
>
> Heinz Guderian *Panzer Leader*

The Allies still assumed that any German invasion would follow the pattern of the 1914. The French High Command continued to cling to the belief that no attack with armour could be launched through the Ardennes, despite the evidence of one of their own pre-war exercises in 1938 which successfully demonstrated that such an attack was entirely feasible. This unexpected result was dismissed by the French Supreme Commander, General Maurice Gamelin, on the grounds that it could never happen in a real war because reserves would be available to contain any breakthrough.

When real war did come, however, crack front line troops had been moved from the Ardennes sector and its defence had been entrusted to a mere seven cavalry regiments and ten infantry divisions of mostly reservist troops. During the Phoney War these forces had singularly failed to impress General Alan Brooke* of the BEF with their lack of discipline and esprit de corps. There were no reinforcements in the sector.

In fact there were many roads in the Ardennes suitable for tanks. Even where trees had been felled to obstruct some routes, the typical thoroughness of German planning ensured that their pioneer battalions were equipped with chain saws to deal with

---

* Later Field Marshal Viscount Alanbrooke, Chief of the Imperial General Staff.

any blockages the Panzers could not push aside or bypass. Far from being an insuperable barrier, the hills held some advantages for the Germans. Their massive build-up of forces was masked from aerial surveillance by tree cover. More importantly, once through the hills and across the river Meuse, the relatively flat roads of northern France offered ideal tank terrain compared to the marshes and canal networks of Flanders.

In 1938 the German army was relatively small. But by May 1940 there had been massive expansion. Facing Belgium and Holland to the north were two armies in Army Group B under General von Bock. To the south behind the Siegfried Line*, which faced the Maginot Line, were another two armies under General von Leeb.

But, thanks to Manstein, the greatest change had occurred in the centre to the east of the Ardennes. The main Army Group A under General von Rundstedt now had four armies consisting of forty-four infantry and seven armoured Panzer divisions. This huge force built up (causing massive traffic jams on the roads) without apparently causing any undue alarm in the French General Staff. It seems that Gamelin believed that any German attack was unlikely to take place before 1941 – and even then would be made through Belgium. So confident was he of this judgement that large numbers of French soldiers were allowed to go on leave in the first few days of May.

On 10 May German Army Group B under von Bock attacked Holland and Belgium in a classic demonstration of the effectiveness of *blitzkrieg*. Bombers, troop-carrying gliders and a relatively small number of paratroopers combined in a daring assault. Half the Belgian air force was destroyed on the ground, key bridges were secured before they could be blown up and Rotterdam was heavily bombed.

The Allies reacted immediately in accordance with the French plan and moved forward to the Dyle to link up with the Belgian army. The move revealed a further crucial complication. Allied pre-war planners had failed to anticipate the

* Known in Germany as the *Westwall*.

importance of adequate communications. Both armies continued to rely on antiquated field telephone lines together with despatch riders and even flags and heliographs. These methods were supplemented by the use of a public telephone system considerably more primitive than today's.

However effective such systems might have been in the static conditions of 1914–18 , their shortcomings were cruelly exposed in the dynamic battlefield of the new German strategy. Even where signallers had time to set up new lines they were torn apart by artillery or tank treads. Despatch riders had the daunting task of navigating strange roads congested with refugees while seeking units forever on the move. Their vulnerability to enemy action meant that critically important messages might never arrive.

A more fundamental problem was that the underlying system of pre-planning and transmission of orders through an over-complicated and ill-defined command structure was still geared to the more leisurely pace of a static war. For security reasons messages were sent in code, which caused much time to be wasted in encrypting and decoding. (It was said that it might take forty-eight hours for Gamelin's decisions to reach his commanders in the field.) French and British cooperation was further bedevilled by lack of fluency in each other's languages. The overall failure of communications has to be considered a major contributory factor in the subsequent debacle.

To make matters worse, when Guderian's Panzers from Rundstedt's Group A started pouring through the Ardennes and over the Meuse, indecision and confusion ensued in the French High Command. In the rapidly developing crisis both Britain and France had major leadership changes which were to prove decisive in differing ways.

When Winston Churchill took over as British Prime Minister on 10 May he found himself in an unenviable situation. Nowadays it is easy to forget how much he was distrusted by the establishment of the time and how little backing he had even within his own party. He was faced with a stream of depressingly bad news from France, which led to a general atmosphere of defeatism. Britain was committed to helping France, her principal ally. However, there was considerable doubt in the War Cabinet as to the strength of the French resolve. Nevertheless, the longer the German advance was delayed in France, the better chance Britain had of preparing for the expected invasion. Britain therefore had to support France as long as possible. At considerable personal risk, Churchill made the first of several air journeys to France within days of taking office in a vain attempt to bolster visibly flagging morale.

By 19 May, when the increasingly ineffective French Commander-in-Chief Gamelin was replaced by the 73-year-old Maxime Weygand, the situation was already slipping out of control. Weygand soon became pessimistic about his chances of fighting a war in 1940 with a 1918-standard army still heavily reliant on horse-drawn transport and cavalry in the front line.

The Allied move to the Dyle had left the way clear for Guderian's Panzers to race past Amiens to the Channel ports of Boulogne and Calais. With Army Group B advancing into Belgium from the east and Army Group A following Guderian to the west in France, it became clear that the BEF and French forces in Belgium were about to be trapped in a pincer movement.

The entire BEF was technically under the command of the French General Georges. However, its commander Lord Gort had a get-out clause in his standing orders which permitted him to appeal directly to the British government if the safety of the BEF was threatened. Gort took full advantage of this loophole to withdraw his troops to Dunkirk. The famous evacuation of 338,000 men was accomplished thanks to the heroic feats by the Navy and a flotilla of assorted civilian craft. However, massive quantities of arms and support equipment had to be abandoned.

These major losses included 82,000 vehicles, 7,000 tons of ammunition, 2,300 pieces of artillery (including nearly all the new 25lb heavy guns) as well as millions of gallons of fuel. Losses of smaller weapons included 90,000 rifles, 8,000 Bren guns and 400 anti-tank rifles. Although much equipment was disabled, significant amounts fell into grateful German hands.

In order to maintain civilian morale in Britain at the time it was necessary to portray Dunkirk as a heroic achievement and that is how it is remembered today. Understandably, many in France saw it as a betrayal by the perfidious British 'willing to fight to the last French breast'. German propaganda seized every opportunity to exploit this view. However, even in France it is now increasingly recognised that Gort's assessment of the BEF's hopeless situation was accurate and his action in withdrawing his men to fight again another day was justified by later events.

Gort was a convenient scapegoat for a disaster that was largely due to peacetime neglect of the army. Later in the war his reputation was redeemed. Heroic work as Governor General during the siege of Malta earned him belated promotion to Field Marshal. However, the keenly-felt disgrace of Dunkirk undoubtedly hastened his early death in 1946.

The Tank War

As already discussed, the importance of the tank in war had not been fully appreciated by the Allies despite the warnings of Liddell Hart in Britain and de Gaulle in France.

The BEF set out for France with only two divisions of Matilda 1 and 2 tanks. The 11-ton Matilda Mk1 had been designed with an operating speed of 8mph so that the infantry could keep up with it! Furthermore, its car engine was to prove unreliable and it was armed only with a machine-gun which was useless against Panzers. Although its 60mm armour plating was sufficient to deflect German tank shells, it was still vulnerable to heavy artillery. Its successor, the 26-ton Matilda Mk2 was a more formidable weapon capable of twice the speed. In addition to its machine-gun it carried a two-pounder cannon – although this was not capable of firing high explosive shells. It is indicative of the expected role of the Matildas within a static war that they were designed to cover a mere ten miles between overhauls. The intention was that tanks should be transported by train or other means to the front. However, they covered 60 miles on their tracks in the hurried advance to the Dyle – and then had to return.

In 1940 the French had even more tanks than the Germans. The French Char B1 was an impressive sight, weighing in at a massive 32 tons and carrying a 75mm howitzer as well as a 37mm and a machine-gun. However, its maximum speed was only 17mph and the 75mm gun could not be traversed. The consequent need to manoeuvre the tank itself to train the howitzer was a fatal flaw in such a cumbersome machine. Even more significantly, there was only room for one man in the turret, which meant that the tank commander also had to load and fire the guns. This not only led to an unacceptably slow firing rate but also substantially degraded his ability to command the tank. Despite these drawbacks the Germans had considerable respect for the Chars.

The German Panzers were extremely efficient fighting machines armed with 37mm or 75mm cannon plus two or three machine-guns. Their armour was typically less than half the thickness of the Allied tanks but this lighter weight contributed to their ability to reach speeds of over 25mph. In theory they were not supposed to fire their guns while in motion but Rommel's advancing tanks behaved like a naval squadron in line astern, firing broadsides left and right. Rommel found that the alarm and confusion thus created more than made up for any loss of accuracy. The Panzer regiments were also supplemented by large numbers of lighter Czech 38(t) tanks captured after the occupation of Czechoslovakia.

The use of radio was of fundamental importance to the Panzer operation. Both Guderian and Rommel could travel with their leading formations and keep in contact with their unit commanders while being on the spot to take key decisions. Command vehicles can be identified in war photographs by the rather ungainly horizontal frame aerials they sported. The few Allied tanks fitted with radio were bedevilled by defects and flat batteries. The use of signal flags was hardly an acceptable substitute.

But on 21 May there was a counter-attack at Arras by the 4th and 7th Royal Tank Regiment with the support of the Durham Light Infantry which remains an intriguing example of what might have been. This should have been a combined operation with 250 tanks of the French 3rd Light Mechanised Division but they were short of fuel and, with their men exhausted, had trouble getting into position in time.

The British tanks had just completed the round trip of 120 miles to the Dyle line and back without a servicing break. Nevertheless, the attack with forty-five Mk1 and twenty Mk2 Matildas caused panic and confusion among an unblooded battalion of the SS.

Rommel's 7th Division Panzers had their first shock of the campaign when they found that their rounds just bounced off the British armour. It was reported that one Matilda took fourteen hits without a single penetration. Rommel thought he had been attacked by a much greater force but, ever resourceful, decided to bring divisional artillery and 88mm anti-aircraft guns to bear. These latter had armour-piercing shells as well as flak rounds and proved capable of destroying tanks at a range of 2,000 metres. They continued to pose a threat to Allied tank formations for the rest of the war.

Rommel was living proof that fortune favours the brave. On 14 May his tank had been hit and he was very nearly captured by the French. In this engagement at Arras his aide was killed by his side as they examined the same map. In post-war debriefings General von Rundstedt confessed to Liddell Hart that this was the most critical moment in the drive to the coast:

> '. . . for a short time it was feared that our armoured divisions would be cut off before the infantry divisions could come up to support them. None of the French counter-attacks carried such a threat as this one did.'
>
> Liddell Hart *The Other Side of the Hill*

However, the main difference between the opposing armies was a strategic one. The French had scattered their armour in small units throughout the front in support of the infantry. The Germans concentrated theirs in highly mobile divisions which could operate at speed independently of infantry. Had the French been able to make a concentrated attack on the vulnerable and over-stretched flanks of the advancing Panzer divisions then the whole history of the campaign might have been changed. When interviewed by Liddell Hart after the war, Guderian said:

> 'The French tanks were better than ours in armour, guns and number, but inferior in speed, radio-communication and leadership. The concentration of all armoured forces at the decisive point, the rapid exploitation of success and the initiative of the officers of all degrees were the main reasons for our success in 1940.'
>
> Liddell Hart *The Other Side of the Hill*

The Air War

> Often unseen by those you helped to save
> You rode the air above that foreign dune
> And died like the unutterably brave
> That so your friends might see the English June.
>
> John Masefield's tribute to the Spitfire pilots

The lack of defensive air cover is a recurrent theme in naval and military reminiscences of the time. Yet the RAF took heavy losses during the period before and immediately after the fall of France. In order to understand the apparent discrepancy in perceptions, a few facts may be helpful.

Fighters such as the Spitfire and Hurricane were at their best at high altitude and so conducted their dogfights at heights where they were invisible to observers on the ground – save for the contrails produced in certain meteorological conditions which, for example, hallmarked the skies during the Battle of Britain. Because they were designed to defend the United Kingdom their maximum endurance was about ninety minutes – considerably reduced at combat power settings. By the time they had crossed the Channel, their fighting time was inevitably brief. It was only with the arrival of long-range North American Mustangs much later in the war that bomber squadrons could be provided with a fighter escort into Germany.

These early British fighters, armed only with machine-guns*, were useless in the ground-attack role. This was delegated to fighter-bombers such as the lumbering Blenheim and the obsolescent Fairey Battle. These were deployed away from the front line in an attempt to slow the advancing German columns and damage bridges and communications. But their bomb-load was small and its effectiveness much reduced by primitive bomb-aiming methods and high failure rates. Neither France nor Britain had realised that bombers diving almost vertically out of the sky could deliver their load against small targets with much greater precision. A Vickers test pilot who had flown the Junkers 87 dive-bomber in 1938 reported so enthusiastically on it that Vickers management tried to persuade the Air Ministry of the need for such a machine. They were told that their pilots should mind their own bloody business!

Many Luftwaffe pilots were already battle-hardened veterans of the Spanish civil war and the Polish campaign. The *blitzkrieg* typically opened with waves of Ju87 Stukas hurtling out of the sky from fifteen thousand feet to drop their deadly load. The psychological terror effect on troop morale was further reinforced by sirens fitted to their undercarriage legs, which created the screaming sound so often heard on old newsreels.

Not only did lack of speed make RAF bombers extremely vulnerable to enemy fighters but they also had to deal with a level of anti-aircraft fire far in excess of that available to the Allies, whose leaders had not anticipated the crucial importance of anti-aircraft weapons. The French Supreme Commander, General Gamelin, believed that air forces would fight one another, leaving the proper business of war to the armies. By contrast, German divisions had flak batteries of the formidable 88mm guns which were also used with great success against tanks.

Bombers forced to attack precision targets at low level in order to achieve any accuracy also took heavy punishment from German small arms fire. Not only did German divisions have

* The eight Browning machine-guns of the Spitfires and Hurricanes fired .303 bullets – the same ammunition as the standard army rifle.

many more machine-guns per unit than the Allies but they also used tracer ammunition which allowed the 'hosepipe' system of targeting and better concentration of fire. By comparison, the chances of damaging (or even hitting) an aircraft with a .303 rifle were small.

In terms of sheer numbers, the French Air Force was probably superior to the Luftwaffe. However, many of these aircraft were obsolete and more were lost in training accidents than through enemy action. Their most promising fighter, the Dewoitine D.520 (not unlike a Spitfire in appearance), had been ordered in thousands but fewer than forty had been delivered by May. For reasons difficult to understand, many hundreds of their other aircraft were held in reserve and never committed to operations at the front.

In the later Battle of Britain the ultimate success of the RAF owed much to the newly developed radar network. The early systems were at their best in picking up aircraft approaching coastlines. When RAF fighter and light bomber squadrons were based in France at the outbreak of war, mobile units went with them; but these were primitive by today's standards and largely ineffective over land. By the time a threat was identified, even single-seat fighters had little time to get airborne and climb to the necessary altitude to engage the enemy. As a result many aircraft were caught on the ground. Bombers were even more vulnerable. On 11 May nearly all of 114 Squadron's Blenheims were destroyed in a bombing raid by Dorniers of the Luftwaffe.

Worse was to come. On one day, May 14, over a hundred aircraft attacked the pontoon bridges the assault forces were building across the Meuse at Sedan. But by then the Germans had their flak batteries in place. Forty-five RAF Battles and Blenheims and forty-seven French LeO 45 aircraft failed to return – clearly an unsustainable level of loss, which effectively ended daylight bombing raids. The heroic sacrifice did delay German crossing of the Meuse but not for long enough to influence the final result. To make matters worse, twenty-seven Hurricanes were lost in dogfights with Me 109s.

While this was the worst day of the entire war for RAF

aircraft losses, a much more serious problem was the attrition rate amongst some of the most experienced aircrew in the service, who should have formed the core of the subsequent defence of Britain. These losses were aggravated by failure to fit any armour plating to fighter cockpits – because it might affect aircraft balance! On their own initiative, No. 1 Squadron salvaged some from a wrecked Battle and put it in their Hurricanes. The modification was soon extended to other aircraft and later proved to be another decisive factor in the Battle of Britain.

By the 19 May, the rapid German advance posed such a threat to RAF forward bases that squadrons had to be progressively withdrawn to home bases in England. The disruption caused by this move temporarily reduced fighting capability.

It is probably true that inter-service cooperation could have been a lot better before and during the early stages of the war. Even with today's infinitely more sophisticated communications, 'friendly fire' incidents still occur. In the Second World War it was accepted by RAF pilots that flying close to Navy ships was a dangerous thing to do. At Dunkirk they were even fired on by British troops because a rumour had spread that the Luftwaffe were using captured RAF aircraft. The problems were aggravated by pre-war planners' failure to appreciate the importance of adequate radio communications. Even within the RAF, there were several incidents of Blenheim bombers being attacked by Hurricane fighters.

Germans were not immune from 'friendly fire' incidents. Guderian records being attacked by the Luftwaffe on the 20 May near Amiens. He promptly ordered his flak batteries to shoot the offending aircraft down!

Troops being evacuated from Dunkirk were particularly critical of the perceived lack of air cover. The fleet which so heroically rescued the majority of the troops suffered heavy losses. Yet there was a standing fighter cover of up to forty-eight RAF aircraft over the beaches. Bearing in mind that Goering had promised Hitler that the destruction of the BEF could be left to the Luftwaffe, the fact that 338,000 men were taken off speaks for itself. It is obvious that Allied losses would have been considerably more had his aircraft been allowed free rein to attack the troops and the armada of little ships that saved them.

Legendary Luftwaffe ace Adolf Galland shot down his first Spitfire over Dunkirk, but in *The First and the Last* made this comment on the operation.

> It merely proved that the strength of the Luftwaffe was inadequate, especially in the difficult conditions for reinforcement created by the unexpectedly quick advance and against a determined and well-led enemy who was fighting with tenacity and skill. Dunkirk should have been an emphatic warning for the leaders of the Luftwaffe.

In particular, Dunkirk was to be the beginning of the end for the Stukas which had proved so devastating in the early days of *blitzkrieg*. Their dive-bombing tactics had considerable success against the assembled flotillas, due mainly to the failure to anticipate the need for anti-aircraft weapons. Very few Royal Navy ships of the time had guns which could be elevated enough to deal with dive bombers. However, the slow speed and high 'greenhouse' cockpits of the Stukas made them very vulnerable to RAF fighters. In the later Battle of Britain their losses were such that they had to be withdrawn from the action.

At the time of Dunkirk, however, Air Chief Marshal Sir Hugh Dowding did have to point out to the War Cabinet that he was losing twenty-five Hurricane fighters a day to Messerschmitts, while the number emerging from the factories was only four. It was fortunate for Dowding and Britain that Lord Beaverbrook was appointed Minister of Aircraft Production. Beaverbrook's robust attitude to cutting red tape made him a hated figure to bureaucrats but greatly increased the rate of aircraft delivery to the squadrons.

However, the loss of experienced pilots when many potential replacements had yet to fly in a frontline fighter was the more serious problem. In the first half of June 1940 the French made frequent appeals for more RAF fighter cover but Dowding argued that he would be unable to defend Britain against the likely German invasion if his fighting strength fell below 25 squadrons.

Churchill's secretary, Sir John Colville, was clearly persuaded by the logic of Dowding's case: 'the effective range of our fighters will not enable them to go far up the Seine, but it would be suicidal to send them to aerodromes in France where they will be destroyed on the ground.' Subsequent events in the crucial Battle of Britain later that year were to vindicate Dowding's judgement. By denying the Luftwaffe the prerequisite mastery of the skies the RAF effectively blocked the threat of invasion – but it was a damn close-run thing.

The Highland Division

I can tell you that the comradeship in arms experienced on the battlefield of Abbeville in May and June 1940 between the French Armoured Division, which I had the honour to command, and the valiant 51st Highland Division under General Fortune, played its part in the decision which I took to continue fighting on the side of the Allies unto the end no matter what may be the course of events.

General Charles de Gaulle at Edinburgh 20 June, 1942

This summary of events leading up to 12 June is of necessity brief. However, a detailed account of the many actions involving individual units can be found in Eric Linklater's The Highland Division *(HMSO 1942) or Saul David's* Churchill's Sacrifice of the Highland Division *(Brassey's 1994), which is more comprehensive and a much better book than its catchpenny title would suggest.*

In September 1939 the 51st was a Territorial division and its three brigades consisted of nine infantry battalions drawn from such famous regiments as the Black Watch, Seaforth Highlanders, Cameron Highlanders, Gordon Highlanders and Argyll and Sutherland Highlanders. In addition, there was one anti-tank and three field regiments of Royal Artillery, Royal

Ordnance, four companies of Royal Engineers, Divisional Signals and three field ambulance units of the RAMC. Supply and transport were provided by the RASC. Significantly, there was no anti-aircraft provision.*

In command was Major General Victor Fortune, who had fought with distinction with the Black Watch in the First World War. He soon established a reputation as a commander who cared about his men and made every effort to get to know them.

After the division assembled in Scotland, the few weeks of preliminary basic training in drill and weapons were hampered by a shortage of equipment. At this stage many men were still wearing uniforms of 1918 vintage, with some of the newer conscripts still in civilian clothes.

Pre-war Highland regiments wore the kilt and there was considerable resistance when battledress was introduced a few months later. (The regular battalion of the 1st Camerons was credited with being the last Highland unit to go into action in kilts when they fought at the river Escaut in May 1940.)

The Division then moved to the Aldershot area in the south of England where the full time Regular Army training had to be compressed into a period of two to three months. After being given a week's leave just after Christmas they sailed for France in January 1940. As their accounts reveal, the men were not impressed by the quality of their billets.

Further drilling and training continued, despite the Arctic weather of one of the worst winters in living memory. In February, when the Division moved to join the rest of the BEF near the Belgian border, conditions varied from snow and extreme cold to continuous rain and mud. Initially the 51st was held behind the main front line near Béthune because the other divisions intended for the sector were kept in reserve to help Finland against Russian invasion.

Accommodation was only marginally better but there were compensations. The pay of a private soldier of the time was

---

* For the full order of battle in May 1940 see Appendix 1.

about four shillings (20p) a day. Even then, that was not much –
but it was twice as much as their French equivalents earned.
The men soon discovered that a plate of eggs and chips could be
washed down with *vin ordinaire* for about four pence (less than
2p!). Evenings in the café were an attractive alternative to the
boredom of the billets – even if the unaccustomed level of
alcohol consumption gave rise to the odd fracas.

Training continued, although it had to be combined with the
arduous work of constructing the defences of the so-called
'Little' Maginot Line. However, every opportunity was taken
to use the five pipe bands in public relations exercises in local
towns. Early in March it was decided to strengthen the Division
by replacing some of the TA battalions with Regulars who had
been in France since the early days of the war.

The 1st Black Watch, 1st Gordons, 2nd Seaforth and 17th
and 23rd Field Artillery Regiments replaced the 6th Black
Watch, 6th Gordons, 6th Seaforth and 76th and 77th Royal
Artillery. The 1st Lothians and Border Horse replaced the Fife
and Forfar Yeomanry as the light armoured brigade.

On 28 March the Division took over the section of the
Belgian frontier between Bailleul and Armentières. Conscious
that many of the troops had no experience of facing the
enemy, the BEF had been rotating small units of officers
and men to the front line at the real Maginot line in the Saar
region. The 1st Black Watch had already had a tour of duty
over Christmas in the area but in the middle of April it was
decided that the 51st should be the first full BEF division to
be deployed there.

Supplemented by ancillary units, the division now mustered
about 22,000 men. Under French command, they were allotted
a sector of the German border between Luxembourg and the
little town of Bouzonville. The intention that this was to be just
a short posting was to be overtaken by events.

The famous fortifications which had absorbed so much of the
French military budget had several lines of defence in an area
which had been evacuated of civilians.

a) The *Ligne de Contact* (Line of Contact), approximately seven miles in front of the forts, faced the equivalent German Siegfried line across no-man's-land.
b) The *Ligne de Soutien* (Support Line) was non-continuous and did not feature in the Highland Division's sector.
c) The *Ligne de Recueil* (Recoil Line) was a defensive line in front of the forts.
d) The *Ligne d'Arrêt* (Stop Line) behind the forts was intended to be the final 'backstop' position. It had not yet been completed.

Officers and men were disappointed at the poor quality of their accommodation and the lack of defences in depth.

> There were many things to admire about the French Army, but their preparation of proper defences in the front and rear of the *Lignes Maginot* was not one of them . . .
>
> *Return to St Valery* Sir Derek Lang

It is probably true that every military unit taking over from another would find much that they would like to change but the Scots were particularly unimpressed by the log huts which formed part of the forward defences. These may have been built because the wetness of the ground did not favour the usual dugouts but they had the crucial drawback of not being bullet-proof.

This was still the period of the Phoney War; both Britain and Germany were concentrating on building up forces and weapons for the conflict still to come. Hitler had wanted to commence the war in the west in November 1939 but the unusually severe winter was a major factor in causing a postponement. The Scots were surprised to find that the French troops they were relieving seemed to have settled into a comfortable accommodation with the opposing Germans; every effort was made not to engage in any action that might disturb the status quo and so risk escalation of the conflict.

Initially, therefore, there was very little action on the frontier apart from some light skirmishing by night patrols – as Angus Campbell records. The 7th Argylls seem to have been particularly active but units were cycled between the various lines of defence in order to expose the maximum number to front line experience. In one incident, Donald Bowie, a member of my own family and close friend of Donald John MacDonald, was among the first to be taken prisoner when an isolated forward post of the 4th Camerons was overrun.* However, the Camerons found Gaelic better than any code when it came to frustrating German tapping of their telephone lines.

As has been mentioned, Gamelin's complacency about the imminence of any attack from Germany led to permission being given for many men to go on leave at the beginning of May. As the 51st were under French command, this generosity also extended to them. Donald John MacDonald was one of the islanders who benefited, but by the time they reached Glasgow news had broken of the German attack on 10 May. To their surprise, there was no recall and they were allowed to complete their leave.

Meanwhile, although Guderian's divisions bypassed the Maginot Line when they broke through to the north near Sedan, the men of the 51st found the temperature of conflict in their sector rising rapidly as forces from the Siegfried Line made feint attacks on the Maginot Line to distract from the main thrust through the Ardennes to the north.

On 13 May an early morning artillery barrage announced a major German assault on the whole front. It was the turn of the 1st and the 4th Black Watch and the 5th Gordons to be in the front line; on their right, the 4th Seaforths had just relieved the 4th Camerons. The Black Watch took the brunt of the early attacks and suffered heavy losses around their outpost at Betting. However, the Division gave a good account of itself and General Condé of the French 3rd Army praised their fighting qualities and high morale as 'renewing the tradition of Beaumont-Hamel.'†

As French divisions on either flank were driven back, the 51st positions in front of the Maginot line became untenable and they were withdrawn – initially to the *Ligne de Recueil*.

---

* Donald John Steele and Finlay MacDonald were also captured.
† A famous action of the 51st in the First World War.

The rapidly developing main German two-pronged assault soon threw French military planning into disarray. Orders were conflicting and travel arrangements chaotic. Initially the French assumed the German attack would be directed at Paris and the 51st were to form part of the defence force. The Highlanders were first ordered to Varennes with a view to assisting in dealing with that threat. When Guderian's divisions swept past to the north heading for Amiens, the troops were redirected by rail on a circuitous route towards Rouen via Orleans and Tours, far to the south and west of Paris. The trains were so old and slow that on up-gradients men had to get out and push!

Meanwhile their motorised vehicles took a more direct 300-mile northerly route but ran into their own problems. German propaganda radio broadcasts in French had caused thousands of civilians to flee to the west using every possible kind of transport for their precious possessions. Vehicles abandoned when they ran out of petrol added to the congestion and chaos. The subsequent jams provided easy targets for the Luftwaffe, who seemed to have a deliberate policy of attacking the pathetic refugee streams in order to obstruct military movements.

It took six days to reunite men and machines but by then Guderian's high speed thrust had cut them off from the rest of the BEF, which was being hounded towards Dunkirk. On 28 May they reassembled along the line of the river Bresle and on 2 June moved towards Abbeville on the left flank as part of the French IX Corps to help repulse the German advance across the Somme.

They were to be assisted by the 1st Armoured Division, newly arrived from England. This division was far from full strength and had arrived without its infantry or artillery. It had 250 light tanks and cruisers which were more suited to reconnaissance than any duel with Panzers. Being lightly armoured they were extremely vulnerable to anti-tank weapons. The division had few spares, no bridging equipment and serious deficiencies in wireless equipment. On 27 May, after a series of conflicting orders, it was thrown against the German bridgeheads west of the Somme and nearly half of the tanks were lost to enemy guns and mechanical breakdowns.

On 29 and 30 May the much more powerful French 4th Armoured Division under the command of the up-and-coming General de Gaulle had more success but without adequate artillery and infantry support was unable to dislodge the enemy.

On 4 June the 51st together with the French 31st Infantry Division and 2nd Armoured Division made a new attempt (described by Angus Campbell and Gregor MacDonald) to take back the high ground overlooking Abbeville and the Somme. Due to inadequate intelligence as to the real strength of the enemy, the Division suffered heavy casualties with 152 Brigade losing twenty officers and 543 men – mainly from the 4th Seaforths and 4th Camerons.

There were some successes. The 1st Black Watch and 1st Gordons pushed the enemy back in their sector; but without corresponding success on either side they were in danger of being isolated. To their great disappointment they had to fall back to their original positions.

The following day the Germans launched their main assault across the Somme and the whole division was slowly forced backwards. The 5 June was a particularly hard day for the Argyll & Sutherlands as companies of the 7th Battalion were isolated and cut off. By the end of a day distinguished by many heroic actions against a far more numerous enemy, twenty-three officers and 500 men had been killed, wounded or captured. Three days later Major Lorne Campbell managed to lead the remnants of A and B Companies back through enemy lines to rejoin the Division at the river Bresle.

However, these losses left no option but further withdrawal to the river Béthune south of Dieppe. By 8 June, with the situation becoming desperate, the War Cabinet wanted them to fall back towards Rouen so that they could be taken off from the port of Le Havre, where many of them had originally landed.

The remains of the 7th and 8th Argylls, the 4th Black Watch, 6th Royal Scots Fusiliers and supporting units of sappers and artillery were detached under the command of Brigadier

Stanley Clarke. This so-called 'Ark' Force was ordered to hold a line south of Fécamp in order to cover the retreat of the rest of the Division and the French IXth Corps.

Weygand, apparently oblivious of the speed and power of the German advance, had wanted the line at the Bresle to be held at all costs. Initially, permission for the 51st to withdraw was refused and Major General Fortune did not have Gort's power to challenge French authority. This delay was to prove fatal for Rommel's 7th and elements of the 5th Panzer Divisions were now sweeping round to the south cross-country towards Rouen. By 10 June this remarkable high-speed advance had cut the road to Le Havre and reached the Channel coast at Petites Dalles. Yet Weygand's orders for the 10th still insisted the 51st should fall back to cross the Seine close to Rouen!

The Navy had already begun to organise a flotilla of ships for the anticipated evacuation. It was clear that speed was of the essence but the plan hit a final snag which was to seal the fate of the 51st. While immediate movement was feasible for the Division (which had mechanised transport), the French needed more time to organise the move and their speed was restricted to the marching pace of their troops. They also intended to move only under cover of darkness so the short summer nights would restrict the maximum distance achievable to about 20km a day. Independent withdrawal of the 51st would have exposed the left flank of the French 31st Division.

On 9 June the Luftwaffe bombed Le Havre and destroyed the Division's stores with consequent food and ammunition shortages. The German bombers also hit oil refineries and storage dumps. The resulting pall of thick greasy smoke spread across Normandy, creating further difficulties for transport drivers struggling with congested roads.

When it was clear that the road to Le Havre had been cut, Ark Force was released to act on its own initiative. As a result, most of them were subsequently evacuated safely from Le Havre or Cherbourg to arrive back in England by 16 June. The remainder of the Division was rapidly running out of options. An alternative move to Dieppe was ruled out for it was reported that the approaches to the port had been mined and the harbour installations damaged. In any case, German troops were approaching from the east.

The last chance was the small coastal town of St Valery-en-Caux, although, as a tidal harbour set in a niche between towering cliffs, it would normally have been deemed quite unsuitable. Furthermore, roads into the town soon became congested by abandoned and wrecked equipment and conditions within it degenerated into chaos through raging fires and destruction as it came under attack from Rommel's 7th Division.

A perimeter was set up around the town. Facing east were 2/7th Duke of Wellington's and 4th Seaforths near Veules-les-Roses and 5th Gordons at St Pierre-le-Viger. Facing south were the 1st Black Watch at Houdetot and 4th Camerons at Néville with French troops in between. Facing west were the 1st Gordons at Ingouville, a company of the 7th Norfolks at St Sylvain and the 2nd Seaforths at Le Tot.

These last units took the brunt of Rommel's attack from the west, as will be seen in Angus Campbell's story. Many of the Norfolks were killed when the Panzers literally overran their dugouts. Meanwhile, another four and a half German divisions were approaching from the east supplemented by the 5th Panzers.

The Navy had assembled no less than 207 vessels to attempt another Dunkirk-style evacuation but the task was complicated by shallow approaches to the harbour. The ships actually approached St Valery on the 10th but the Division had not yet arrived; however, some wounded were rescued. They were already being fired on from the cliffs to the west. On the morning of the 11th small boats were used to take some men off from Veules-les-Roses further east. By a cruel twist of fate, heavy mist and rain on the night of 11 June delayed the rescue and also created major communication problems due to the reliance on visual signals. Only sixteen out of the 207 ships were equipped with radio and, of course, the army had little compatible equipment. By the 12th Rommel's guns commanded the cliffs to the west of St Valery, making further rescue by sea impossible.

Rommel himself paid tribute to the stout resistance put up by the 51st but the disparity in weaponry was too great; the gallant British and French effort was doomed as food and ammunition ran out. The French surrendered at 0800 on the morning of 12 June and the 51st had no option but to follow suit two and a half hours later.

Four thousand French were captured together with eight thousand men of the Division. To Rommel's delight, these included the headquarters staff and Major General Fortune, who had fought his men's corner with Whitehall till the bitter end.

> Rommel never forgot General Fortune and often spoke of him to his wife and son Manfred with sympathy, as the gallant leader of a good division who had had bad luck.
>
> Desmond Young *Rommel*

During the subsequent imprisonment, the General's commitment to his troops was further underlined when he refused a transfer to a special camp for senior officers and then, despite failing health, an offer of repatriation for himself; he chose to remain with his brother officers. After the war he was knighted by King George VI for his defiance of the Germans and his leadership of his fellow prisoners.

> It is safe to say that he is the only prisoner of war ever to be knighted for his services as such.
>
> Bernard Fergusson *The Black Watch, a Short History*

Not everyone was captured. Some vessels had made it inshore to the little port of Veules-les-Roses further east along the coast. After the order 'Every man for himself' was given, many men made their way there by descending the cliffs. Numbers fell to their deaths in the attempt or were gunned down on the beaches and some of the gallant little ships were lost. Nevertheless, 1,350 British and 930 French were taken off. To these numbers must be added the men of Ark Force.

In reading the graphic accounts of the long march of over three weeks which the prisoners undertook to the barges on the Rhine it must be remembered that most of these men had been constantly on the move for the preceding month. During that period they had inadequate supplies and very little sleep. The stress of battle was compounded by the back-breaking chore of digging defences in each new location.

By the time they arrived at St Valery they were suffering from hunger and exhaustion and yet these part-time soldiers had upheld the finest traditions of their famous regiments. Soldier after soldier confirmed that the order to surrender came as a complete shock to them. As Donald John MacDonald recounts, the order to the Camerons to lay down their arms had to be repeated. In 1999 the 89-year-old Archie Macphee could still describe it as '. . . the saddest day of my life.'

One of the finest unsolicited tributes to the men of the BEF came from the enemy. While the invasion of Britain was being planned in 1940 the German IV Corps drew up a briefing based on their own experience. (The use of 'English' for all Britons continues to upset Scots to this day, but it was as common a practice then as 'Yanks' for all Americans.)

> The English soldier was in excellent physical condition. He bore his own wounds with stoical calm. The losses of his own troops he discussed with complete equanimity. He did not complain of hardships. In battle he was tough and dogged. The English soldier has always shown himself to be a fighter of high value.
>
> Certainly the Territorial divisions are inferior to the Regular troops in training, but where morale is concerned they are their equal. In defence the Englishman took any punishment that came his way. During the fighting, IV Corps took relatively fewer English prisoners than in engagements with the French and Belgians. On the other hand, casualties on both sides were high.

The Highland Division was to rise again from the ashes of St Valery and went on to earn new battle honours in North Africa, Italy, France and Germany. When St Valery was liberated in 1944 the 5th Camerons under Derek Lang and the 5th Seaforths under Jack Walford vied for the honour of being first into the town where, as Derek Lang recorded in *Return to St Valery*, they were received with 'wild delight'. He was to go on to command the 51st in 1962.

The people of St Valery continue to remember the men of the Highland Division. A street in the town bears the name Avenue de la 51st Highland Division. In 1950 a fine granite monument was erected on high ground to the east. Its Gaelic inscription, '*Là a' bhlàir is math na càirdean*', translates as: 'On the day of battle it is good to have friends.' It faces another on the west side of town dedicated to the French defenders. In June 2000 it was a privilege to be present when the eighty-six-year-old General Sir Derek Lang led a proud group of his veterans in commemoration of the sixtieth anniversary. There were many moving moments as wreaths were laid at monuments and services were conducted at the immaculately tended graveyards which hold so many young men of the 51st – some known only to God.

> Tread lightly with care
> On the fresh earth of Europe
> For this soil was once
> The still eyes of young men.
>
> Donald John MacDonald *The War Memorial*

Escape

All four of the major contributors to this book made attempts to escape, with varying degrees of success – as will be seen. Many other attempts by men of the 51st have also been celebrated in print.

General Sir Derek Lang, adjutant of the 4th Camerons at the time, has left us a highly readable account of his own adventures in occupied France and eventual return to active service in *Return to St Valery*. Richard Broad's even more impressive venture, leading seven men of the 2nd Seaforths, is documented in *The Long Way Round* by William Moore.

Some ordinary soldiers also pulled off spectacular escapes. Neil Campbell and Hugh Oliver of the Camerons got away in the early days of the march and, after surviving on their wits for over two weeks, managed to 'borrow' a sailing boat from the harbour at St Valery and leave under the noses of the sentries. Campbell, who had been a fisherman in South Uist, navigated his way by the stars until they were picked up by a navy minesweeper. For this achievement they were both awarded the Military Medal.

Three men from the Argylls were also decorated after escaping from the march. After over a month of adventures, Cpl John MacDonald, L/Cpl James 'Ginger' Wilson and Willie Kemp reached the Spanish frontier and eventually returned to Scotland by ship from Gibraltar. At one point they were arrested and famously managed to baffle all the interpreters their captors could throw at them by speaking Gaelic. When asked to point out their homeland on the map, Kemp pointed vaguely towards Russia!

Those that escaped often owed much to the courage and generosity of ordinary people in France and Belgium (and even Germany) who were aware they were risking their own lives. Many did pay the ultimate penalty.

Camps such as Stalag IXc and XXa were massive holding centres containing as many as 20,000 men at times. They had numerous satellite work camps in the surrounding areas where POWs could be used virtually as slave labour.

Treatment in the camps themselves seems to have been much dependent on individual commandants. However, it seems that for all the suffering and lack of food and basic amenities, many guards made some attempt to follow the rules of the Geneva convention – at least where British and American prisoners were concerned. As will be seen, other nationalities such as Russians and Poles were not so lucky.

Treatment by the SS and Gestapo was a different matter altogether. As Donald John MacDonald's story makes clear, soldiers of the Wehrmacht often felt it was their duty to protect prisoners against these monsters from their own side. There are also stories of guards trying to set up no-escaping agreements with their charges so that all concerned might have an easier life. The atmosphere is reported to have worsened considerably in the last winter of the war when Himmler's SS took over responsibility for the POW camps.

Most of the best-documented escapes from the camps involved officers, for the simple reason that they could not be made to work. Ordinary soldiers, exhausted by twelve-hour days of forced labour and malnutrition, did not have the time, energy or resources to plan and carry out elaborate schemes. Many of their escapes – from camps hundreds of miles from the nearest neutral border – seem to have been motivated by sheer bloody-minded refusal to be cowed by their captors.

Apart from notorious episodes where escapees were shot – usually by the Gestapo – punishment of recaptured prisoners usually involved periods of solitary confinement and postings to punishment camps. The defence that it was 'a soldier's duty to escape' was recognised by military courts and those recaptured often earned the grudging respect of their guards.

Exact figures for the number of POWs held by Germany are difficult to come by, but it is estimated to have been in the region of a quarter of a million British and Americans alone. In the depths of the winter of 1944–45, with the Russians closing from the east, many of these prisoners had to endure the nightmare marches described by Angus Campbell. It is estimated that thousands lost their lives as a result and many of the survivors were as emaciated as those found in the concentration camps.

When it was realised that these marches were to take place, the Red Cross tried to set up a distribution network despite bureaucratic hurdles and lack of transport. In the end some of these problems were solved – but clearly many of the marching men never received the parcels that might have made the difference between life and death.

If anything positive came of the disaster that befell the Highland Division, evidence may be seen on war memorials such as the simple monument that stands on Ben Corary in South Uist. It records that an island with a population of about

2,000 lost 123 of its finest young men in the carnage of the First World War. The figure for the second conflict is 46. Who knows how many of those who endured five years of harrowing experience in the camps might have failed to survive if they had been returned to the battlefield?

The Myths

As memories of Dunkirk and the heroic rearguard action of the 51st fade, the years since 1940 have been fertile ground for simplistic theories to explain the disaster that overtook the BEF. Beliefs that the 51st had to hold the Germans back while the rest of the BEF escaped or that Churchill had deliberately sacrificed the Division to keep the French in the war fail completely to address the complexity of the situation.

As already suggested, the fundamental problem was that the Allied armies were not equipped to fight a European war against a determined enemy who had the effrontery to change the rules. In the fast-moving, dynamic scenario which developed, First World War timescales were just not good enough. The problem was exacerbated by poor communication at every level which made it impossible to react swiftly enough to events.

While German commanders such as Guderian and Rommel used radio to coordinate ground and air forces while leading their daring assaults from the front, the Allies were handicapped by archaic systems. In Belgium, Lord Gort was out of contact with his HQ at a critical stage and on 8 June General Fortune reported communication problems as he did not have the latest code.

In a situation where units were continually changing positions and affiliations, communication between the French Supreme Command and British forces suffered further from lack of familiarity with each other's languages. Clearly this militated against better cooperation. A tendency to blame each other for the debacle is understandable. For all the criticism levelled at French commitment, it is clear that many French units fought with great courage and inflicted serious damage on the enemy. It was the French Army that held the perimeter for the last few days at Dunkirk and French casualties in defence of their country amounted to 100,000 against the British 68,000. The main fault lay with poor leadership and lack of strategic planning at the very top.

As far as the Highland Division was concerned, it was sheer bad luck that their short-term tour of duty in the Saar coincided with the launch of the German attack through the Ardennes. According to Gregor MacDonald's account, the whole Division was due to be recalled to England for re-equipment The fact that men were allowed to go on leave in May demonstrates an apparent unawareness of the massive German build-up. This failure of French Supreme Command to appreciate the threat remains inexplicable.

As the speed and extent of the German advance took even their own High Command by surprise it is little wonder that Allied military thinking failed to keep up with events. By the time the Division was withdrawn from the Maginot line it was already impossible for them to rejoin the BEF. As they journeyed north on their slow trains to Normandy Guderian was laying siege to the Channel ports of Boulogne and Calais. Boulogne fell on the 25th and Calais on the 26 May but spirited British and French resistance had tied up three of Guderian's Panzer divisions, thereby relieving some of the pressure on Dunkirk. By 2 June, when the 51st joined the French attempt to halt the German advance across the Somme, the BEF evacuation from Dunkirk was already complete (although French troops were still being embarked two days later).

To read detailed accounts of the chaos that prevailed in the month after 10 May is to be lost in admiration of the way individual units continued to operate even when out of contact with HQ or having lost their senior officers. The courage and esprit de corps shown by men of the 51st in the most desperate circumstances lived up to the highest standards of their proud regiments despite the fact that they had been sent to war with pitifully inadequate anti-tank weapons and no anti-aircraft flak batteries.

The final and decisive straw was Weygand's refusal to permit the 51st to withdraw to Le Havre on 8 June. Even after permission was given, the timescale was hopelessly unrealistic because the French 31st Division, lacking transport, could only proceed by night at marching pace. But for that, the 51st could have escaped with Ark Force from Le Havre or Cherbourg. A last cruel twist was that fog and rain on the night of the 11th prevented the Navy from making any further attempt at evacuation.

The theory that Churchill sacrificed the Division in a desperate endgame to keep the French in the war owes much to some deep need in the Scottish psyche to attribute all the woes of the world to one personal villain. (Nowadays that figurehead role has been allocated to Margaret Thatcher). Churchill's liability appeared to be confirmed in 1994 by the title of Saul David's otherwise admirably comprehensive book *Churchill's Sacrifice of the Highland Division*. Despite his publisher's title, David devotes only a few paragraphs to the theory and his conclusions are ambivalent. In discussing the reasons for the delay in withdrawing to Le Havre he had this to say:

> But could these facts be interpreted in an even more cynical light: namely that the British government deliberately sacrificed the 51st Division as a symbol of Allied unity which would silence French complaints that the British had abandoned them? It is not out of the question.

Historian Trevor Royle accepted this interpretation without question in his obituary of Sir Derek Lang in *The Herald* of 11 April 2001:

> . . . the same division had been sacrificed by Prime Minister Winston Churchill when it was forced to surrender to General Rommel's 7th Panzer Division . . . Instead of escaping at Dunkirk with the BEF, in a needless act of Allied solidarity the 51st covered the French retreat and fought to the last round.

Apart from the fact that Sir Derek himself is known to have disagreed with this simplistic explanation, it has already been made clear that from the moment Guderian crossed the Meuse it was impossible for the 51st to have rejoined the BEF.

Churchill recorded his personal dismay at the loss of the Division;

> We had been intensely concerned lest this division (the 51st) should be driven back to the Havre peninsula and thus be separated from the main armies, and its commander, Major-General Fortune, had been told to fall back if necessary in the direction of Rouen. This movement was forbidden by the already disintegrating French command.
>
> Repeated urgent representations were made by us but they were of no avail. A dogged refusal to face facts led to the ruin of the French 9th Corps and our 51st Division. On June 9 when Rouen was already in German hands, our men had but newly reached Dieppe, thirty-five miles to the north. Only then were orders received to withdraw to Havre. A force was sent back to cover the movement, but before the main bodies could move the Germans interposed. Striking from the east, they reached the sea and the greater part of the 51st Division, with many of the French, was cut off. It was a case of gross mismanagement for this very danger was visible a full three days before.
>
> Winston Churchill
> *Their Finest Hour, 2nd World War Vol. ii*

It might be argued that Churchill, writing with the benefit of hindsight, was justifying his own position but the comment that his secretary, Sir John Colville, recorded in his diary is telling confirmation of the reaction in Whitehall at the time: 'The most brutal disaster which we have yet suffered.'

It is true that Churchill was determined to support France as long as possible. This was underlined when General Alan Brooke returned from Dunkirk. He was ordered to return to France immediately to form a second British Expeditionary Force. As part of that force, the 52nd Lowland Division landed at Cherbourg on 12 June – the very day that their comrades had to surrender. But by 14 June Brooke learned from Weygand that French organised resistance was at an end and recommended all remaining British troops should be evacuated to England. Over 50,000 men were embarked from Cherbourg and St Malo as well as Le Havre. In fact evacuations of Allied forces continued from ports further south such as Nantes, St Nazaire, Bordeaux and Mediterranean ports until August. By that time 144,000 British and nearly 48,000 French, Poles, Czechs and Belgians had been rescued in addition to the Dunkirk numbers. Clearly the Highland Division should have been numbered amongst them.

If personal villains are deemed essential then much of the blame must be shouldered by successive French Supreme Commanders who found themselves in situations totally beyond their experience and resources. There is little evidence that the British would have coped any better. Rather should credit be given to German visionaries who reinvented the arts of war and to the audacious generals who were able to take full advantage of the ensuing chaos. The 51st were victims of that chaos.

Blitzkrieg achieved success in 1940 through surprise. Once that element was gone and counter-measures devised, the strategy was to have limited value for the rest of the war.

A Cameron Never Can Yield

A Prisoner of War's Escape from Germany to Gibraltar

GREGOR MACDONALD

The son of a gamekeeper, Gregor Grant Macdonald was born and brought up in Glen Lochay near Killin in Perthshire. Having joined the Bank of Scotland, he was eventually transferred to their branch in Tarbert, Harris – which is where his story starts.

Like many of his comrades, he spoke little of his wartime experiences. In his later years, his daughter Janette urged him to record them and eventually he agreed to do so – provided she won a Gold Medal for singing at the National Mod!

At Stornoway in 1989 she fulfilled her part of the bargain and the result was an engrossing personal account of the campaign of the Highland Division.

This is the major part of his original book, A Cameron Never Can Yield, *published posthumously by the Cameron Highlanders Association in 1999 and dedicated to Janette. Even though it was written over fifty years after the event, his story breathes with the art of a natural story-teller. He maintained that, had he written nearer the time, the account could have been three times as long!*

Apart from the vivid account of the events leading up to St Valery, he is the only one of the contributors to this volume to have made a successful escape immediately afterwards. There is especial interest in his experiences of Free France, the work of the Tartan Pimpernel and, above all, the horrors of Spanish prisons and concentration camps.

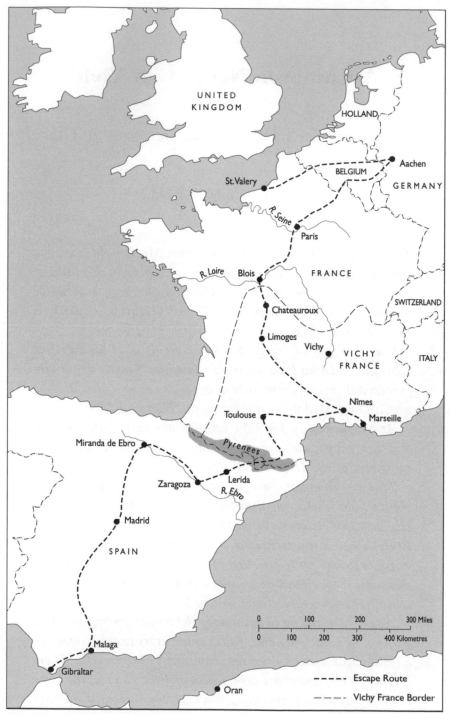

Map 4: Gregor MacDonald's escape route

Mobilisation

I like to think the whole thing started for me on Good Friday 1939. That morning I heard on the radio that Mussolini's troops had invaded Albania but that news made little impression. It was a Bank Holiday and the Bank of Scotland at Tarbert, Harris was closed. I spent the afternoon helping to prepare the football field for a visit by Stornoway Rovers on the following day.

Postman Donald Kennedy brought me a letter from the Territorial Army Association at Inverness advising me, as Secretary of the Leverhulme Hall Committee, that they proposed to recruit a Territorial Company of the Queen's Own Cameron Highlanders in Harris and requesting that the Leverhulme Hall be made available as headquarters for the Company. I called a members' meeting for the following week and duly reported to the Association that the hall would be available.

Sometime in May 1939 the Permanent Sergeant Instructor, Ronald MacDonald, arrived from Lochmaddy and soon contacted some likely recruits. He made his headquarters in the public bar of the Harris Hotel and ridiculed any suggestions that war was imminent. However, a fortnight later Captain Derek Lang,* then adjutant of the 4th Battalion of the Camerons, arrived in Harris, accompanied by Captain Lord Fincastle and very quietly began a recruiting drive.

Initially, they concentrated on South Harris, with encouraging results, and then announced they would hold a meeting in the Hall at Tarbert. It was packed to overflowing and Captain Lang gave a very convincing performance. It was unthinkable that war would break out, but we must show Hitler that we would not be caught unprepared. The adventure appealed to the younger listeners and when volunteers were called to step forward I found to my surprise that I was the first and so became No. 2931066, Private MacDonald.

* Later Lieutenant General Sir Derek Lang, author of *Return to St Valery*. He wrote a warm foreword to Macdonald's original book.

Towards the end of May a huge consignment of service dress
and Cameron kilts arrived by boat from Lochmaddy, followed
by arms and equipment from Inverness. The Sergeant Instructor (PSI) was now permanently resident in Harris and there was
great excitement when we first donned our uniforms and
marched through the village. Everyone turned out to see us –
very quiet – perhaps it brought back memories of 1914.

I'm afraid we did not take our soldiering too seriously and
thoroughly enjoyed ourselves one evening per week – despite
threats from the PSI! We were promised a fortnight's camp at
Barry near Dundee in the middle of June so the PSI encouraged
us in our training, saying that he didn't want to feel ashamed
when we drilled with other experienced companies from Skye,
North and South Uist, Nairn and Inverness.

The summer of 1939 passed quickly and, although we sensed
the threat of war, in our spare time we continued to fish and play
golf as in previous years. So it was quite disturbing to wake up one
morning in July to find an oil tanker, the *Vimiera*, lying at anchor
in East Loch Tarbert and be told that every sea loch in the West
Coast of Scotland was occupied by a ship carrying a full cargo of
oil. The last week of August was very tense and when Germany
invaded Poland we awaited call-up with a sense of relief.

It came on Saturday, 2 September but, as there was no ship
available to take us over the Minch, the company was put on
stand-by. Eventually we were informed that the SS *Clydesdale*
would call at Lochboisdale, Lochmaddy and Tarbert on
the Tuesday afternoon to collect and transport the Cameron
Highlanders to Kyle of Lochalsh, where a train would be
waiting to take them to Inverness.

The appearance of the *Clydesdale* in the East Loch was the
signal for 90 per cent of the Harris population to assemble on or
around the pier. When the ship docked the first person to
appear on the gangway was our PSI – now promoted to
Company Sergeant Major. He strode across the pier to where
the Harris contingent was drawn up and announced, 'Up to now
you've been playing at soldiers, but from now on I'll see you are
made into real soldiers!'

The stores which had been held in the Leverhulme Hall had to be loaded. This took over an hour before the *Clydesdale* cast off at 7 p.m. and the war for us had started. When we had waved our goodbyes a few of us drifted back to the stern where we sat on coils of rope and discussed the big adventure. A corporal from the Uist company informed us that we would get a meal on arrival at Kyle of Lochalsh and by the time the slow cargo boat had crossed the Minch we were quite hungry. Imagine our feelings when we disembarked to be handed two slices of bread, a small piece of cheese and a first-war mess tin, caked with rust and coated with grease. Into the mess-tin a pint mug of black tea was emptied. That was the moment we all realised we were now in the army.

We arrived at Inverness Station about midnight and marched the five miles to Dochfour carrying all our equipment and belongings. On arrival we were issued with a blanket and shown into a concreted stable. By this time we were so tired that all we could do was spread our blankets on the concrete and in ten minutes everyone was asleep.

The months of September to December were given over to intensive training and by the end of October units of the 51st Highland Division were concentrated in the Aldershot area in preparation for their move to France. On 19 December our Battalion were officially presented with the 'Blue Hackle' by the king and from that date every man of the Battalion wore the hackle behind his Cameron cap badge. At the present time it is worn by all ranks of the Queen's Own Highlanders. Two days after Christmas all ranks were granted eight days leave and we knew that as soon as we reported back to the concentration area we would become part of the British Expeditionary Force.

Arrival in France

On 10 January 1940 we left Bordon Camp by train, arrived at Southampton Docks and embarked on the *Lady of Man*, an Isle of Man pleasure steamer well-known to holiday-makers. We docked at Dieppe during the night and when we disembarked

the following day we were given our initial location. We were
expected to march to the small town of Bolbec, a distance of
some ten miles, carrying full equipment plus one blanket per
man. Our billets would be on a small farm near the town and
although it was snowing hard we contented ourselves with the
thought of a nice dry hayshed or barn. Imagine our feelings
when we arrived at a group of broken-down wooden sheds all of
which housed lean, hungry cattle. It was clear that no attempt
had been made to clean the sheds out. After much delay we
finally contacted the farmer, a filthy unshaven individual who
made it clear that we were not welcome. One of our officers
spoke fluent French and after much haggling the farmer eventually produced a cart of damp evil-smelling hay and each man
was allowed his ration.

It was now dark and our company cooks set out their cookhouse, consisting of four sheets of corrugated iron, and soon a
dixie of M & V * rations was heating up on the pressure burner.
The farm cattle had been turned out during daylight hours and
had churned up the mud around the sheds until it was over the
uppers of our army boots so that we had permanently wet and
frozen feet. The three platoons and company headquarters were
each allotted sheds and we set about brushing and scrubbing
until there was some improvement in our sleeping quarters.
When the cattle returned to their stalls in the evening they were
chained a matter of ten feet from where we slept, so we were in
constant danger of being spattered in our beds. The flagstones
were rough and uneven but, having cleaned up as well as we
could, we spread the musty hay and rolled up in our single
blanket. Being very tired we were soon asleep and so ended our
first day in France.

For the next three weeks the snow and rain continued and the
mud round the billets made life very unpleasant. A shed was set
up for weapon-training and we gradually became more efficient
on the Bren light machine-gun and the two-inch mortars with
which the company was equipped. Every second day we went

* Meat and Vegetable.

on a route march through the surrounding villages led by the company piper. As the entire company wore kilts the villagers turned out to see us march past, and we gradually got to know some of them. They were very friendly but when war was mentioned they became silent and even at this early date we got the impression that they did not relish war against the Germans.

At this time B Company was 130 strong and in the evenings we all repaired to the sole café in our area, where the only item on the menu was fried eggs and potatoes. We consumed vast quantities and spent the evening sitting round the iron stove – occasionally sampling a few of the attractive bottles which stacked the shelves.

The weather continued very wintry and we were quite relieved when we were ordered to move to the small village of Lillers near Lille. Once again we occupied a farm and steadings but this time we were housed in a half-built house, work having been suspended at the outbreak of war. Fortunately the cattle and pigs were housed in separate buildings and the roads were roughly metalled. The days were now lengthening and we were employed in constructing anti-tank traps surrounding Lille.

In my rank of company quartermaster-sergeant I visited the company at midday and issued each man with his haversack ration, consisting of two slices of bread and cheese. This kept them going until their return to billets at 6 p.m. There was no heating in the billets and with only one blanket we were often unable to sleep because of the cold.

Two weeks later we moved again to the little town of Hante on the La Bassé canal, the scene of very heavy fighting in The First World War. The billets were reasonable and with improving weather B Company were just beginning to enjoy this so-called war when we were moved once again, this time to an empty textile factory on the Belgian frontier. In our army news-sheets we read of patrol activity on the Saar front and felt that sooner or later we would be bound for that area.

After a week at Rubaix we moved, along with the remainder of the Battalion, to Bailleul, a town that had been totally destroyed in the 1914–18 war. At this time all sorts of rumours were prevalent. According to our French Allies the enemy were preparing for a 'blitz' in the shape of an assault by thousands of aircraft and tanks but the older soldiers explained this was typical German propaganda and we should not let it worry us.

The Maginot Line

A fortnight later we left for the Alsace-Lorraine front where the French-German border follows the line of the Saar River. We occupied a French barracks for two days and then moved forward of the Maginot Line to occupy the support line. Two days later we took over the front line from the 2nd Battalion Seaforth Highlanders.

We found ourselves in densely wooded country where the enormous beech trees shut out the mid-day light. During daylight hours no sounds could be heard but as soon as night fell owls and other night birds hooted and shrieked from every direction. We were confident of being a match for the enemy in this type of warfare until we learned from a prisoner captured by a French patrol that the Germans had recruited a full battalion made up of smugglers whose occupation in peace time was in illicit trade on the Franco-German border. From years of experience they knew all the forest tracks, even in the darkness, and we found ourselves at a decided disadvantage.

There were small farms in the forest clearings but these were now deserted as the occupants had fled to the west on the outbreak of war. The livestock were abandoned in the surrounding pastures and our Uist C Company rounded up two milk cows which they tethered beside the company position. For a few days they supplied the company with fresh milk but then on two successive mornings the cows appeared to have been already milked. The Uist boys blamed the Foyers D Company for this and two of their men volunteered to sleep beside the cows but were shocked on waking up during the night to find two German soldiers milking their cows!

We were gradually becoming used to being in the line although action was very limited – almost non-existent. Then one night a fire-fight developed on our left and next morning we learned the enemy had isolated one of C Company's forward posts, wounding three and taking three prisoners.* At dawn the following morning, enemy artillery blasted our company headquarters, killing three and wounding two. One of the dead was Corporal Neil Macdonald, who had worked with me in the Bank of Scotland in Tarbert, Harris. It was only then that I began to understand what war was all about. In the following week patrolling was stepped up by both sides and we were encouraged when we ambushed an enemy patrol and inflicted some casualties.

One morning we were standing-to at first light when we heard a steady drone of aircraft and shortly afterwards the sky was dark with enemy bombers flying due west at a height of around 4,000 feet. For the next two hours we counted wave after wave of Junkers and Fokkers† flying due west without any fighter cover. This was not surprising as we had not seen a British or French aircraft in the sky since our arrival in France three months before. Half an hour later we heard the enemy bombs being dropped in Western France.

Having completed our spell in the front line we were withdrawn to the support line and replaced by the 4th Battalion Seaforth Highlanders. On their first night in the front line they were attacked by the enemy in strength and suffered considerable casualties. We were stationed in the Ising Barracks for two days amid rumours that the German army was poised to attack all fronts at a moment's notice.

It was with a sense of relief we received the good news that the whole Division was to return to England for re-equipping with new and more powerful infantry weapons.

During the last week in May the rifle companies entrained at Metz and commenced the long and slow journey to Rouen via Orléans. We were conveyed in large railway trucks labelled '40 Men or 10 Horses' and the overloaded train crawled along at 4 mph through the battlefields of the First World War.

* See p. 25.
† Possibly Heinkels or Dorniers at this stage of the war.

The battalion transport left by road at the same time only to find every highway blocked by French civilians with all their belongings fleeing to the west. Every type of transport imaginable from prams, bicycles, carts and horses to cars and lorries jammed the roads and, to make matters worse, when the petrol ran out vehicles were abandoned on the verge. As a result a number of our trucks were caught up in traffic jams and strafed by the low-flying Stukas. In the meantime the train carrying the rifle companies finally reached the outskirts of Rouen, six days after leaving Metz.

In pouring rain we set up tents abandoned by French army units and prepared for a few hours sleep. About three o'clock next morning I heard a despatch rider arrive on his motor cycle with a message for our Company Commander, Captain Fincastle. He called the sergeant major and me to his tent and read the message to us. The German army had broken through the unfinished defences of the River Somme. B Company would parade immediately and would be picked up by French army transport in thirty minutes time. After a wait of three hours, three ancient trucks arrived and the 130 men of the company climbed wearily aboard and we headed for the east.

The Somme

Half an hour later we disembarked at the town of Blangy where our Brigade Commander was waiting. The 4th Camerons were directed to the area around the small village of Limeux some two miles west of the Somme. We dug-in under cover of dense forest, which afforded us some protection from low-flying aircraft. We then made contact with a French Territorial company, who informed us that the enemy had succeeded in crossing the river directly in front of us. The French troops did not appear to take the war very seriously and were more concerned with shooting the owls and rabbits which abounded in the woods. Towards evening they withdrew and B Company were left on their own.

As quartermaster-sergeant I made arrangements for a meal

for the company. On the outskirts of Rouen we had come across two abandoned ration trucks and had taken as much as we could carry so we now had sufficient provisions for two days. I helped the Sergeant Major to check the holding of small arms, ammunition and hand grenades carried by our three platoons. The company piper, Angus Mackay from South Uist, was not in his usual good spirits. He confessed that the gloomy woods got him down and wished that orders for our expected advance would come soon.

I was despatched to an abandoned ordnance dump to collect any suitable ammunition I could find and took with me Corporal Maclean, the company clerk, and John McGlynn the company runner. Just before we left, an order from Battalion HQ informed us that the attack on the German bridgehead would commence at 3.15 a.m. We would have the support of French aircraft and a troop of French tanks. On the way back with the ammunition we saw that the company position was receiving a lot of attention from German mortars but by the time we arrived back it had stopped. With the sergeant major I began to distribute the ammunition and mentioned to him that I had seen the mortaring.

'Any casualties?' I asked.

'Only one,' replied the sergeant major, 'Piper Mackay – he got a shell to himself.'*

At exactly 3 a.m. three French planes appeared – but it was on our position they dropped their bombs. The long-expected tank support arrived soon after – one tank whose commander had been wounded and who retired with his tank to the nearest Aid Post. There was nothing else to wait for and at 3.15 a.m. B Company, 126 strong, emerged from the wood in extended order.

Our objective was the west bank of the Somme roughly one mile away. Our front was a broad expanse of flat ground with a rye crop one foot high, which afforded us little cover, and we

---

* Angus Mackay *Aonghas Ailig Mhòir* was from Kilphedar, South Uist. Apparently when he left home after Christmas leave in 1939 he was unusually sad, as though he had a premonition that he would not return.

must have presented an easy target to the waiting enemy. By the time we were half-way to the objective we had seen a number of our men go down. If the casualties were close at hand we tried to help but our objective was first priority and we were forced to leave as many where they fell.

Then, quite suddenly, there appeared before us what must have been at least two enemy companies which had been lying unseen in the rye crop and only appeared when we were within one hundred yards. They greeted us with a hail of fire from their Spandau machine-guns and huge gaps appeared in our formations. By this time we were getting near our objective and with a final desperate effort we reached the edge of the escarpment bordering the River Somme. In the confusion of battle we had veered slightly to our right and found ourselves very close to our A Company position, which they had previously assaulted.

The last hundred yards had cost B Company dearly and at roll call only forty-one men stood up. Of the officers only Captain Fincastle and 2nd Lt. Robertson survived the advance, the remaining three having been killed or wounded. Two sergeants were killed and three wounded, leaving the sergeant major and me as the only surviving senior NCOs.

Evacuation of the wounded was our first priority and we collected twenty in the orchard overlooking the river while a force of twelve men pushed forward to deal with any enemy counter-attack. It was only then that the sergeant major saw that Captain Fincastle had been wounded in both legs. He applied his own field dressing to the wounds and, seeing me coming in from the right flank, he shouted for my dressing. I made my way to where the company commander lay and was cutting the stitching on my battle dress pocket where the dressing was carried when the mortar battery again concentrated on our position. Unlike artillery fire, mortars give no warning and my first recollection was being thrown to the ground by the blast and trying to regain my feet. The sergeant major, his face covered with blood, shouted, 'QMS, give me a hand – I think the Company Commander has had it.' I moved across to where

Top. 8 January 1940: General Ironside (Chief of the Imperial General Staff), Winston Churchill, General Gamelin (French Supreme Commander), Lord Gort (Commander BEF), General Georges (Commander Allied Forces) (© Imperial War Museum, London)

Right. General Heinz Guderian – framed by the radio aerial of his command vehicle (© Imperial War Museum, London)

Below. General Erich von Manstein, who devised the plan for attack via the Ardennes

Men of the 4th Black Watch in an improvised dugout on the Bresle, 7 June. The soldier nearest the camera is using a captured German machine gun. (© Imperial War Museum, London)

2nd Seaforths Bren gun post at Boencourt, June 1940 (© Imperial War Museum, London)

Captain Fincastle lay to find that the last mortar had landed on him and he was already dead. I hurriedly put a plaster on the sergeant major but he assured me it was not serious.

At that moment another mortar landed between us and I felt a burning sensation in my head. When I retrieved my helmet I found that a piece of shrapnel had gone in below the rim and out through the crown leaving me with an uncomfortable head wound. At the time I did not feel any pain so I turned to examine one of the Harris boys, 2931866 Pte. John Angus MacDonald, who was quite conscious and made light of a painful thigh wound.

By this time a number of the men wounded in the final assault had crawled into the orchard while others were being carried in by their comrades. We used the ammunition truck to take these men to the Regimental Aid Post, packing twenty-five wounded into the 15 hundredweight truck.

During the night the sergeant major received orders to withdraw the remnants of B Company, now numbering twenty-six men, to Battalion HQ in the Chateau at Huchenneville. Here we were met by Major Stanley Hill, second-in-command of the Battalion, who explained that as B Company had no officers surviving I would be required to take the remaining twenty-six men forward nearly one mile to the Oisement railway line, where we would relieve a French platoon under attack from some enemy advance troops.

Although we were very tired we set off immediately, hoping to get to our positions before first light. Our line of approach was a narrow sandy road running at right angles to the railway line, crossing it at a level crossing and continuing across flat hayfields until it disappeared in a forest half-a-mile away. From the railway line we had an excellent field of fire and we started to dig-in without delay, expecting the enemy to appear at any moment. For our defence we had twenty-four rifles, two sub-machine-guns and two Bren guns. The Brigade anti-tank platoon had sited a light Hotchkiss anti-tank gun on our left flank. About eleven o'clock in the forenoon two 15 hundred-weight trucks emerged from the woods on our front. Having the only field glasses I kept them in focus and was relieved to observe that they carried the 4th Seaforth identification plates. However, when they were about 200 yards from our position they suddenly pulled up and two German mortar sections alighted with their weapons and disappeared in the long grass. We immediately opened up with our Brens and one of the vehicles had some trouble getting away. The other one took cover in a depression and we observed the two sections piling into it before heading back to the shelter of the woods.

In the afternoon we repelled three frontal attacks without loss to ourselves and by evening it appeared that the enemy had by-passed us on our right flank and were engaged by French troops on the Bresle front. In the evening we were encouraged by the sight of a French company preparing a defensive position some three hundred yards behind us and awaited orders from our Battalion HQ to withdraw through the French lines, leaving them in direct contact with the enemy.

Suddenly a French colonel appeared with a sergeant and said, 'We are taking up position just behind you – it's a good position – we'll be able to hold the Germans but we'll need to be able to dig in our defences. Would you be able to hold on until tomorrow afternoon?'

'Oh! I don't know about that, sir,' I said, 'but we'll have a try.'

So we held the railway line until next day and the colonel came up with the sergeant again. He told the sergeant to take my name and I asked, 'What's this for?' The sergeant said, '*Peut-être medal militaire.*'

I didn't think much about it but Cpl Peter Martin said, 'Oh! you're OK for a French decoration – whatever that's worth.'

At this time we became aware of a massive build-up of German armour and infantry in the woods directly in front as we waited impatiently for instructions to withdraw. The expected message was delivered by despatch rider after last light and, as we prepared for our departure, I sent Cpl Peter McIntosh to advise the French troops that we were withdrawing at midnight. Imagine our feelings when he returned to report that our allies had abandoned their prepared position and disappeared without trace. Nobody knew where they had gone to and the Germans were swarming through the area. Peter said to me, 'Not much chance of your medal now.'

'No, I don't think so, Peter.' In the chaos of the next few days I thought no more about it.*

Withdrawal

Before leaving our position we planted six anti-tank mines around the level crossing, having obtained them from an RE section the previous day. During the evening German shelling had set fire to a large expanse of forest two miles west of our position. With this as a guide the twenty-six remaining men of B Company set off in an attempt to reach the Divisional front line.

We started off in three sections at thirty yards between formations and although we had to alter direction frequently because of the fires we made quite good time. At one point our leading section stopped and when I went forward to investigate I found them listening intently to a squeaking noise which seemed to be approaching from the opposite direction. In a few moments, out of the darkness and smoke there appeared a single soldier carrying a rusty pail, the handle of which squeaked at his every step. He was wearing a balmoral and as he came closer I could see he sported a red hackle in it.

'What are you doing here?' I asked.

'Looking for a coo tae mulk,' he replied, showing me his rusty pail.

'Well,' I said, 'there's nothing but Germans behind us.'

'OK,' he said, 'there's another ferm further back, I'll try that.' And away he went, completely unperturbed as if he was strolling down a farm road in Perthshire or Angus!

Eventually, as dawn was breaking, we were challenged by

* The incident with the French colonel was not mentioned in the original book and has been taken from an interview Gregor did with D. Ferguson of the Bank of Scotland in 1987. See also p. 143.

sentries and to our great relief discovered they belonged to our Battalion HQ, who were sleeping in an area of open ground near the small town of Le Transloy. Major Hill was on hand to welcome us and advise us to take cover in a hayfield bordering the road. On no account should we move during daylight hours as the enemy dive-bombers would be out at first light to harass any movement on the roads. In five minutes we were all asleep.

After three hours sleep I was awakened by an orderly from Battalion HQ with an urgent message to report to Colonel Cawdor at Huchenneville Château. This was some distance away so it was well into the afternoon when I finally reported to the commanding officer. He was alone in a vast room in the chateau and looked a very worried man.

'Oh, Colour Sergeant,' he said, 'you have just returned from the Oisement railway line which you have been holding with the remnants of B company.'

'That's correct, sir,' I replied.

'Well, I am very reluctantly asking you to return to your former position at last light tonight, acting as guide to a company of the 5th Gordons of 153 Brigade who will take over your former position. When the Gordons are in occupation you will contact our A Company Commander and lead the company back to rejoin the Battalion. Take two men with you and you will contact the Gordons at Map Reference ————, which you will find is the junction of a forestry track and the secondary road to Limeux. You will have to rely on your ears rather than your eyes as the forest will be in pitch darkness.'

I just couldn't believe it possible that an under-strength company of infantry were being sent to contain the enemy advance when at least a brigade would be required. The area around the railway crossing was swarming with German troops who had poured across the Somme in a steady stream since the previous forenoon.

'But, sir,' I said, 'no rifle company could ever survive for any length of time against such opposition.'

I also told him how we had watched the massive build-up of armour half a mile forward of the railway line.

'Well,' he replied, 'these are my orders from Brigade which in turn have come from the French General de Gaulle.'

I rejoined B Company, called for two volunteers and was immediately joined by Cpl Maclean and Pte McGlynn. We got half a loaf and some cheese from the ration clerk and as a great favour were given a tin of 'bully' by one of the Colour Sergeants. As darkness fell we made our way down the Limeux road to the map reference, where we found the Gordon company waiting. Their company commander, Captain Usher, suggested that he and I and his sergeant major should lead the column while the two Camerons took up the rear. We kept to the grass verge and were forbidden to speak so it took us over an hour to cover the three miles to Mareil Caubert.

It was apparent that the enemy were occupying many positions commanding the road and we were very lucky indeed to find a clear way back to the positions we had held on the previous night. When the Gordon company were in position I contacted our A Company Commander and informed him that our CO had instructed me to act as guide in the withdrawal to rejoin the Battalion. By this time dawn was showing in the eastern sky and A Company Commander considered it too risky to attempt a withdrawal in the half light and decided to remain in his present position throughout the day. He gave us his permission to return to B Company, if and when we could find them.*

As soon as permission was given we set out on our return journey, passing through the meadows over which we had advanced on 4 June. We kept as far as possible from the Caubert-Limeux road as we could hear the enemy armour advancing west on the line of the road. We passed through German advance posts, being fired on three times without damage and finally reached the chateau, where I intended to report to the Battalion Commander. To our surprise the whole area was deserted and shortly afterwards the building was

---

* These two companies were isolated and surrounded by tanks and snipers. Despite heavy casualties, they held out till 11 a.m. on the 6th before eventually having to surrender.

shelled. We were very tired but decided to push on westwards, although our water bottles were empty and we had not eaten since we left Le Transloy the previous afternoon.

Even more disturbing was the sound of German armour from the direction of the chateau and we hoped they would not use the narrow track through the forest in their advance. We had progressed about two miles when McGlynn, who was leading our group at the time, reported we were overtaking two men. These proved to be the last two signallers who had manned the communications equipment at the chateau and had been the last to leave. They assured us that they were only half an hour behind the remainder of Battalion HQ who were also heading back to Le Transloy.

One young signaller was weighted down with his personal arms and equipment and a bulky radio set. Balanced on top was a Boyes anti-tank rifle. This weapon weighed over twenty pounds and was very awkward to carry so when I offered to give him a rest he was glad to hand it over. To make conversation I asked him where he came from and he replied, 'Beauly.' I continued, 'If there was no war what would you be doing now?'

He thought for a few seconds before answering, 'Probably posting the ledger in the Bank of Scotland, Beauly.'

'That's amazing,' I said, 'for I too am in the Bank of Scotland – teller at Tarbert, Harris.'

I then asked him who carried the ammunition for the anti-tank rifle and he confessed he didn't know as the Signals Platoon had been divided up between five different companies. As I reckoned we had still six or seven miles in front of us without food or water, I decided against all regulations that we must abandon the useless weapon. When we came to a part of the forest carpeted by beech leaves we dug a hole with an entrenching tool and said farewell to our burden. As the signallers were moving off I asked, 'What's your name?'

'Charlie Leggatt,' he replied.

'I'll remember that and we'll meet again somewhere in the Bank of Scotland.'

'The sooner the better!' he shouted back.

For the next two hours we continued on the forest track and, on coming to a small stream, made contact with a section of Royal Engineers who had waited behind to blow up a bridge when all the stragglers were safely across. Their water bottles were full of cider and this put new life into us and we finally rejoined the remnants of our unit at last light.

St Valery-en-Caux

The following afternoon (probably 8 June) we edged back in a north-westerly direction taking advantage of any cover in an effort to reach the Channel. We had not seen any Allied aircraft in the past month and were beginning to doubt if we had any left. On the other hand, from dawn the sky was never without enemy planes. At first light close formations of heavy bombers at around four or five thousand feet were heading for the Channel ports and lines of communications in Western France. An hour later we heard the crump as they unloaded their bombs. Escorts of fighters now accompanied them on all raids but, so far as we could see, they were never challenged by Allied planes.

The next three days were very confusing and it is now very difficult to remember what happened. Each night as darkness fell we retreated in the direction of the Channel until we came to a defensive position where we dug-in to await the enemy advance, which usually came at first light. I doubt if we inflicted many casualties – at best we only delayed them for an hour or two at each position. When night came we repeated the previous night's procedure and on the morning of 10 June we could see the Channel at a distance of about two miles. This greatly cheered us, for we had been told that the Royal Navy would embark us from the small town of St Valery-en-Caux, a few miles down the coast from Dieppe.

The following night as soon as darkness fell Sergeant Major MacDonald, who had rejoined us the previous day, sent me down to the beach to see how the evacuation was proceeding. It was only then that I came to realise the full gravity of the situation. The small town was situated on the only flat ground at the base of cliffs. The main road descended from the escarpment by a very steep hill and running parallel to the road were numerous tracks and paths down the rock face.

Every square foot was occupied by troops, some dead, some wounded, but most sound asleep in the torrential rain which had started at dusk. To make matters worse, fog was rolling in from the sea and there was no sign of any Royal Navy ships. A steady concentration of shellfire was coming from a south-westerly direction and I concluded that the enemy were in possession of the cliff tops between St Valery and Fécamp. All the houses round the harbour were in flames and chimney pots were rolling about the streets. Stretcher bearers were carrying bodies to the town square where a huge heap was steadily growing.

There was nothing further to learn and I attempted the return journey through the solid mass of bodies on the narrow tracks. Fortunately they were so tired that they didn't protest when I tramped over them. I finally reached the cliff top but found it very difficult to locate the Camerons in the darkness and confusion. When I stopped to take my bearings a soldier standing in a doorway invited me into the building.

'We're the 1st Black Watch; come in and get a cup of tea, Jock.'

I then discovered I'd landed in a schoolroom which about a dozen men of the Black Watch were defending with two Brens firing from the windows. A wood fire was burning in the grate and an elderly French woman was calmly toasting bread and spreading jam from a large container. The Black Watch had rescued the foodstuffs from a blazing ration truck and a corporal was making tea in a huge pot. He handed me a mug of boiling tea and a piece of bread with jam. That proved to be my last meal for four days.

I finally found B Company sleeping soundly on the eastern outskirts of the town. The rain had continued throughout the night but the island boys did not seem to notice it. I reported to the sergeant major that no boats were to be seen but he did not appear to be too concerned and asked me to help him bury the Company box, which contained all the Company funds and records. On second thoughts he distributed all the funds amongst the survivors – the equivalent of twenty-five shillings per man.

The company clerk reported he had spoken to some of the Battalion HQ staff, who informed him that we were surrounded by the enemy; they were giving us one hour to surrender. I refused to believe this and sought out Major Hill, who agreed that the position was critical and asked, 'How are you off for ammunition?'

'Very little left, sir,' I replied and knew then that the ammunition factor could decide whether the 51st Division would be forced to surrender.

Suddenly the shellfire ceased and everything was quiet. Then three German tanks appeared with a high-ranking officer in the first vehicle. At the time we did not recognise him but later learned that it was Brigadier General Rommel. Following the tanks came battalions of infantry, with many of the officers speaking fluent English. Without fuss they instructed us to place our rifles and bayonets in one pile and the remainder of our equipment on a grassy bank above the road.

To say we were shocked would be an understatement. As infantry soldiers we had at some time imagined ourselves wounded or even killed but now our only thought was the humiliation of the Highland Division surrendering. Some time after our arrival in France a French Liaison Officer was attached to the Battalion. He held the rank of Lieutenant and was very popular with all ranks because of his ability to obtain almost anything the Battalion requested and to sort out the many problems arising with the French authorities. On the morning of the surrender he calmly walked towards the German tanks and was given a very enthusiastic welcome by the enemy officers. Our troops soon let him know our thoughts and the island boys reverted to Gaelic to express their opinion of him.

The March

The following days are very difficult to record. So far as I can recollect we were formed into a large crocodile nearly one mile long and comprising possibly six thousand prisoners. I made my way up the column until I saw Major Hill, who had taken over command of the Battalion in the last few days. He told me that all prisoners were free agents and if they wished to attempt an escape they were at liberty to try. German guards now accompanied the column, one every five yards on either flank. They were for the most part elderly men who behaved very well towards us. However, they warned us that in a few days the Hitler Youth Movement would be taking over from them and we would need to be on our best behaviour.

For the first three days we were escorted cross-country through crop fields and meadows with huge barbed-wire enclosures constructed along our route at the points where we were timed to arrive each evening. We had our water bottles filled each morning for the day's march but it was 15 June, the third day of captivity, before we were given anything to eat. This consisted of a slice of rye bread and one of our own tins of M & V rations between two. I should explain that the trucks containing our rations had been driven west during the retreat but any that had reached Dieppe had been looted by the French Army, most of whom had given up fighting about the end of May. They also rifled our NAAFI supplies and attempted to sell them to us at inflated prices whilst on the march to captivity.

On the afternoon of 13 June we were encouraged by the sight of a solitary Spitfire which flew down the column at a height of 100 feet. We assumed it was from a Canadian squadron as it sported a maple leaf on the wings.

By the third day of captivity we were all feeling pretty low. The small towns or villages through which we passed were now crammed with German infantry and, as the French inhabitants had already fled, the enemy troops were busily engaged in looting the houses. In the main square of one town the invaders had set up a wooden platform and on it strutted an exact replica of Mr Chamberlain, complete with heavy black moustache, top hat, morning jacket, striped trousers and carrying a rolled umbrella. The guards halted the column opposite the platform while the spectating troops roared with laughter and shouted, 'So you hang out your washing on the Siegfried line, *Schottlander*!' This went on for some time until the spectators fell silent. Then, all of a sudden, loud and clear came a voice which could only have belonged to a Gordon, demanding, 'Dis this feel loon nae ken we've got Churchill noo?' This gave us a great lift and we cheered for some minutes until the guards decided that their joke had fallen flat and re-started the column, leaving the spectators scratching their heads.

During the first three days the French prisoners were twice fed on tins of sausage and black bread but no attempt was made to feed the British. By this time we were feeling very weak, for it must be remembered that for the past fortnight we had had very irregular periods of sleep and no regular meals. We were usually allowed to fill our water bottles each evening but by noon on the following day they would be empty and by evening our throats were parched and swollen. There were several wells in each village but any attempt to reach these water points brought a fusillade of shots from the guards, although it was clear they aimed above our heads.

On the eighth day of captivity the guards were changed and we found that the Hitler Youth had taken over. Their efficiency scared us and we wondered how the Allies would ever be a match for them. In the afternoon two prisoners made a break for a dense wood some thirty yards from the route but were gunned down when only half-way to cover. In spite of the obvious danger the temptation to reach a well seemed worth the risk.

B Company runner, John McGlynn, was marching in the file behind me and seeing a well some way ahead said, 'What about it?' and handed me his mess-tin. I took my own from my haversack and together we made a dash for the well. Bullets rattled on the winding gear but John got hold of the handle and started to wind up the bucket. When it appeared it was full of rusty water with green slime floating on the surface but I filled the two mess tins and we fled back to the safety of the column, which we reached just as three additional guards appeared. One of them used his rifle to smash the containers to the ground, spilling our precious water. The green slime remained in the mess tin and I was so angry I flung it in his face. He screamed in anger and we were fortunate to reach the column where I found myself directly behind a Gordon piper or drummer who was wearing a glengarry. I grabbed his hat and thrust my balmoral into his hand whispering to him that the guard was after me and the exchange would probably save my life. The guard had by this time taken up his former position and I watched him search the ranks, but I was now wearing a glengarry so he paid no attention to me.

Escape

My companion was very keen to make a break at the first opportunity and this came sooner than expected. When passing through the small village of Béthencourt-sur-Somme the column was halted for a ten-minute rest and as we lay on the roadside McGlynn spotted a deep ditch overgrown with nettles. A few minutes later, undetected by the guards, we crawled along the ditch until we were five yards from the road. At that moment we heard the prisoners being formed up for the march. Some of the sentries led Alsatian dogs and we feared the animals would discover us but eventually the column moved off and the route was deserted.

We climbed through a hedge to find we were in an overgrown garden with bushes of ripe red currants – how good they tasted. After a few minutes we heard voices and a French woman with her little boy appeared in the garden. I asked her if it was safe to hide in the bushes but she told me that all the houses were occupied by enemy troops and that a curfew was in operation during the hours of darkness. She sent the little boy to their house and he re-appeared with six eggs and a jug of milk. We swallowed the raw eggs and drank the milk while the lady pointed out a group of buildings about a mile away which she called Bachimont Farm. As it was far from the route nationale she did not think the Germans would visit it for at least a few days.

As soon as darkness fell John and I set off across the fields and reached the farm just before dawn. Approaching it with great care we made our way to the barn where we soon fell asleep in the warm dry hay. I awoke in broad daylight to the sound of milking pails being carried to the byre, which contained about twenty cows. They were being hand-milked by a man and a girl, and they were quite shocked when we emerged from the barn.

They turned out to be a Belgian brother and sister, Victor and Marta d'Hayer, who had been tenants of Bachimont Farm for a number of years. When the milking was finished we were taken to the kitchen and given *soupe* (bread and milk) and coffee. Afterwards Victor produced some of his old working clothes which we exchanged for our battle dress. Then we proceeded to dig a hiding place in the nearby woods and another hole in which we buried our army equipment. During the day we lay in our hiding-place in the thick undergrowth and, as instructed by Victor, returned to the farmhouse after dark. Marta had prepared another pot of *soupe* and we both consumed a bowlful before returning to our hiding place to sleep peacefully until the sun was high in the sky.

The following morning Victor instructed us to fell three fairly large trees and saw up the logs for the kitchen fire. Each morning Marta handed us a flask of coffee which she had ground from a few coffee beans and a large quantity of acorns. The following day Victor announced that we could help him harvest a field of sugar beet as he was sure the Germans were so intent on reaching Paris and the Channel coast that they would not take time to search isolated farms. That day we discovered we were only three miles from the main road bridge over the River Somme south of Abbeville.

John and I had seen a few roe deer in the woods and Victor brought a roll of wire from the farm from which we fashioned a few snares and attached them to low trees on the many deer tracks. The following morning we went round our snares and discovered a well-conditioned roe in one of them. After bleeding it, we carried it to the farmhouse where we had an enthusiastic reception as food was generally becoming scarce. Once at the farm we skinned the carcase and hung it up in a fly-proof room. Victor could not understand why I was so knowledgeable in the skinning and cutting-up of the roe until I explained I was a gamekeeper's son and as a schoolboy had assisted with the skinning of red deer at the larder.

In addition to the milk cows Victor and Marta kept two bullocks, half-a-dozen calves and a fully-grown pig which they planned to kill the following week. One day they told us that German troops had been visiting neighbouring farms taking away their best stock and hoped they would keep away from Bachimont.

However, it was not to be and one evening when we arrived for supper we found Victor very angry and Marta in tears. The Germans had arrived in the afternoon and gone off with one bullock and the pig, which was to have provided meat for the coming winter. Fortunately, they had not discovered the roe, which by this time had been salted in a tub. The officer in charge of the raiding party issued Victor with a very complicated receipt which promised payment immediately the Army of Occupation became organised. When I visited Victor in 1968 he was still waiting for payment and his remarks about the Boche were most uncomplimentary. About this time we both felt that, should we be discovered by enemy patrols, we would be endangering Victor and Marta, so we decided to move on. We planned to make for the Channel coast round about the mouth of the Somme on the chance that we could acquire a small boat or dinghy to take us across to England.

However, the day before our intended departure we heard explosions from the direction of Amiens. Three workers who were helping Victor with his harvest became very excited. According to them the Australians had landed in France and were advancing westwards. The Aussies had created a tremendous impression on the French in the First World War but I was of the opinion that their report was just wishful thinking.

The explosions increased in volume and John and I set off in an easterly direction. We were soon convinced that it was not gunfire and indeed this proved to be only too true. When we approached a route nationale we found German troops demolishing all roadside buildings which had been damaged by shellfire and flame-throwers in their recent advance. We were both very disappointed but set off on our return to Bachimont as it was near curfew time.

To make matters worse it had started to rain heavily and we were thoroughly soaked and very hungry. We reached the farm about midnight but found the barn and all sheds locked up so we had to return to our retreat in the woods, where we found an inch of water in our sleeping trench. There was nothing else we could do so we lay down in the water and tried to get some sleep. John had made some joke about tightening our laces to keep our hearts from getting down to our boots, when something made me ask, 'John, do you ever pray?'

After a long pause John replied, 'My mother was a very good-living person and she insisted that my sister and I attend church and Sunday School until we were eleven or twelve years. I suppose some of the teaching rubbed off on me but I'm afraid I can't remember when I last prayed.'

'Well,' I said, 'what about praying now for some encouragement in the days which lie ahead?'

'Right,' he replied, and we lay together in our dripping wet hiding place and prayed that we might have the way pointed out to us.

It was so cold and we felt so hungry that I doubt if we slept at all so I was glad when the first signs of daylight filtered through. During the night we heard aircraft fly over at a very low altitude but I had forgotten about it when I forced myself to rise and pull back the groundsheet which had kept the worst of the rain off. In the clearing round our hiding place I was amazed to see thousands of leaflets scattered on the grass and bushes, every one showing a map of France with the area in the south shown as *France Libre*.

'John,' I shouted, 'our prayers have been answered!'

For the next couple of hours we pored over the message dropped from the skies and decided that we would make for Free France and the south the following day. Later on we made our way back to the farm, showed Victor and Marta the leaflets and broke the news that we would be leaving next morning. Marta started immediately to bake bread and cook a haunch of venison for our journey. They were both sorry to see us go but, although they did not mention it, I think they were quite relieved as the Germans had visited them twice in three days and they would have been severely punished had they been discovered harbouring British soldiers. Victor produced a torn map and advised us to pass St Ouen and then strike south for Amiens.

Re-captured

On the second night we made good progress over rolling green fields and lay up in a wheat field as dawn was breaking. From this position we had a grandstand view of an early morning attack on Amiens airfield by six Blenheim aircraft. Six enemy fighters engaged them, but the battle only lasted five minutes; we counted five bombers crashing in flames, but thought that the sixth, flying at tree-top height, probably escaped.

The sight really depressed us and we lay all day in the wheat, only venturing out when darkness fell. We made for the nearest forest, but the moon had now come up and we felt we would be clearly visible to any sentry. We made for the safety of the trees and were within five yards of our goal when there was a loud shout – '*Hender Hoch*' – and there stood two sentries in the shadows pointing their Schmeisser machine pistols at a range of two yards. There was nothing we could do so we raised our hands and were prisoners again. I felt a bit depressed but John insisted, 'We escaped once so we can do it again.'

Our captors shut us up in an army transport with a sentry at each door. They appeared to be an anti-aircraft unit and had posted their guns at the comers of the wood. The sentries gave us bread and water and, as there was nothing we could do, we

lay down and slept until daylight. In the morning we were interviewed by the unit Intelligence Officer, who spoke quite good English. At first we tried to convince him that we were Belgian refugees but he was having none of it and said he knew we were English. He showed us a poster in English stating that we were liable to be shot for wearing civilian clothes, and then gave orders that we sweep out the barn on a near-by farm with two guards watching over us.

Later in the day we were uplifted by a German army truck and our journey into captivity continued. In the evening we were deposited at a barbed wire enclosure which contained about thirty men of the Rifle Brigade, who had defended Calais until caught up in Rommel's advance. Some of them had escaped after a short time in the bag, but had been picked up after a few days freedom.

Our fellow prisoners reckoned we were just inside Belgium, not far from the German border, so John and I decided that the sooner we made a move the better. However, the guards gave us little opportunity and for a week we marched steadily eastwards. We felt the inhabitants of the towns through which we passed were sympathetic to us; occasionally some of the older women would give us a scrap of bread or an egg. Suddenly the atmosphere changed and when the children began to spit on us we knew we were in Germany. Three days later we were uplifted by civilian transport and in the afternoon were herded into barges which took us through a network of canals and waterways. While waiting to disembark I noticed a pencil marking on the woodwork and found this was the names of two of the 4th Seaforths – at least the Division had come this way and the thought cheered us up. The following day we continued our march into Germany and were surprised and heartened to meet a huge column of men in civilian rags, heading in the opposite direction. I asked a fellow prisoner, a Frenchman, who these poor chaps were, and he said he believed them to be displaced persons from eastern Europe who were being taken to industrial areas of the Saar where they would be used as slave labour in the munitions factories.

I felt that if we could join this column we would at least be marching in the right direction and when I explained this to John he agreed that if we could escape from our column we could lie in wait for the next slave labour detachment.

The Second Escape

Two days later we were herded into an enormous farmyard and steadings, where we spent the night in fairly comfortable conditions, apart from the fact that we were only fed every second day and were permanently ravenous. In the morning, when we lined up to have our water-bottles filled, we spotted a high pile of sawn logs and brushwood in the corner of the yard. This looked a likely place so we both edged towards it and while the guards were busy supervising the water distribution we managed to climb the log pile, pull some brushwood over us and lie still.

From the German commands we knew they were preparing the prisoners for the day's march and were soon thankful to hear the sound of marching feet die away in an easterly direction. Three or four men continued to work in the yard and spoke to one another in a language we couldn't recognise. About mid-day they appeared to knock off so we descended from our hiding place and made for a line of trees and scrub about three hundred yards away. No one was to be seen and we were delighted to find the trees and scrub were on a railway embankment. It was very similar to any found in the UK with a tangled mass of ash and red-stemmed dogwood giving ideal shelter.

We lay in the thicket for half-an-hour and could hear a never-ending stream of traffic somewhere beyond the railway line. This proved to be from a highway running parallel to and about two hundred yards north of the railway. A constant stream of military traffic, mostly travelling west, continued throughout the day, and we recognised many British military trucks, which had possibly been captured by the enemy at Dunkirk or St Valery.

About half-a-mile along the railway line there appeared to be

a station with considerable sidings and two spare engines. In the afternoon a train from the east passed along above us but did not stop at the station. John was keen to lie up nearer the station on the chance that a train might stop and we might be able to stow aboard a wagon. I was not too happy at this idea as the cover appeared to thin out near the station, but we finally decided it was worth the risk and were making our way towards the sidings when a train from the east pulled in to the station and stopped.

Encouraged by the fact that few railwaymen were to be seen we made our way along the track, taking cover between the wagons. John noticed that the fifth rear wagon was a different type with long girders, on which what we took to be gun barrels were stacked crosswise. We climbed on to the girders directly below the barrels, praying that they were securely in place and prepared for our journey to the west. Although the day had been very warm the light was now fading and the sun disappearing down the railway line. Fortunately the girders had raised edges and we were able to grip them as we lay on the cold iron surface.

Round about midnight we heard shouts and whistles then the sound of brakes being released and in a few minutes we were on our way. For the first hour we were reasonably comfortable but then our hands began to feel numb and by the time we had been three hours on the journey we decided to abandon our transport. The train was travelling very slowly and we doubted if we had covered more than fifty miles. Then, quite unexpectedly, we heard the brakes being applied and the train ground to a halt. We descended from the girders and could see enemy soldiers on the platform. We knew there would be no time to lose so, keeping in the shadows, we made our way to the rear of the train. Luck was with us and soon we were amongst signal boxes from where we made our way along an embankment to a field of stooked grain, where we pulled some sheaves over us and went to sleep.

When we awoke we felt weak with hunger as it was now two days since we had eaten. We decided we must be near the Belgian or Dutch border and in the afternoon we set out for a wooded area some two hundred yards north of the highway.

Once again our luck held and we walked into a gooseberry bush
laden with ripe red gooseberries. I could hardly believe our
good fortune as we stripped the branches and crunched the
juicy fruit. As we filled our pockets John remembered he had
seen an empty tin on the railway crossing and went back to
retrieve it; we filled it with the remaining berries and set out
again for the west.

During the night we made good progress and did not meet
with any guards or curfew breakers. Although the national route
was still crammed with empty transport there was no sign of the
civilian population. When we came to an isolated farm we found
it was deserted, with the cattle abandoned in a nearby field. We
managed to corner a cow beside the steading and I was able to
milk about two quarts into the tin which John had used to carry
the gooseberries. After this he went in search of the henhouse
and returned with a dozen eggs. We broke one of the farmhouse
windows and were delighted to find the kitchen with its
contents intact so we lit the wood stove and were soon sitting
round a pan of fried eggs. After our meal we hard-boiled the
remaining eggs and found two tins of meat and some rice in the
kitchen cupboard; all this we put in a sack in preparation for the
following day. That night we slept on real beds for the first time
for months.

The following morning we rose at dawn and after a splendid
breakfast of meat and eggs we set off in high spirits. We had no
further worries about food as we relied on the deserted farms to
provide us with milk and eggs. About mid-day we came to
another lonely farm and after watching it for some time we tried
the door and found it unlocked. Entering the kitchen we found
an elderly man making scrambled eggs. He was very frightened
but looked much happier when we told him who we were.

I asked in French if the farm was in Belgium, Germany or
France and we were relieved to hear it was Belgium. He pointed
to the direction from which we had come and said 'Aachen',
then turning to the west he said 'Namur', and turning to the
south said 'Luxembourg'. On hearing that we wished to return
to France he advised us to keep to the open country parallel to

the national routes and this would eventually take us to the Cambrai/St Quentin region. He stressed that we should not use the main roads, but he did not expect the Germans to raid the isolated farms until they became hungry. His last piece of advice was that we both collect a small bundle of firewood and carry them on our backs, hoping the enemy would take us for farm workers and if we could pick up a spade or a hoe so much the better. As we left he wished us '*Bonne Chance*' and said we would make St Quentin in about two weeks.

Occupied France

The next ten days are very difficult to sort out. We kept heading west through marshes and scrub country and I doubt if we averaged more than fifteen miles a day. One night we landed in a sewage farm and after falling into innumerable ditches and canals we wondered why we were doing all this. John declared that the enemy would be able to smell us long before they could see us. Finally, after a two hour struggle with barbed wire, we got clear. Next day we came to a slow-flowing but clean stream where we stripped off and washed ourselves. As we lay on the bank waiting for our clothes to dry we could not decide whether it was the River Aisne or the Oise but we agreed if we followed it we would be bound to be getting nearer Free France.

We were again getting short of food, but one afternoon as we were resting on the bank of a river overlooking a deep muddy pool I saw the mud being disturbed and suggested to John that there were fish in the pool. Right away he proceeded to separate a strand of the rope which he had used to carry his bundle of firewood, and in a few minutes he had a ten-foot line. A staple from a near-by fence was fashioned into a rough hook and we obtained half-a-dozen earthworms under some riverside stones. John then cut a willow wand and we were in business. The baited line was dropped in the deep water and we sat down to await results. After a few minutes we saw the line slowly cutting the surface and I called John to give it plenty of time. Suddenly he swung the pole round his head, and an eel measuring nearly

three feet was wriggling on the bank behind him. I took out my
knife, cut the eel's head off, recovered the hook and passed it to
John to rebait. In a very short time another eel joined the first
one so I cut them both up and packed pieces into the tin we had
picked up on the railway crossing. A short way down the river
we came to an island and, wading through shallow water, we
reached a good hiding place. There was plenty of dry grass and
sticks and soon a small fire was burning, on which we boiled our
can of water and the eel steaks. In a short time they were cooked
and tasted delicious. Although a pinch of salt would have
improved the feast we were not complaining. That night we
slept on the island and next morning continued down river.

When the Germans overran France the French authorities
removed all signs and direction boards, hoping to confuse the
invaders by their being unable to identify smaller towns. By the
time half of France was in German hands they did not consider
their precautions served any purpose. The signs had been
replaced and we were greatly encouraged when we reached
the small town of Pontoise. It confirmed we had followed the
River Oise and were certain we could not be far from the River
Seine.

Just south of Pontoise a French farm labourer pointed out to
us the line of the Seine, but warned that there were German
checkpoints on every bridge. Having crossed a route nationale,
we took a small side road which led us to Meulan. Just outside
the town we bought bread and cheese at a small café and
counted our worldly wealth; John had 120 francs and I had
90. From here we could see the river, which looked very wide
with a strong current; but it held no terrors for my companion,
who was a powerful swimmer. We spotted a shingle bank about
mid-stream and reckoned we could make it by resting for a time
at the half-way stage.

It was now the middle of summer and as there was no
question of the cold affecting us we tied our clothes round
our necks and set out for the south bank. We took off from well
up-stream but soon found the current was much stronger than
we anticipated. It carried us downstream until we were opposite

the tail of the shingle and it was only a desperate effort that eventually took us there.

We lay on the filthy gravel for twenty minutes and then prepared for the next leg. John had gone to look for a likely taking-off place when I heard him calling, 'Come to see this'. I found him in a little backwater which had cut into the shingle, looking at three bodies – one woman and two men. The female had her throat cut and one of the male bodies was minus a head.

The second leg of the crossing was surprisingly easy. The main channel had a very strong current but when we took off we allowed the stream to carry us downriver, swimming at an angle of 45 degrees and in a matter of minutes we found we were being carried to the south bank and were able to scramble ashore at the base of a railway embankment. We spread our clothes on a narrow concrete ledge and lay in the sun for nearly two hours until they dried out. We then crossed another route nationale by a railway bridge and in the distance could see what we took to be the palace of Versailles.

We took care to bypass any sizeable towns lest they be occupied by enemy troops and finally stopped at a small country café due west of Versailles, deserted except for the proprietor. He supplied us with bread and cheese and a tin of horsemeat, but when he heard we were on the run refused our offer of payment and insisted that we accept a large bag of cherries and apples. He also informed us that Hitler was expected in Paris the following day to gloat over his prize. Our friend had a torn map of northern France which he was glad to offer us and, with rising spirits, we set off for Free France. Before sleeping in an empty barn that night we reckoned we had covered forty kilometres and swum the Seine in the one day.

From the map given us at the café we took advantage of the narrow side roads and followed the Seine in a south-easterly direction. The enemy had apparently completed their dash to the Channel and were now occupying all the towns and villages in central France. They made every effort to make friends with the local population, many of whom had given up hope and were prepared to fall in with German wishes. We found the majority of the gendarmes were sympathetic to the Allies and were prepared to assist us. They directed us from the Seine Valley to the course of the River Yonne, where we had our first major contact with the German army since the capitulation at St Valery.

Pay the Ferryman!

The River Yonne, a tributary of the Seine, was only a matter of forty or fifty yards wide and we were prepared to swim it should there be a checkpoint at Pont-sur-Yonne. When we arrived there we found the bridge had been blown and a huge barge which now bridged the stream had been substituted. On the barge sat three German officers with three or four clerks, who stamped the passes of the French civilians if they considered they were on legitimate business.

John and I had no identity papers so we walked down the bank looking for a suitable crossing place. We had found a small wooden jetty when suddenly a small coracle emerged from the rushes of the far bank. At the oars was an elderly priest, clad in a long black cloak and black headgear and, as the current was not very strong, he had no difficulty in manoeuvring the craft to the landing stage below us. John jumped down and held the boat until the old man scrambled ashore. He looked at us and asked, '*Anglais?*'

'*Ecossais,*' we replied and then, pointing to the boat, he told us to take it back across the stream and tie it to a tree on the far bank. He would cross by the checkpoint in the afternoon and recover the boat. At that moment the entire personnel manning the checkpoint were engaged in manhandling a German staff car on to the barge at the far side.

Our boat did not appear to be very sound and the oars were barrel staves but we both got aboard and I remember thinking it was exactly like what the South Harris folk use to ferry their peats home on the Lochs Morracha and Steisevat at Leverburgh. We had barely reached half-way when there were loud shouts from up-stream and a German officer and a sergeant came running down the path. Our hearts sank; we were convinced they were coming to check our papers but to our great relief they only wanted a passage to the other side. I back-watered the boat to the landing-stage and John helped our two passengers aboard. On the way across the sergeant offered John a cigarette, which he accepted with a smile, but for my part I was scared to look at the officer. However, when we reached the far bank he climbed ashore, put his hand in his front pocket and produced a handful of loose change. Taking a chance I said, '*Dix francs, Monsieur,*' whereupon he took two coins from his collection and threw them on the floorboards. John was after the coins in a flash and reappeared from the boat with twenty francs. Although our passengers were still very near us he announced, 'Twenty francs, what a gentleman, we'll drink his health at the next café!'

By a strange coincidence Captain Lang, our adjutant, escaped from Belgium and made his way south some six weeks later. He was contacted by the same priest, who told him how the two Scots had charged the Germans and it was only when he finally reached Marseilles that he learned from the Rev. Donald Caskie that the two 'Jocks' involved were from his own battalion. He took very much pleasure in recording it at some length in his book *Return to St Valery.*

There was now a very strict curfew imposed by the enemy on the country villages and from this point we took care to be off the roads by nine o'clock, when their motor-cycle patrols covered all routes. One evening we had a further encounter with occupying troops which gave us considerable confidence.

We were very tired, having covered some forty or fifty kilo-metres, and were approaching a group of farm buildings when, in the gathering darkness, we came on a capsized farm cart and horse lying on the tarred road. The horse was struggling to get to its feet and the shafts of the cart were in real danger of being reduced to matchwood. The two teenage girls in charge were reduced to tears. John knelt on the animal's neck and the girls and I set about 'lowsing' the horse. We had just succeeded and were endeavouring to withdraw the horse from between the trams when, with a roar from their motor-cycle combination, two German soldiers arrived. Taking in the situation at a glance they leapt off their machine and dragged the cart clear of the horse. While John and I got the horse to its feet the girls made a great show of thanking the soldiers and edged them away from us and, when one came forward to recover the horse, she loudly thanked us and said goodnight.

We continued on our way and the soldiers, having yoked the cart, started up their motor-cycle and passed us at speed, giving us a friendly wave in passing. At the farmhouse we found one of the girls waiting at the roadside and we were invited in for a very good meal, followed by a good night's rest in the barn.

Vichy France

At this stage we decided that it was becoming dangerous to travel on routes nationaux as every town was occupied by enemy troops, who accompanied the gendarmes on all check-points and bridges. After ten days travelling we found ourselves on the outskirts of Orleans, where we were fortunate to be picked up by two gendarmes on cycles. They insisted that we accompany them to their station where we had visions of being handed over to the Germans. We were surprised when, in the safety of their headquarters, they explained they were anxious to help escaping British troops and gave us an excellent meal and fifty francs each. They advised us that the enemy were making use of the rivers Loire and Cher to establish the demarcation line between Free and Occupied France and that it would be very difficult to get through the checkpoints.

After much discussion they advised us to make our way to Blois on the Loire where a railway and a road bridge crossed the wide river. Blois railway station was being used as a collection point for thousands of Belgians who had fled when their country was invaded and the Germans were now rounding them up and returning them to their homeland. Our friends thought we might mix with the refugees and in the confusion might make our way across the railway bridge. They insisted that the crossing of the Cher was still our major obstacle and suggested that we should try the checkpoint near the town of Vierzon. They were a mine of information and before we bade them goodbye they advised us that if we managed to make Free France we should make for Châteauroux where the French army, on German orders, were demobbing all French farm workers.

Two days later we were making good progress towards Vierzon and were proceeding along a long straight road bounded by poplar trees when a German troop carrier drew up beside us. The driver, a bareheaded youth, jumped from his vehicle, saluted smartly and politely asked if we could direct him to Mont Vitesse. I had no idea where it was and my only wish was to get rid of him so I replied, 'Fifteen kilometres, straight on'. He saluted again, stepped into his truck and drove off. As usual John had the last word, 'A nice chap, but I nearly put him on a charge for saluting without a bunnet on!'

At Blois everything turned out according to plan and, mixed with the Belgian refugees at the crossing, we found it very easy to cross the bridge. John nearly upset our plan by getting slightly involved with a very pretty fair-haired girl, who pleaded with him to return to Belgium with her. Uncertain of what was in store for us when we reached the Demarcation Line, we bedded down early that evening in a wheat field that had recently been cut. It had been a very hot day and the sheaves were dry and warm so we used four of them for a mattress and pulled two others apart and covered ourselves with straw.

The sun was well up when we awoke and set off on the five kilometre walk to Vierzon. The town was very busy and all roads seemed to lead to the river crossing but we were allowed to cross the bridge without our papers being asked for – which was fortunate as we had none. Just beyond the far end sat four German officers with some clerks and half-a-dozen police interviewing those who wanted to cross.

We stood in the queue for some time until we realised that everyone, including even farm servants, had papers and concluded that our chances of being allowed through were slim indeed. Across the street John spotted a café and suggested that we should have a glass of beer there and think it over. On entering the doorway we discovered to our horror there were a dozen enemy infantrymen sprawled on rough benches drinking beer. It was too late to turn back so we picked a bench as far as possible from the enemy troops and when the attractive girl approached us I ordered two beers.

From where we sat we could look into the café kitchen and could see the girl in earnest conversation with a middle-aged woman. We saw her point towards us and when she came with our drinks she said in a whisper, '*Etes-vous Anglais?*' I nodded and she went to serve a noisy German who was shouting for more beer. When she returned we had finished our drinks and as she collected the empties she whispered, '*Suivez moi.*' We waited for a couple of minutes and then wandered towards the kitchen, where the elderly woman appeared to be in full control. She ordered us to follow the girl through a door leading from the café.

'*Vite, vite!*' she said and we followed our guide down a long earthen passage which we could feel sloped downwards. It got darker and she took my hand while I reached back to hold John's jacket and we proceeded in this way for quite a distance. Then she climbed over a large stone block and we could see daylight ahead. A few yards on we came to a flight of rough stone steps which climbed steeply to an overgrown garden filled with shrubs and nettles. When we reached the high garden wall she signalled us to climb over and drop some six or seven feet to a sunken road on the other side.

She looked over and said, '*Bonne chance, maintenant vous êtes en France Libre.*' John said to me, 'I wish I could speak the lingo. Tell her I'll come back to see her some day.' I relayed John's message to her and she flashed him a smile, '*Mais oui Monsieur – apres la guerre fini,*' and she was gone.

We were elated – hadn't we covered one thousand kilometres of enemy and enemy-occupied country and were now in neutral territory where we could expect help from the inhabitants? John was singing songs of Bonnie Scotland at the top of his voice and we felt it was only a matter of keeping going and we'd soon be back in Blighty. We were passing a small cottage on the roadside and when we reached the far gable we were horrified to see two German motor-cyclists doing maintenance on their machines. They regarded us with suspicion so we strolled casually on until we were out of sight and then crawled into a hayfield. Minutes later we heard the motor-cycles start up and they passed by our hiding place heading south.

It was a bitter blow to us when we realised that the Demarcation Line was a sham and we decided not to continue our journey until after dark. We slept for a few hours in the tall grass and later heard men and women passing along the road. Satisfied there was no longer a curfew, we set out on the road to Châteauroux as advised by the friendly gendarmes at Orleans.

The next day was very hot and we were exhausted by the time we reached the town in mid-afternoon. At the outskirts we came across a vast conglomeration of wooden shacks and army tents, which we rightly guessed was the Agricultural Demob Centre. We reported to the Guard Commander, who asked some questions which we must have answered to his satisfaction, for he called a corporal who took us to the cookhouse where we were given a tin of French 'bully', a bunch of dandelions and a small black loaf between us. For three francs we purchased a tin of sour red wine and were told by the corporal to find an empty tent where we could stay for the night.

New Friends

We found one near the main gate and passed the time watching new arrivals. We were about to turn in when two men approached our tent to ask where shelter was available. They were an odd-assorted pair, one tall and strapping with a mass of golden hair and very well dressed while the other was a very small fellow, dressed in very dilapidated working clothes. The taller one appeared to be in charge and spoke very correct French and, while I was trying to direct him to the cookhouse, I heard the small man addressing John.

'I think you're Jocks,' he said.

'Sure,' said John, 'we're Camerons.'

'That's great,' said the small man, 'I'm Jimmy McGowan from Greenock and the 7th Argylls.'

We invited them to share our tent, and after they had eaten we talked long into the night. The immaculate Frenchman was Sergeant André Varnier of the French Engineers and he was determined to join the Free French forces in Britain. When the French Army ceased to exist in June 1940 he avoided capture and fell in with McGowan at a French military hospital, where the latter had been taken after being wounded on the Bresle front. Varnier appeared to have all the answers and, although McGowan was rather suspicious of him, he reckoned it was in his interest to throw in his lot with him.

Next day we discussed the situation and, as neither McGlynn or McGowan spoke French, I had to relay the conversation as best I could. We finally agreed that Varnier and McGlynn would proceed about two hundred yards in advance of wee Jimmy and myself and that we would head for Limoges via Argenton, a good three days' journey away.

I was a bit annoyed at the pairing suggested by Varnier. While I did not dislike McGowan, he proved to have complaints about everything in general and I missed the happy-go-lucky atmosphere prevailing when I was with McGlynn. On the other hand, John had to listen to accounts of Varnier's prowess on the football field. He appeared to have been a star at left back in the French league team, Côte du Midi, and he never tired of relating his experiences. On the second day, just as light was beginning to fade, we came to a farm where three young boys were kicking a football about. Although we were very tired the attraction proved too strong and we joined them until darkness fell. It was obvious that André was quite an experienced footballer but what puzzled us was that he was completely left-footed. I asked him if he had had a right-leg injury at any time but he assured me that he always preferred playing on the left side of the field.

When we finished, André went to the farmhouse to ask

permission to sleep in the barn while John and Jimmy lay down on a heap of straw in the cart shed. When I entered and asked, 'Well, what do you think of the Côte du Midi?' They were almost asleep; but after some time John replied, 'He's got a grand left fit.' But wee Jimmy chipped in, 'That's right, but his right leg is only for staundin' on!'

This happened fifty years ago and it was the first time I had heard the expression so I was very amused. Months later this was repeated in Whitehall when two sergeants named André Varnier were being interrogated by British Intelligence.

The following day McGowan gave me a very interesting account of what had happened when he and Varnier were passing through Orleans about ten days before they fell in with us. Jimmy explained that they were very short of money but Varnier informed him that he had an aunt living in the town and was sure she would provide him with funds to help them to Marseilles or to cross the Pyrenees into Spain. Jimmy was left in a dense thicket on the outskirts of the town and his companion promised he would collect him in the late afternoon or early evening. McGowan spent a miserable day, tortured by clegs and midges until he could stand it no longer so he walked into the town centre and parked on a seat opposite the German Kommandantur.

He watched the comings and goings of many senior officers until suddenly at the top of a long flight of steps appeared Varnier, accompanied by what McGowan took to be a German major. When Jimmy joined him some time later he mentioned he had seen him leave the German HQ. Varnier explained that the building had belonged to his aunt before the invasion and he had gone to enquire if they knew of the whereabouts of the lady.

'The Germans,' said Varnier, 'were not interested.'

Jimmy concluded his story by telling me that from that day his companion had plenty of money and they never went hungry again.

With Varnier acting as spokesman we were accepted at a French Demob Centre at Limoges, where we stayed for two days. We then resumed our journey into the barren, hilly country south of the town. There were occasional commercial vehicles on the roads but, although we tried to flag them down, none stopped. One morning Jimmy and I were proceeding up a steep hill some two hundred yards behind John and André when a heavy lorry loaded with stone chips passed us at a fair speed but began to slow down as the hill became steeper. We started to run and after a few hundred yards I managed to haul myself on to the tailboard to find John and Varnier already aboard. However, the effort proved too much for wee Jimmy and he collapsed on the roadway. I jumped down hoping to get him to his feet but just at that moment the truck reached the top of the hill and as it accelerated away Jimmy and I were left behind. Once we had rested, Jimmy announced he was ready to carry on and we set out on the road again.

Some months later when I finally contacted John at the Cameron barracks in Inverness, he filled in all the blanks. After the truck had reached the summit the road ran due south for three or four miles. As it was driven at breakneck speed, they were both unable to leave the vehicle until it turned off on a side road. They then made their way back to the main highway and, finding a piece of chalk stone in a quarry, they scratched a message on the road showing the route they had taken. Meanwhile Jimmy and I continued on our way.

I was very annoyed at losing John and was inclined to blame Varnier. Jimmy had not much to say and did not appear to have any interest in his surroundings but, although he was not good company, I had to admire his courage for his feet from the ankles downwards were red raw but I never heard him complain of the pain.

Two days later we were feeling very tired and hungry when we came to an enormous truck with trailer attached, parked in a lay-by. It appeared to be fuelled by charcoal and carried at least thirty bags on the trailer; a huge turbine took up all the body space. The driver was a friendly old chap who had been in the French Army Transport Corps in WW1 and was very sympathetic towards us. He gave us a slice of bread and a sip of cognac and we began to feel better. After he had had two hours sleep he would clear a place amongst the charcoal sacks for us to lie down on a tarpaulin.

On no account should we allow ourselves to be seen as the Vichy Police in some areas were favourable towards the Germans. He had come from Lille in northern France and his destination was Nîmes, which he reckoned might take four days to reach. Before setting off he persuaded us that Marseilles would be a better bet than the Spanish frontier as a mail boat service was still plying on the North African routes.

At this time I had about fifty francs left and Jimmy had twenty. On the evening of the first day the driver parked in a small town and went round the shops buying provisions to last us for the next two days. In return for our share we insisted that he accept twenty-five francs; when we had eaten he made up our beds amongst the sacks and we were happy to bed down for the night. Sleep was no problem and at six o'clock next morning we were on the road. The driver insisted that we remain hidden when passing through Arles and Nîmes as the RAF had bombed the French Navy warships lest they be handed over to the enemy and had caused many French casualties from that area. This had not yet been forgotten.

The Tartan Pimpernel

At Nîmes we said goodbye to our good friend from Lille and left by a small third-class road which later skirted the Camargue in the delta of the Rhone. It was a vast stretch of swamp and scrub and I was very interested in the wild cattle and horses which seemed to roam at will. I only wished the circumstances were different but I reminded myself that the first priority was to reach Marseilles.

On the long, dusty road into the city there were numerous hamlets and a few small towns. In case the gendarmes were not well-disposed towards us we skirted the towns and on the second evening arrived at a small farm in the suburbs. The owner was very kind and after giving us bread and cheese led us to a cave in a steep bank near the farmhouse, where we slept on some musty hay. Although very tired I couldn't sleep and lay awake wondering what was in store for us. I kept thinking of the way our prayers were answered when the way to Free France was indicated by the leaflets dropped from an Allied plane and had since prayed regularly each night before sleeping. I think this gave me confidence, and never at any time did I doubt that I would eventually make my way back to Britain.

Jimmy and I were up early the following morning, and were directed to the city centre by a street cleaner. Unfortunately he had no idea where the American Embassy was and we eventually reached La Canebière, one of the main streets of the city. We were afraid to ask the gendarmes for directions so we wandered along some of the more prosperous streets without success until we came to a low wall where we rested.

Quite unexpectedly, our prayers were answered. The pavements were crowded with every nationality one could imagine. Suddenly the crowds thinned out, and walking towards us was a pleasant looking man of middle age, dressed in a light cream suit, wearing a soft hat and carrying a walking-stick. On seeing him approach I was convinced he was reliable so, putting on my best French accent, I asked if he could direct me to the American Embassy. He looked me up and down, smiled, and then said, '*Bheil Gàidhlig agad?*' (Have you the Gaelic?)

I paused to consider my reply in French and, suddenly realising he was speaking Gaelic, replied, '*Beagan*' (a little). That was how I met the Rev. Donald Caskie, the Islay man who had been Church of Scotland Minister in Paris before the outbreak of the Second World War. In a few quiet sentences Donald Caskie explained how he made his way south on a bicycle on 18 June, the day Paris fell to the Germans. With help from the American Embassy he took over the British Seamen's Mission at 36 Rue de Forbin, Marseilles, and at the moment was hiding eleven soldiers of the 51st Highland Division. He was ever on the look-out for Scottish soldiers and always addressed them initially in Gaelic.

Jimmy and I accompanied him to the American Consulate where we were well received and given 200 francs each. He then directed us to cross the street and continue for over one mile until we came to Rue de Forbin. He was leaving as soon as possible and would arrive at No. 36 before us. Jimmy and I had not eaten since the previous night so we each purchased a sandwich at a café and were feeling much better when we reached No. 36, where the door was opened by Donald himself. He had two local boys employed in the kitchen, tea was already prepared with two large sandwiches filled with tomato and lettuce – probably the best meal I have ever had.

Once we had eaten, Donald explained the circumstances under which he was prepared to give us temporary lodgings. At the moment his only legitimate lodgers were seven ship-wrecked sailors who could not be interned under international law, made up of two brothers Logan from Kessock Ferry, two deckhands from Glasgow and three Australians. Escaped prisoners of war were in a different category, however. Every few days the Vichy police raided No. 36 and took all military personnel to Fort St Jean, the Headquarters of the French Foreign Legion, where they were interned in an empty part of the twelfth-century fort for the duration of the war.

That evening we were given another meal – a fairly substantial one – and when I asked Donald how on earth he was able to feed them all, he said very gently, 'If you sincerely ask God to provide for you he will never let you down. Since I left Paris some months ago I have ceased to be amazed how I've been delivered from many dangers and tribulations that beset me at every corner.'

He was the most attractive man I've ever met, gentle, good-tempered, completely unflappable and with a wonderful sense of humour. As one Highland soldier said, 'He gave us hope when we had none.'

Jimmy and I slept soundly that night but at five o'clock next morning Donald awakened me to ask if I would accompany him in search for the day's food. Carrying two large sacks we made our way along the Quai Joliette to where the Cypriot boats were berthing after their night's fishing. In his friendly way Donald approached the skippers and in five minutes we had our sacks filled without any money changing hands. The fish were very small – only four to five inches long and many had been squashed by the crews tramping on them but Donald accepted them gladly and announced we would have tasty fish soup for at least three days. On the way back we purchased a sackful of bread, although it was becoming scarcer and was very dear.

When France capitulated in June 1940 one of the first actions the enemy took was to establish a German and Italian Harbour Commission to control Marseilles harbour, through which most of the food and materials arrived in France. This enabled the Axis forces to take exactly what they required from the warehouses on the docks. When the British forces withdrew they left a large stock of M & V rations and hard biscuits, which Donald was anxious to obtain before the Harbour Commission confiscated them. By discreet enquiries amongst sympathetic dockers he was able to acquire more than half of the food stored.

After a week in Rue de Forbin I was awakened at three o'clock one morning by knockings and shouts to open the door. This proved to be a squad of Vichy police led by a Gestapo officer from the Harbour Commission. Leaving the shipwrecked sailors in their beds they marched the soldiers, now numbering twenty-two, to Fort St Jean, a forbidding building commanding the harbour.

Here we were shown into a vast, stone-built barrack room where each man was given a ragged blanket. At six o'clock we woke to the sound of the Legion bugles and watched their early morning drill parade through locked iron gates. We then entered the so-called dining room for a breakfast of black bread and horsemeat washed down by red wine. Here we were surprised to find a further thirty soldiers from nearly every regiment in the British army – most of whom had been wounded in the fighting and were interned by the French on their recovery. I suspect that quite a few were deserters.

Amongst the internees were two sergeant majors of the Pioneer Corps who had arrived in France at the beginning of June. They were elderly and refused point-blank to accept responsibility for the discipline of the internees. It was left to Colour Sergeant Leiper of the West Yorks Regiment and me to make a register of all inmates and to take particulars of all new arrivals. It took us a few days to complete the task and from then we posted a detail each morning showing the names of those who would be employed in the cookhouse and in cleaning up the barracks. Usually enough turned up to carry out the different fatigues.

The discipline administered by the French was very lax and soon we were all allowed to leave the barracks for two hours every afternoon on condition that we report back to the draw-bridge guardroom at 5 p.m. prompt. In addition to this, Donald Caskie informed the senior French officer that his only link with the internees was Clr/Sgt MacDonald and that he would require to see him at Rue de Forbin almost every day. This permission was given immediately and soon afterwards I was furnished with a pass signed by the French officer and was able to come and go as I pleased.

The Work of Rev. Donald Caskie

I was amazed at the amount of work Donald packed into each day. He rose at 5.30 each morning and spent the next two hours in search of food, which was becoming increasingly difficult to obtain. By the autumn the numbers of British wounded discharged from French hospitals were steadily increasing and on some nights he would have to provide food and beds for an additional twenty men. Twice a week the French police, accompanied by a Gestapo officer, would raid the premises at about 3 a.m. and all military personnel would be removed to Fort St Jean.

His forenoons were taken up with visits to the American Consulate and long discussions with the French authorities, some of whom proved very helpful to the Allied cause. One day in September 1940 he told me of a visit he had had from a Polish priest who was anxious to obtain a safe retreat for over two hundred Poles who were arriving in southern France in ten days time. They had fought in the German invasion of Poland for six weeks, and had then escaped through Czechoslovakia, Hungary, Austria and Switzerland and finally made it to France. After incredible hardships they found temporary shelter somewhere in the Rhone Valley, but of the seven hundred who left Poland only two hundred and twenty survived.

Anyone else in the circumstances would have considered the Polish request impossible – but not Donald. In three days time he had taken possession of the empty Queen Alexandra Hospital on the eastern outskirts of Marseilles and a week later the Poles were smuggled in under cover of darkness. Donald kept in constant touch with them and they in turn contacted a Greek and a Corsican in the Marseilles underworld who owned a Liberian-registered freighter, the SS *Storm*, which was sufficiently coaled and provisioned to make Gibraltar should the opportunity arise. The Polish padre approached Donald with a view to him furnishing a four-man guard on the ship from among the internees of the fort.

Three days later Donald selected PSM Sandy Moir of the 1st Gordons, a Welsh gunner named Chris and two others who were duly ferried across to the *Storm* on a dark night in the middle of a rainstorm. They lived on board for ten days while Donald bargained with the Poles that the British internees should join them in the escape bid. They were agreeable, but when the owners were informed the price was doubled. Donald was confident that he could raise the additional cash by having a diplomatic messenger sent from Lisbon to Marseilles, but while arrangements were pending a strong force of harbour police boarded the *Storm* and Sandy Moir and his guard were fortunate to escape by swimming to the opposite side of the harbour. Apart from a ten-mile walk back to Fort St Jean they were none the worse.

All the internees in the fort lived for the day when they could return to the UK and many hours were spent discussing escape plans. We actually considered taking over the excursion boat which plied between the Quai Joliette and the Chateau d' If in Marseilles harbour but one of the would-be escapers met some of the crew in a dockside café and learned that the boat was strictly rationed for fuel so our dream of making Gibraltar had to be shelved.

Donald Caskie had been in touch with a British agent who thought it would be possible to reach the Spanish frontier by using the railway line which ran from Marseilles to the frontier via Montpellier, Narbonne and Perpignan, leaving the train when the steep incline between Port-Vendres and Cerbère forced the engine to reduce speed. If the escapers' nerve failed they were arrested when their papers were checked at Cerbère on the frontier and they were escorted back to France for a spell in prison at Toulouse. Those who made it were picked up by the Spanish police and were given a jail sentence at Figueras before being sent to the Concentration Camp at Miranda de Ebro. This route proved very successful over a long period and many escapees who were able to survive Miranda finally made it to Gibraltar and the UK.

About this time a Captain Martini of the Polish Intelligence informed Donald that he suspected the Germans were making use of the French shipping line who ran a thrice-weekly service from Marseilles to Oran and Algiers to ferry men of the enemy Afrika Korps to North Africa. He was of the opinion that the Germans were using the run-down Hotel Britannique as a base. Hundreds of military personnel collected there and were then transported to the docks just before the mail ships were due to sail.

Donald made his plans with attention to every detail and arranged that PSM Moir, a Sergeant Cole of the Royal Artillery Signals and I would meet him at Rue de Forbin on the following afternoon; he explained he had chosen us for a very important task. Each evening, as the light was fading, we would stroll down the pavement to a café exactly opposite the Hotel Britannique, buy a *Paris Soir* evening paper and a glass of beer each. This would have to last until eleven o'clock when we would be free to return to Rue de Forbin. In that time we were required to make a mental note of anything unusual happening at the hotel. Donald supplied us each evening with five francs to cover the beer and the evening paper.

The café proprietor was well aware that we were not French and appeared puzzled as to what our intentions were. He suggested '*Anglais*', but Sandy Moir and I protested and I think we remained a mystery to him. Nothing happened and we concluded we were wasting our time until, at 10.30 p.m. on the fifth night, a large blacked-out coach moved quietly along the street and turned in at the rear of the building. At ten-minute intervals a further four coaches followed and we reckoned that about two hundred and fifty Afrika Korps men had been transported from northern France or even Germany. Two nights later a further five coaches arrived at the hotel.

Captain John Garrow of the Glasgow Highlanders, who by this time was a trusted agent of the French Resistance, volunteered to hang around the docks for the next few nights to check if the occupants were being transferred to the ship. Sure enough, on the third night following their arrival, the five coaches drove through the open dock gates, which the guards closed immediately they were inside. After an hour the gates were opened and the coaches drove out. Captain Garrow thought they looked empty.

These operations were carried on for a few weeks and Donald made a very meticulous note of our reports each time we returned to Rue de Forbin. All the information was contained in a small green notebook in abbreviated Gaelic, which he called 'shorthand Gaelic', and he laughingly declared that no enemy intelligence organisation would ever decipher it. The book was kept behind a loose tile in the living-room fireplace. We were never told where Donald disposed of his reports and we did not ask. He never mentioned British Intelligence to us, but we thought that reports were probably deciphered during his many lengthy visits to the American Consulate, and were possibly passed on from there.

One afternoon about the beginning of November I called at Rue de Forbin to tell Donald I wanted to make arrangements to cross the Pyrenees to Spain before the worst of the winter had begun. To my surprise I found him entertaining Captain Derek Lang, Adjutant of the 4th Cameron Highlanders, who had also been taken prisoner at St Valery and who had escaped from German custody in Belgium. He had always been a great favourite with the Jocks and I was delighted to see him again. We exchanged accounts of our escapes and he recalled how he heard from a priest of the two Scottish soldiers who ferried two Germans across the river Yonne. When I informed him that it was B Company runner John McGlynn and I who were involved he was amused and delighted. 'If I survive to write my story I shall certainly include that', he said.

True to his word, our crossing of the River Yonne was fully reported in his book *Return to St Valery*. In his wanderings through France he had made contact with some influential French families, who had helped him on his way to Marseilles. Here the American Consulate passed him on to Rue de Forbin and he finally managed to persuade the crew of a freighter sailing between Marseilles and Beirut to accept him as a stowaway. After incredible experiences he finally made it to a British base somewhere in Palestine. After serving throughout the desert campaign he commanded the 5th Camerons when in 1944 they retook St Valery and thereby fully avenged the disaster of 1940. After commanding the 51st Division he was in 1966 appointed Army Commander in Scotland and later that year was installed as Governor of Edinburgh Castle. The following year he retired with the rank of Lieut. General. When he left us in Rue de Forbin I wished him good luck and said I would have liked to accompany him.

'Don't worry about that,' said Donald Caskie, 'I think I'll require your services for a very special task sometime around Christmas and it should prove quite exciting.'

Voyage to North Africa

When Captain Lang left I returned to the fort to be told that a Foreign Legion officer wished to see me and had left a note pinned to our dining room door. It was typed in very stilted English, to the effect that the Legion personnel were shortly to be posted back to Sidi bel Abbas. As their numbers were depleted the CO would be grateful if twenty of the internees would assist in carrying down the vast quantity of stores and equipment, initially to be stored at the drawbridge and later loaded on the ship for the journey to Oran. The note stressed that only volunteers would be required.

Next morning I reported to the Legion guardroom with twenty men and was escorted to the office of the sergeant-chef (RSM). In French, he detailed me to report the following day at 8 a.m. and then, to my surprise, lapsed into broken English. He explained he had been a sergeant in the German army in the 1914–18 war and had been taken prisoner on the Somme. He was held for two years in Essex, where he was very well treated by his guards. On repatriation he could not find employment so he returned to France to enlist in the Legion.

'So, you see, *Englander*, I am now a soldier of France.'

'*Schottlander*,' I corrected him and he then went through the motions of playing the bagpipes.

The following day we turned out at 8 a.m. and apart from one hour off at mid-day we worked very hard carrying heavy furniture and all kinds of equipment down a flight of eighty steps and stacking them neatly in the courtyard beside the drawbridge. At noon we returned to our quarters for a meal and were back on duty at 1 p.m. This continued for one week, at the end of which the sergeant-chef told me he had no idea when the actual move would take place.

Taking a chance, I said I was very anxious to cross to North Africa and make my way to Gibraltar and would it be possible to travel with the Legion to Oran?

'Not possible, but you might be able to stow away on the ship.'

This gave me some hope and when I returned to the fort that evening I pondered over his reply and considered all the different methods by which I could make the journey across the Mediterranean.

Next day I went to the Rue de Forbin to tell Donald of my plans to escape to north Africa and he encouraged me to go ahead. I then returned to the Legion quarters and offered to help at the cookhouse. The corporal in charge detailed me to help an Armenian NCO to issue the daily ration of *vin rouge* to all legionnaires and then help prepare the morning coffee. After that I could spend the rest of my day scrubbing and burnishing hundreds of dixies and mess-tins which looked as if they had not been cleaned since the Beau Geste era. I seem to have given a degree of satisfaction in these tasks for after four or five days I was promoted to feeding and cleaning out three pigs which were housed in the rampart.

Every day fresh rumours were in circulation regarding the timing of the departure of the draft for Sidi bel Abbas. The majority of the legionnaires were anxious to return to north Africa but a few wished to remain in France. At this time I got to know about half-a-dozen of the draft and they were indeed a motley assortment. One elderly man spoke and wrote beautiful English and assured us that he had been educated at Cambridge. He left there in disgrace, fought through the Boxer Rebellion in China at the turn of the century and later saw service as a colonel in the Uruguayan Army in the Gran Chaco War. He also served in the 1914–18 War but in 1930 was forced to join the *Légion Etrangère* as, he explained, he was then beginning to run out of wars.

Another character was an Irishman from Limerick who had joined the Metropolitan Police in the early thirties. His name was McPartland and after a few years in the service he became involved with a London gang, led by an Irishman, which specialised in jewel robberies. He was on beat duty around Buckingham Palace when he got the tip that enquiries were being made into his connections with criminal circles, so he took off immediately and landed in France the following day. He finally made his way to Marseilles, crossed to Oran and joined the Legion there. He had a good record of service in Africa but the physical conditions were too demanding and he was now regarded as being mentally off-balance. His special friend was a very handsome young Norwegian who made no secret of his past life. He had been employed by a Norwegian bank, and in broken French he explained he had somehow managed to get the bank's money mixed up with his own!

About this time I was put in a section of ten men commanded by a Corporal Feyt, a Czechoslovakian, who explained to me that so long as I was present on muster parade at 6 a.m. each morning I need not attend any further parades. He was a very smart soldier who seemed to be a cut above the average legionnaire and we became quite friendly.

One day when the entire company were off duty and he was orderly NCO he visited the cook-house. Over a glass of *vin rouge* I learned that he fought against the German army when they overran his country at the beginning of the war. He had been imprisoned for some time but escaped to the west, joined the Legion and fought on the Saar front. He, too, wanted to get to the UK and was most anxious to find out if there were any organised Czech forces in Britain. I had no means of getting this information for him but promised I would make enquiries at the American Consulate.

I do not remember praying for an answer but one evening shortly afterwards I visited Rue de Forbin. I found Donald on top of the world. Having just received a modern radio from an American friend, he was able to get the BBC 6 o'clock news. As we listened it was announced that six Hurricanes had made a sweep over northern France and a Junkers had been shot down by a Czech pilot. When I told Corporal Feyt the following day he was delighted and said he now had no doubts as to where his future lay.

At the beginning of December 1940 the Legion were advised that their move to north Africa had been sanctioned by the German Command. This was the signal for a dozen legionnaires who wished to stay in France to desert and from that time the 70th Company were always about ten below strength. Some drifted back, but two days before embarkation the sergeant-chef sent for me and insisted that I sign my name on a complete register of the company. At the time I felt that nothing could prevent me reaching Oran and Gibraltar so I signed as ordered. The following day the SS *Jebel Druse* docked within one hundred yards of the fort and with the help of some horse-drawn vehicles we conveyed all the equipment and stores to the foot of the gangway. These were put under guard until next morning when the whole company proceeded to carry them aboard and stack them in an open space between decks. Six of us were detailed for guard duty for the duration of the voyage.

We were informed that the *Jebel Druse* would sail shortly after midnight. The Legion officers, whom I had not previously seen, came aboard about 10 p.m. and a muster parade was held on the deck shortly afterwards. It then appeared that some of the would-be deserters had had a change of mind and had rejoined the company on the short journey between the fort and the ship so that as a result there were three surplus bodies on the draft. The Italian Harbour Commission insisted that three men be withdrawn so the Register which I had previously signed was produced and the last three volunteers struck off.

I was told of this decision by the sergeant-chef and was returned to sentry duty at the gangway. The duty was shared by a crew member with whom I tried to make conversation without much success. Then, to my astonishment, four blacked-out coaches drove in through the dock gates and parked at the foot of the gangway. They were identical to the vehicles we had seen at the Hotel Britannique and I knew they contained Afrika Korps troops. This was confirmed when my fellow sentry spat over the rail and muttered, '*les sales Boches!*'

I spent a very miserable day crossing to Oran, which we reached round about midnight, tired, hungry and very cold as the Mistral was blowing very strongly and it was impossible to keep warm between decks. By 2 a.m. the Legion stores were unloaded and we then had to help the dockers load the vessel for the return journey to Marseilles. Before we left on the return journey I managed to have a word with my Czech friend Corporal Feyt and we vowed to meet again in the UK.

We were given hammocks and allowed three hours sleep but were awakened by crew members at 7 a.m.; they issued us with scrubbing brushes and soap and set us to scrub a very filthy and very long companionway. This lasted until the afternoon when we were given coffee, *vin rouge* and a small black loaf. During the night we disembarked at Marseilles at the same quay where I had so hopefully embarked two days previously. I was very disappointed at the outcome but consoled myself with the thought that few Jocks had the experience of crossing the Med in company with three or four hundred soldiers of the Afrika Korps.

Three French gendarmes took charge of us and we were escorted to the chief Marseilles prison and thrown into a large cell containing upwards of two hundred prisoners. Never at any time had I imagined I would ever be in the company of such an assortment: cut-throats and thugs of every nationality and the noise and smell was foul. I remember thinking, 'Surely this is the bottom.'

It was impossible to sleep under such circumstances. To make matters worse I made the acquaintance of an English-speaking Algerian who informed me he had been two years in the prison and the only crime he had committed was attempting to stow away on the Algiers-Marseilles mail boat.

However, two days later, when in a queue for bread, I heard two fellow prisoners speaking English. They turned out to be two NCOs from the Royal Artillery who had been picked up by the Vichy police and charged with having no identification papers. They had been sentenced to two weeks' imprisonment and were due for release the following day. They had spent three days at Rue de Forbin and promised to let Donald Caskie know that I was in custody. For the next three days I waited rather impatiently until Donald turned up accompanied by a high-ranking Vichy policeman. I was released on condition I reported back to Fort St Jean.

The Traitor

For two days after my release I remained at Rue de Forbin helping Donald with records and reports, which he disposed of by handing them in to the American Consulate. At that time he was quite worried because his schemes for getting RAF personnel back to the UK were not working as well as he would have wished. One evening he informed me that Pat O'Leary*, John Garrow and he had been accepted into the French Resistance movement. Their main task was the repatriation to the United Kingdom of RAF pilots and navigators who had been shot down over France.

By this time Pat O'Leary and John Garrow had established a number of safe houses in the area around Lille and Roubaix and the Resistance had arranged a team of agents or couriers who were responsible for the safe collection and passage of the escapees down through France until they reached Marseilles. Here Donald Caskie took over and saw they were well-provided with food and clothing for their crossing into Spain. The final part of the journey was becoming particularly hazardous as the Gestapo had strongly reinforced their presence in the Toulouse, Narbonne, Carcassonne and Perpignan approach to the Pyrenees. Lately, quite a number of escaping British personnel had been apprehended in this area and, after serving a sentence in Toulouse jail, were returned to Marseilles to be interned once again in Fort St Jean. For the most part these were military personnel and were not accompanied by guides. Donald made a point of personally interviewing these men on their return to the fort and came to the conclusion that there was a traitor in the French Resistance who was passing on to the Gestapo information regarding the escape routes to Spain.

One afternoon in early December I called at Rue de Forbin and found Donald looking very worried. He went on to explain that a priest from Avignon, l'Abbé Carpentier, with whom he was very friendly, had disappeared and was believed to be in a concentration camp in Germany. L'Abbé originally came from Abbeville in northern France and was in the habit of visiting Donald at the Seamen's Mission. He was a very small, very gentle man with a love for his country which prompted him to leave his home at Abbeville and join the Resistance movement.

* 'Lt. Cdr. Pat O'Leary RN' was in fact Dr Albert Guérisse (later Major General), a Belgian national who took the name of a Canadian friend. Betrayed in 1943, he survived the notorious Dachau concentration camp. Awarded the George Cross and DSO by Britain, he was one of the most highly decorated officers of WWII.

When it was discovered that he was an accomplished printer and artist the Resistance leaders employed him to produce forged passports and ration cards. One evening I had the pleasure of meeting him. Donald gave me a few francs and instructed me to get a small snap of myself, which was passed on to l'Abbé Carpentier. In due course I was the proud possessor of a forged French passport made out in the name of 'Grigore Mansois'.

On my next visit to the Mission I made the acquaintance of three members of the Australian merchant navy whose ship had been torpedoed somewhere in the Indian Ocean. The two seamen and the Chief Engineer, Ross Dunshea by name, had been imprisoned in an enemy escort vessel. After a nightmare journey lasting many weeks, during which time they were kept in the hold, they were finally put ashore at Bordeaux en route for a German prison camp. On the journey to captivity they escaped by jumping from a moving train in pitch darkness somewhere on the German border east of Metz and, although they were all injured, they managed to find one another in the darkness and set out for Marseilles.

Dunshea was in charge and he made an excellent job of leading his party to the American Consulate where they were referred to Donald Caskie. They were treated as ship-wrecked sailors and were not interned in Fort St Jean, so they remained in Rue de Forbin until the spring of 1941 when they successfully crossed the Pyrenees and finally made the United Kingdom. I was very interested in their capture and escape; it was so very different from our experiences.

On a later visit to Rue de Forbin I found Donald with important visitors from the Resistance: Pat O'Leary and an Australian by the name of Dowding. They were all very concerned by the recent losses of trusted agents and after Donald had vouched for me they discussed the matter in my presence. Donald insisted that he was very suspicious of an Agent No. 11, and they all agreed there was a traitor in the movement who was an enemy collaborator. However, the other two pointed out that No. 11 had a very distinguished record and had recently arrived in Marseilles with nine escaped prisoners whom he had collected on the Belgian frontier.

At this juncture Donald enquired if I had come across a Royal Engineer sergeant by the name of Cole.

'Oh, yes,' I said, 'but I think he's a Signal sergeant in the Royal Artillery. You must remember him as one of the three you sent to watch the Hotel Britannique. He's a Devon man, and is a first class chap.'

'I'm afraid that's not the one I'm thinking of,' said Donald. 'The one I suspect says he was a sergeant in the Royal Engineers but from what he let slip I think he must have been a deserter. My second sight warns me that he cannot be trusted and to my horror I now learn from Pat that he has been working as a trusted agent with the French Resistance for the past three months. He appears to have a very elementary knowledge of the French language, but in spite of this he has recently taken a party of escapees from the Roubaix area to Marseilles. I have told Pat and John Garrow of my suspicions but they point to his excellent record as a courier. At the present moment there are four pilots and a navigator in hiding in northern France and both our friends think that Cole, with his excellent past performance, may be entrusted to see them safely to the Spanish frontier.'

The internees at Fort St Jean had very few duties to carry out – other than keep the billets tidy and clear the so-called dining area after meals. One day I was making out details of duties in the small room which served as an office when I heard two persons outside the door having a long discussion in fluent French. They spoke so quickly that I could make little of the conversation but when they moved away I had a good view of them from the window. When I went across to the dining-room for my meal I noticed one of the two men was eating at the next table. When I asked Corporal Masson of the 1st Gordons who the stranger was he replied, 'He says he's Sergeant Cole of the Royal Engineers but I think he's a pretty fly man and worth the watching.'

When Cole rose from the table I said, 'By the way, I'll want your particulars to enable me to draw your rations from the French authorities.'

'You'll get no particulars from me,' he said, 'I'm on special assignment – in any case I'm leaving here tonight and won't trouble you again.'

'That's OK,' I said.

In the evening I hurried down to Rue de Forbin to tell Donald that Sergeant Cole was a fluent French speaker. He was very angry but his first thoughts were for the escaped airmen. 'I'll get Pat O'Leary to liquidate Cole this very night,' said Donald.

Unfortunately Cole had left by train for northern France before O'Leary could catch up with him but in ten days time he re-appeared at Rue de Forbin, accompanied by four pilots and a navigator. The escapees were loud in their praises of Cole, who seemed to be able to charm the German military and the Gestapo alike. However, Donald was determined to have a showdown with him and he, O'Leary and Garrow had a stormy interview when Donald accused him of being an enemy informer and of taking his orders from a society lady in Paris who was well-known to the French police as a German spy. Cole remained unperturbed; his record was there for all to see but if the three Resistance members were not prepared to trust him he would step down and allow another agent to guide the RAF men to the Spanish border.

This is exactly what happened and the new courier set off with his party the following night from Marseilles. Acting on Resistance instructions they planned to travel by rail to Carcassonne where they would leave the train and make their way on foot to the small village of Formiguères on the Andorra border, where the link would pick them up and wait for an opportune moment to cross the mountains.

The courier in charge was well satisfied with the arrangements and all went well until the party reached Narbonne, where a railway employee handed him a typewritten letter. This purported to be from Donald Caskie and contained details of an altered plan. Instead of passing the RAF men to the link agent on the Andorra border the party would remain on the train until it reached Perpignan, where they would take shelter in the stables of an isolated inn ten kilometres west of the town. They would remain in hiding until contacted. The courier had already used the stables in a previous instance, so his suspicions were not aroused by the change of plan.

The proprietor of the inn was well-regarded by his Resistance friends and could always be depended on to see that the travellers had a good meal before leaving for the mountain crossing. The courier led the airmen to a hayshed attached to the stables and when they had bedded down in the warm hay he walked across to the inn to collect food for them.

He was returning when there was a prolonged burst of fire from the area of the stables and about six armed men emerged from the building and disappeared in the semi-darkness. A grenade was thrown by them, and the courier was wounded in the shoulder but he and the inn keeper were able to reach the stables where they were shocked to find four of the airmen dead and one seriously wounded. The latter gave an account of the massacre before he died, and it was afterwards established that it was carried out by a Gestapo death squad acting on information received from Cole.

Even worse was to follow. In the next week over seventy of the Resistance were put to death by the Gestapo. Amongst the victims were Dowding, the Australian, and Carpentier, the priest who produced the forged passports; they were both beheaded in a Paris prison. The latter was a great friend of Donald's and I think he never really got over his death. By this time it was obvious that the enemy were receiving up-to-date information from a traitor in the Resistance and many escapers were shot on the escape routes which had proved so rewarding in the early days of the Occupation.

After the Perpignan massacre Cole disappeared from the French scene and it was assumed he had gone over to live in Germany. I had almost forgotten the matter until 1965 when Donald visited me in Grantown-on-Spey and filled in the blanks. It appears that the French police did not forget and kept a constant watch on his lady friend in Paris. They were rewarded in 1946 when Cole returned to France and occupied apartments in Rue de Greville. After a considerable time eight gendarmes surrounded the building and in the shoot-out that followed Cole was killed – but not before he had wounded two of the police. By this time Donald Caskie was engaged in the reconstruction of his church in Paris and was asked to identify the body – a task that gave him a certain amount of satisfaction. He was later asked to give evidence at a Court of Inquiry in London but declined when he learned that Cole had a widow and family living in the south of England.

Leaving Marseilles

On my next visit to Rue de Forbin I found Donald very disturbed. The previous evening he had been visited by a friendly Vichy police superintendent who warned him that the Gestapo were becoming increasingly suspicious of the establishment at Rue de Forbin. They had asked the Vichy police to close it down and deport Padre Caskie to a region far removed from Marseilles. Donald was not worried as to his own fate but was very concerned about how the escapees would fare with no one to supply them with food and clothing for the mountain crossing. He had an urgent meeting with O'Leary and Garrow and stressed that new, safe routes over the Pyrenees had to be found as soon as possible.

Two of these routes had already been partially planned. The first one ran parallel to the Mediterranean coastline and finally to the small town of La Preste some thirty miles south-west of Perpignan, where a Resistance link would pick up the escapees. The second would cross the frontier twenty miles south-east of Andorra, but in fact this plan was abandoned when it was discovered that the Gestapo had recently established their main depot at the town of Puigcerda, over five thousand feet up in the mountains.

When I left Donald he said, 'I think you told me that your father was a gamekeeper at Killin in Perthshire.'

'That's right' I replied, 'and I've spent all my spare time in the Perthshire hills.'

'Good, I think you're just what I'm looking for to find a route about one hundred miles south-west of Andorra. I'll see you in two days time.'

I had now been several months in Marseilles and had managed to save up nearly £4 from the very small allowance paid to us at the American Consulate. I spent the lot on the purchase of a cheap compass and a small map of the Pyrenees, while Donald assured me that he would provide sufficient food for the crossing of the mountains. When I attended the arranged meeting I found a staff sergeant in the RASC was also present. He had impressed Donald with the story of his escape from a camp at Besançon by way of a sewer which ran beneath an enemy parade ground. He was very anxious to take part in the venture but stressed that, being a native of Romford, he had no experience of mountains, especially snow-covered ones.

It was now 21 December and the frost was becoming very severe. I explained to him that some of the mountain passes we would use would be at a height of anything from five to seven thousand feet. He finally decided he would go, although I felt he had some misgivings regarding the conditions he would experience on the mountains. His name was Edward Patrick and he had served as a baker in the regular army, including a spell in India.

In view of the warning which he had received from the friendly Vichy superintendent of police, Donald was anxious to find if the route we were planning to use was passable during the winter months. If not, then he would have to concentrate on the coast route by Perpignan and La Preste. He took much pleasure in showing us a variety of exceptional clothing he had received from American residents in Nice and Monaco and we selected a jacket and a pair of trousers each, along with two pullovers, two wool blankets and two pairs of socks. Our only worry was obtaining suitable footwear. I was fortunate in acquiring a half-worn pair of French army boots whilst employed in the Legion cookhouse but Ted's present shoes were very slight and useless for climbing. However, Donald produced a pair of boots which he had used on his journey down from Paris and a shoe repairer at the docks obliged Ted by studding the soles.

On our last night in Marseilles we slept at the Mission and when we rose at seven o'clock we found Donald was away on a shopping expedition. He returned for nine o'clock breakfast and presented Ted and me with two second-hand bags for carrying our food, which he had purchased in a pawnbroker's shop. Into the bags we packed the food which we hoped would take us over the frontier. We each carried:

> one tin Bully (horsemeat)
> two tins M & V Rations
> two packets hard biscuits
> one long loaf
> about 3lbs potatoes
> 1/2 lb tea

We fitted a wire handle to a tin for boiling our tea and Ted, being a smoker, carried a box of matches. Our blankets were tied with string and slung over our shoulders.

We spent the day poring over maps of the frontier which Donald had acquired from, I think, the Resistance movement. It was agreed that we would catch the midnight train from the Marseilles main station and travel west by Nîmes, Montpellier and Narbonne, where we would change trains for Carcassonne and Toulouse. There would be a long dangerous wait at Toulouse for the evening train to Bayonne, which we would leave it at St Gaudens some sixty miles south-west of Toulouse and about forty miles from our goal, Bagnères de Luchon on the frontier.

We realised that our identification papers would be checked and re-checked many times en route, sometimes by Gestapo and sometimes by Vichy police; the fact that Ted had only a few words of French made the situation particularly hazardous. Donald then produced two blank postcards which he filled with small writing in French, with an odd Gaelic phrase thrown in.

They conveyed the impression that the writer had gone to the Pyrenees on a climbing holiday; one of them describing the weather conditions as very reasonable and the other as impossible. They were addressed to Donald at his Rue de Forbin address and were correctly stamped. Depending on the conditions, we would post one of the cards as soon as we were in Spain. As it happened Donald was informed by the Vichy police the day after we left Marseilles that they were closing the Mission in ten days time and he was being deported to Avignon.

All our arrangements were now complete and Donald presided over a very good meal and then said a prayer. At the Mission door he shook hands and I can still see him standing on the step. 'God be with you,' he said.

The night was clear and frosty as we set out for the station, nearly two miles away. We stood in a queue at the ticket office, tendered the exact amount of the fare and then produced our identification papers to a Vichy policeman before boarding the train. We were fortunate to get two seats in a crowded compartment and shortly afterwards the train pulled out and we were on our way.

The compartment was without heating of any kind and to start with the cold was intense. However, by the time we reached Montpellier it had warmed up and we were fairly comfortable, apart from the fact that the wooden seats had no covering of any kind. We were obliged to change trains at Narbonne and again were lucky to get seats together. Once more our papers were checked by the Vichy police and, although they looked twice at Ted's photograph, we were allowed to proceed. At Carcassonne came another check and a male passenger sitting next to Ted was dragged from his seat and taken away by three armed men. The lady sitting next to me whispered, 'Gestapo!' and afterwards I didn't feel so comfortable. I understood from the general conversation that the train was running late and it was long after dark when we arrived at Toulouse.

Even before the train drew up we could see that the platform was swarming with armed Gestapo. I was first out and handed over my forged papers to the guard who had taken up position at the door of our carriage. He looked at the photo and ordered me to take off my beret. This seemed to satisfy him and he handed me back my papers. In the meantime Ted was involved in a struggle to reach the door with a big stout woman who was dragging behind her two huge heavy cases. As she attempted to produce her papers from a carrier bag she was forced to release the cases so Ted picked them up and carried them to a seat on the platform. At that moment a rush of passengers descended from the carriage and the guard was so busy I think he forgot to check Ted's documents.

We strolled leisurely down the platform and then crossed to a siding where an engine with snow plough attached was being stoked by one crew member while the other had drawn hot water from the engine and was making coffee. We looked so longingly at the bright red coals in the firebox that the stoker took pity on us and invited us on to the footplate where we soon warmed up. When they had finished their coffee they poured what was left in the bucket into the mugs and handed them to Ted and me.

We had hardly finished when a train from the north drew into another platform and a number of passengers descended on the Bayonne train. Our friends hurried us off in case we might lose our seats. I had previously asked the stoker how long we would take to reach St Gaudens and he replied with a shrug, '*deux – trois heures.*' About three hours later the train drew up at St Gaudens and when we opened the carriage door we were immediately engulfed in a blizzard. Ted and I were the only passengers to leave and we made our way with some difficulty to the exit where our tickets were collected. Two gendarmes demanded our papers but when they were offered they didn't even examine them, but motioned us to carry on.

Crossing the Pyrenees

Once outside the station we found ourselves on a wide flat road covered in snow to a depth of one foot. On either side were high buildings but the whole area was devoid of lighting of any kind. Fortunately, the wind was from behind us and this made walking easier, but after stumbling into ditches we decided that unless we found shelter we would be forced to return to the station.

At that moment Ted reported he had seen a light to the left of our route but by the time we had stopped to investigate it had disappeared, only to appear a few minutes later. We both shouted and in reply a voice demanded, '*Qui va là?*' This turned out to be a farmer carrying a lantern, making his way from the farmhouse to a byre where a sick cow was housed. He returned with us to the house where he refuelled the kitchen fire and heated a large pan of milk which he laced with cognac.

When we had drank the milk he took us to the barn, where we were soon asleep in the dry warm hay. In the morning we had *soupe* and coffee for breakfast. Our friend advised us to use the railway line in our journey to Luchon as the railway authorities always kept the line clear of snow, even if no services ran. We thanked him for his kindness and he replied that no veteran of Verdun, as he was, could ever forget the British troops of the 1914–18 War. Following his directions, we reached the railway line after an hour's walking and then made good time in our journey to the south.

Round about mid-day the snow stopped and a soft drizzle developed, which soaked our clothes and the two blankets we carried. Late in the afternoon a sharp frost came on and when we came to a ruined church beside the railway we decided to have some food and bed down on the stone floor. There were small pieces of scorched wood attached to the stone walls and after gathering a large pile we soon had a cheery fire going. As our food stocks were disappearing at an alarming rate we rationed ourselves to one tin of M & V Ration, a packet of hard biscuits and a large can of strong tea. After our meal we felt much better and prepared for sleep by wrapping our wet blankets around us and laying a wooden beam on the fire. After a short time I awoke to find the fire had gone out and the cold was intense. When I tried to replenish the fire I found my damp clothes were frozen to the wet blanket which in turn was frozen to the stone floor. Ted was in a similar situation and it was over an hour later before we managed to relight the fire.

The following day was even colder and after a breakfast of bread and tea we set out for Luchon. During the whole day we never saw a single person and finally reached our goal as darkness was falling. We were fortunate to come across the town's football stadium and, as there was no one to be seen, we climbed the locked gates and curled up under a pile of wooden seats in the grandstand.

Ted reported that his matches were down to about a dozen so we did not attempt to light a fire but contented ourselves with a slice of bread and three army biscuits before proceeding into town in search of a café. It was still very early but as we were approaching the main square we spoke to a schoolboy who invited us to visit his father's café. He then ran on ahead and soon appeared at the café door with a pleasant-looking middle-aged man whom he introduced as his father. The latter satisfied himself that we were genuine British escapees and we were served with a very substantial meal of cheese and anchovy sandwiches with as much coffee as we could drink.

The proprietor was a very good type. He told us to call him Alain and his son Jean Pierre but they would not give us their surname and warned us that they were living in very dangerous surroundings. In the summer months of 1940 they had guided more than thirty British escapees over the Spanish frontier. The twelve-year-old Jean Pierre was fast becoming an outstanding courier whose ambition in life was to become a member of the Resistance. His father informed us that only madmen would attempt the crossing during the winter months but on the other hand the Gestapo and the Vichy police were very thin on the ground in such appalling weather and with luck we might reach Spain in about ten days.

Accompanied by father and son we left Luchon about 11 a.m. and for the first two hours climbed steadily upwards through beautiful pine trees. In the afternoon the trees thinned out and we were soon among the juniper bushes of the upper tree limit.

Alain pointed out tracks which he said were made by '*les loups*'. Ted took a poor view of this, saying, 'As if these bloody mountains were not enough, we now have wolves!'

Our guides seemed to know every track and pass on the mountains, even although the snow was beginning to drift in the strong wind. About three o'clock in the afternoon we arrived at a small ski hut to find it occupied by two young French soldiers who had been wounded in Belgium and were now recuperating in southern France. They belonged to the Carcassonne area and this was their first ski outing for over a year. After a good meal our friends from Luchon gave us clear instructions for the following day and reckoned we should be on the way to Lerida in a week's time, provided the weather got no worse. They then shook our hands and wished us good luck and, along with the two soldiers, set out for home. In the meantime Ted and I stoked up the fire and settled down to a good night's sleep feeling dry and warm. Two or three times during the night I heard Ted putting more wood on the fire – he was taking no chances with the wolves!

The following morning we rose at dawn and prepared a good meal – our last tin of bully and two boiled potatoes each. Breakfast over, we locked up the hut, hung the key on a nail at the rear of the shed and set out for the pass as instructed. The snow was fairly soft and although walking was difficult we made quite good time. As we climbed higher we picked our way over patches of short grass and flat rock slabs where the fierce wind had blown the snow away. When we finally reached the summit of the pass we found ourselves looking down into an enormous basin possibly three thousand feet below us. From our map I guessed we were on the edge of the Valle de Arán.

It looked as if the valley had been scooped out by a giant shovel and the rock band round the rim topped a perpendicular drop of up to one thousand feet. Directly in front of us reared the gigantic Pico de Maladetta, shown on our map as being between eleven and twelve thousand feet with surrounding peaks averaging seven thousand feet. It was a sobering enough sight for me but for Ted, brought up on the fertile plain of East

Anglia, it was horrific. From the edge of the basin we looked down on the vast white hollow and could see a medium sized town on our right. Using our map and compass we rightly concluded that this was the town of Viella, some two miles on the Spanish side of the frontier, but our immediate problem was how to descend through the rock band to the valley.

The weather had now improved and a warm sun was shining from a bright blue sky, making the top layer of snow softer and easy to walk on. Keeping well back from the rim we discovered the road from Luchon ran through a narrow cleft in the rock band and emerged on the floor of the basin. We had great difficulty in descending through the deep snow to the road but by mid-afternoon we were approaching the outskirts of Viella.

By the time we had reached the main square of the town we were accompanied by about two hundred of the inhabitants, who were very curious as to who we were and how we had managed to cross the mountains. Ted had sufficient francs left to purchase a box of matches and two cigarettes, while my last coins just covered one loaf of black bread. The people were quite friendly and spoke a mixture of French and Spanish. When we left the baker's shop we were picked up by two frontier guards, easily identified by their triangular three-cornered hats. They then escorted us to the town's police station, where they took our particulars and informed us that '*mañana*' we would be returned to the French frontier guards and probably would be escorted to Toulouse to serve a prison sentence.

This was bad news indeed, and Ted was a bit depressed. 'What are we going to do now?' he asked.

'Get down on your knees and pray for snow,' I answered.

It was now dark, and when we were taken to the cells the senior guard gave us to understand that we would start our return to France at nine o'clock the following morning. He then returned with a flagon of coffee and the cooked ribs of what we took to be goat – so with part of the loaf we had purchased we made quite a good meal. The guard impressed on us that the food was good only because the two officers and their families were celebrating Christmas and the New Year.

We now examined our cell to find the floor and walls were of concrete but there was a small heap of straw in one corner. It was very difficult to get our bearings in the darkness but Ted shook up the straw while I checked the window – only to find there was no glass in it and a bitter wind blew through the iron bars. I suggested that Ted move the straw to the only sheltered spot beneath the window but he declared the straw to be filthy and that he would prefer to sleep on the stone floor.

We tried to sleep but the cold made it impossible and we debated whether we could survive the night. However, around midnight we heard a key being inserted in the lock and the younger guard appeared carrying an iron bucket of glowing charcoal. We were delighted, but he reminded us that we were returning to France at 9 a.m. the following morning. To keep the charcoal alight one of us had to rise every five minutes to swing the bucket from side to side and keep the fire glowing. Once we warmed up, the vermin in the straw came to life and thereafter we spent an uncomfortable night.

At eight o'clock next morning we were given coffee and bread and told to prepare for the thirty kilometre march back to France. From outside the police station our guards pointed out the route and I was very pleased to see the sky thickening and the snow beginning to fall. We all set out together but by the end of two hours the younger guard and I were two hundred yards ahead of Ted and the older man, who were making very heavy weather of the steeper slopes. Finally, my companion waited for the other two to join us and after discussion they agreed that the attempt was dangerous and we should return to Viella. This is what Ted and I wished and we were quite happy to return to our cell. We complained about the lice in the straw but the guards only laughed and assured us that all Spanish prisons were alike in that respect. In any case, that same straw had been there for about a year and had been used by many different nationalities.

By the time we arrived back in Viella we were on very good terms with our guards. They arranged that we be allowed to use what appeared to be a public washhouse and when we arrived there we found a large tin bath filled with icy water with a fire of tree roots and dry turves kindled beneath it. An hour later the water was just lukewarm and when Ted got into the bath I scrubbed him with a piece of rough sacking and he later repaid the compliment. We asked for some soap but the guards explained that the local people were starving and that soap was a thing of the past.

When we had dried ourselves with some more sacking, we were grateful to find that one of the officer's wives had bought two vests and two shirts from a shop in town. They were of poor quality but at least they were clean. The senior guard explained he was allowed to spend from a tiny fund which had been set aside to provide for destitute unfortunates. That night they gave us some fresh straw and allowed us to sleep on the washhouse floor.

Another Winter Trek

We were roused at dawn the next morning and given instructions for the next leg of our journey to the small town of Esterri, about twenty-five miles to the south-east of Viella. Our friends furnished us with a letter for the police at Esterri, informing them that they had attempted to return us to France but found the frontier passes impossible and it was unlikely they would be passable for a week or ten days. At first the going was favourable but in the early afternoon the road climbed up the steep side of the basin and it began to snow heavily.

It was a very lonely road and we were relieved to see a figure approaching us from the direction of Esterri. We were sure he was a frontier guard but he turned out to be a postman on his way round from Esterri to Viella. He spoke excellent French and proved to be very helpful, informing us that we could not possibly reach Esterri before nightfall. He advised us to follow the snow-covered road past the village of Salardu and then tackle the pass where the road rose to a height of nearly two thousand metres. On the very summit of the pass there was a small hut beside the road in which he always sheltered if the conditions were bad. It had a fireplace and a supply of wood and he explained that beneath the snow behind the hut we would find an axe hidden under a sheet of corrugated iron, which we should use to eject the iron bolt keeping the door closed.

We thanked him for his help and he remarked that he might see us again as he was due to return to Esterri in two days time. Before leaving he shared out his food with us, explaining that the local inhabitants were very generous to him every Christmas. He wished us good luck and we set out for the village of Salardu but when we arrived there it appeared to be deserted and we did not see a single soul. From that point the road climbed steeply and when we approached the summit we found ourselves in blizzard conditions. To make matters worse, Ted appeared to be very lame and I suspected he was suffering from frostbite – for he complained of his feet feeling numb while a short time later they felt on fire.

It was impossible to see more than a few yards and when the road began to descend I knew we had missed the hut. We were becoming increasingly concerned about our food supplies as we reckoned we still had forty miles to cover before we reached the small town of Sort, where we might be fortunate to get transport to Lerida.

Close to the summit two large birds of prey rose from the road two hundred yards in front. I remarked they looked like buzzards and wondered what they found to eat in such surroundings. Further on we came across the carcase of a large rabbit. The blood had stained the snow but was not yet frozen so I knew it had only recently been killed. It was of the same colouring as a normal rabbit but was as big as a mountain hare. The head and the inside were already missing but the back and hindquarters were intact. I skinned the hindquarters with my army knife and wrapped it up in my scarf.

The blizzard continued unabated and Ted had slowed until he was no longer able to keep up with me. Any time we stopped he would take out a photo of his wife and two-year-old twins and I had difficulty in getting him started again. I explained to him that I thought we had missed the hut in the snowstorm but when I added that we would need to retrace our steps he sat down in the snow and told me that he found it impossible to continue. I told him that unless we could find shelter in the hut it was unlikely that we could survive the coming night.

Just at that moment the snowfall ceased and I set out again for the summit. I had only gone two hundred yards when I spotted the hut standing forty yards above the road. I scrambled up the steep slope on hands and knees, found the corrugated sheet and the axe and knocked out the bolt holding the door closed, as instructed by the friendly postman. Once in the hut I went down on my knees and thanked the Lord for my deliverance. I then hurried back and found Ted fast asleep in the snow, still clutching his photograph.

The following two hours were probably the most frustrating of our whole journey. Ted was only partially conscious and did not appear to understand that I was trying to get him to his feet. Sometimes I managed to get him to his knees but his feet were so numb that he couldn't stand. On one occasion we both fell in the snow. While attempting to get up, the string on Ted's rolled blanket came adrift and the blanket rolled down the steep slope and disappeared over the edge in spite of my effort to salvage it. All I could do was listen as it plunged five hundred feet to the floor of the basin.

In the semi-darkness I scrambled back to the road and picked up Ted's photograph, which he had dropped in his fall. I put it in my pocket and said nothing about it. He showed some improvement for when he got to his feet he managed to progress for about twenty yards. The next time he fell I encouraged him by saying that the hut was only one hundred yards away. I put my arm round his waist but he was so much bigger and heavier than me that we invariably fell down together. As we lay in the snow we debated whose turn it was to attempt getting up first.

We had reached the summit of the pass when he suddenly said, 'Jock, I'm going back for my photo; I lost it at the time my blanket disappeared.' I assured him that it was safe in my pocket. He wanted it returned but at that moment the hut became visible and we climbed the steep slope on our hands and

A piper playing outside HQ near Le Caudroy on 8 June (© Imperial War Museum, London)

Men of the 51st marching along the sides of the road near the Bresle to minimise risk of detection by aircraft (© Imperial War Museum, London)

Left. Group in Stalag XXa (date unknown). Angus Campbell is fourth from the right, middle row (© D.J. Campbell)

Below left and right. Angus back in Lewis after the war (© D.J. Campbell)

knees and soon were safely inside. Exhausted, we both fell asleep on the floor.

When I came to, the cold was intense and it was five minutes before I was able to stand. There was no light but after I found the fireplace I raked out the ashes and tore up part of the map which had served us so well, putting the tiny scraps of paper into my hat. In the darkness it was very difficult to find dry branches to light the fire, but by this time Ted was awake and lit one of his precious matches. We could then see a pile of sawn wood and a box of dry grass and twigs. We were not long in getting a fire going and then used the axe to break up the branches. By the time we finished we were so tired we lay down and slept until well on in the night.

When we woke we filled our can with snow and proceeded to boil the remains of the rabbit. Ted discovered three hard biscuits and two shrivelled-up potatoes in his bag so we consumed the biscuits and put the potatoes in the can with the rabbit meat. After what seemed hours we decided that the rabbit was cooked and we each took a leg and a portion of the back. It tasted delicious and, although a pinch of salt would have improved it, we finished every scrap of meat and then sucked the bones. The sun was now showing above the peaks but it was so cold that we shut the door again and stoked up the fire. Just then we heard shouts and knockings on the door and, half-fearing a visit from the Gestapo, we opened up to find it was our friend the postman on his return journey to Esterri. He was delighted to see us again and produced a fresh loaf, some goatsmilk cheese and a tin of so-called coffee. We had a leisurely meal and about mid-day set off for Esterri.

On the way I asked him how he was able to have so much wood stored in the hut and he explained that during the summer months the postal authorities made a pony available for the task of re-stocking the hut with wood. He was allowed to collect all branches at a sawmill in the pine woods near Esterri and, having sawed them into suitable lengths, he packed them into the two panniers carried by the pony. He also explained that most of the Gestapo were to be found on the French side of the frontier but

Franco's troops, who were equally bad, were mostly on the Spanish side. As the light was fading we finally arrived at Esterri and reported at once to the police headquarters. When I produced the letter from their Viella station they were relieved as they did not relish a journey across the border to France.

Spanish Prison

We said goodbye to our friend the postman and I gave him the postcard for Donald Caskie, informing him that the Bagnères de Luchon-Viella route was impossible before the coming of spring. He promised to post it the first time he was on the Viella-Luchon delivery. We had no means of knowing that, two days after Donald had said goodbye to us in Marseilles, his establishment at Rue de Forbin had been closed on Gestapo orders and Donald himself had been deported to Grenoble.

The guards then showed us to a bare but clean cell where we spent a very cold night. Before locking us up they informed us that a truck was leaving Sort for Lerida in two days time and that they would escort us to Sort, leaving at 8 a.m. the following morning.

The distance to Sort was around fifteen to twenty miles and, while I felt I could probably make it in one day, I was not very confident that Ted could last this distance. We were both affected by frostbite: both my feet had bled a good deal and I had permanently lost three toenails; Ted's feet were now a dark blue colour and very painful indeed. Three months later when we were examined at the Military Hospital in Gibraltar the Medical Officer was of the opinion that the bleeding had probably cleared away the frozen blood in my feet and lessened the chance of gangrene.

Our two police escorts proved to be very reasonable and helpful. They carried Ted's rucksack over the worst sections of the route and when we had covered half of our journey they stopped at a small village where we were given a meal of beans and potatoes and some black bread and wine. In the afternoon we set out on our ten-mile trek to Sort and after a nightmare journey finally arrived there as darkness was falling. We were shown to a very bare but clean cell where our only covering was two threadbare blankets; we were unable to sleep because of the cold.

We got no further food that night but in the early morning were given a sort of porridge made from ground beans and a cup of acorn coffee. Just before mid-day our transport appeared and we set out on our eighty-mile journey to Lerida with one of the Esterri guards and a fresh one from the Sort staff. We were told to take with us the two blankets we had used at Sort as snow was lying in depth on the road and they did not expect to reach Lerida before the afternoon of the following day. By this time we were both in a bad way, with our footwear giving very little protection from the freezing snow. In fact both of Ted's boots had shed their soles and his feet were completely numb. The guards, although sympathetic, had no encouraging news for us. According to them there were over one million Republican prisoners in jail in northern Spain and the main Lerida prison was bursting at the seams.

When we finally reached there, just as darkness was falling on the second day, we were directed to a half-completed building which housed about four hundred Republicans who had fought against Franco at the battle of the Ebro. The conditions they lived in were appalling. Many of them had been wounded two years previously and hardly a morning passed without bodies of men who had died during the night being carried out for burial.

That was bad enough, but when we saw the sanitary arrangements we reckoned we had reached rock bottom. On one side of the cell was a large sunken square measuring about ten feet by ten and about six feet deep and this was spanned by three wooden sleepers. Two large water pipes led into the square from outside the building, but according to the prisoners no water had ever come through the pipes and the excreta in the pit had built up to within six inches of the top. Urine was welling over the top and running across the sloping floor to the lowest side.

As Ted and I were the latest arrivals the only vacant floor space we could get was at the bottom of the slope. We remained standing for most of the night but in the early hours of the morning we collapsed through sheer fatigue, and woke in the morning with dripping wet clothes. When an orderly officer appeared I protested as strongly as possible and he promised we would be moved to a better cell '*mañana*'. However, *mañana* took some time to materialise and we spent five nights in that dreadful place before being removed to a cold dry cell. Ted declared that another two nights there would have seen him being carried out for an early morning burial.

Life, it is said, is full of surprises and in the next week we began to feel that the tide was beginning to turn in our favour. In our new prison we found that our Republican fellow inmates had all been prisoners for two or three years. Life in Spain held no attraction for them, so their dearest wish was to eventually emigrate to America. With this in view they held classes every day to learn or improve their English. They hated the Italians and somehow or other they knew in detail exactly what was happening in the Eritrean and Western Desert campaigns in spite of the fact there was no radio or newspaper communication in the entire prison. We were the first British soldiers they had seen and they could not do enough for us. After a few days, one of them who worked in the prison cookhouse took away our filthy-smelling clothes, washed them out with real soap and returned them the following day.

Nearly all the prisoners were originally from the Lerida area and every Thursday their mothers, wives or sweethearts were allowed to visit them in prison with a basket of provisions. After our arrival the first thing our fellow prisoners did was to come to us with their baskets and ask us to take our choice. There is no doubt but that these additional rations helped to keep us alive. I must confess I was near to tears to see little children kissing their fathers through the prison bars. After a week in our new surroundings we both agreed that we would try and sleep each afternoon as it was impossible to do so at night. The Spanish prisoners were in a dreadful state and each night they would cough, cry in their sleep and generally relive their experiences of the past three years. When one of their friends passed away during the night they held a sort of wake until the body was taken away for burial.

One afternoon we saw one of the guards unlocking the enormous steel doors and suddenly about twenty British troops burst into the cell. They were all known to Ted and me, for we had been together at Rue de Forbin and Fort St Jean and we had a hilarious reunion. They had escaped by the rail route from Marseilles when the Seamen's Mission had been closed by the Gestapo but had been picked up at different places on the frontier. It was intended that they be returned to France but weather conditions made this impossible so they were locked up in the Spanish town of Figueras for ten days.

I was very anxious to hear of Donald Caskie but they could only tell me that he had been arrested by the Vichy police and had been taken away to Avignon or Grenoble. It was ten years before I saw Donald again. He told me everything in the Mission had been confiscated by the police so I assumed my postcard from Luchon had gone the same way.

The day after the arrival of the batch from Figueras we were given a quantity of straw. I hoped it was clean but soon after we had bedded down the straw became alive with vermin and soon everyone was scratching. So far as food was concerned, Lerida was probably the best prison we had been in. At 9 a.m. we got a mug of acorn coffee and a small black loaf weighing about three ounces and about six o'clock in the evening we had our supper, consisting of about one pint of soup made from beans and potatoes.

This was supplemented by what we received from our fellow prisoners. All our lives we had been brought up to regard Communists with suspicion but here were men very much like ourselves, who were intent on learning our language and who were only too pleased to share their meagre rations with us. They had been in prison for up to five years and their outlook was indeed bleak, yet they remained very cheerful in the hope that the Axis armies would eventually declare war on Russia. They never at any time discussed politics with us. Several of them had been in prison at Zaragoza, which they labelled the 'hell prison' of Spain and they hoped we would not be sent there when we were moved on.

Amongst the contingent from Figueras was a young Black Watch soldier whom I had admitted as an internee to Fort St Jean three days before I left Marseilles. The following day he was allowed out on pass to enable him to have a bath in the public baths at the Vieux Port. On his return he and I were held up for a few minutes at the drawbridge while the guard commander checked our passes, and he appeared to be interested in a huge escutcheon emblazoned with heraldic bearings and the following motto: '*Tu as demandé la mort – je vais te la donner.*'

'What does that mean?' he asked me. I translated it for him, 'You have asked for death – I will give it to you,' but he did not appear to be very impressed. 'A cheery bunch – they French,' was his only comment.

There were now about two dozen British troops in Lerida prison and we decided that we must notify the British Embassy at Madrid of our plight. We managed to raise sufficient pesetas to buy a postage stamp and, having asked our men to search their pockets for any partially smoked cigarette papers, we proceeded to roll six fairly presentable cigarettes. We then contacted a Canadian national who had volunteered to fight in the Republican Army at the outbreak of the Spanish Civil War and he agreed to approach a friendly guard, who would post a letter for us. A sheet of paper and an envelope were donated by a Republican prisoner and our postman was rewarded with three cigarettes. A week later we received a reply from Colonel Drummond Wolfe, the British Military Attaché at Madrid, informing us that he would visit Lerida Prison within ten days. This gave us tremendous encouragement and for the next week we counted the days till his arrival.

Zaragoza

On the eighth day I was instructed to report to the prison reception office where the Military Attaché awaited. He was shocked at our condition but we soon recovered when he produced a large carton of cigarettes and paid us each a small amount to enable us to buy bread at the prison canteen. He explained that food was very scarce but promised that he would return the following week with something better. Everything depended on whether the Spaniards would barter our release for oil or wheat.

However, before his next visit the British contingent were warned to prepare for a further move. Although we had heard bad reports of the Concentration Camp at Mirando de Ebro, we knew we would have to endure at least a month there before our final release. Our Communist friends were in tears as they said goodbye and we felt equally sad leaving them in such appalling conditions with no real prospects of ever being freed.

We were marched to Lerida railway station, each man carrying a bundle of straw to serve as a bed in the cattle trucks into which we were herded. The bare minimum of food was placed under guard in a separate wagon and twice a day we were issued with just enough to keep us alive. Late at night on the third day we were handcuffed in pairs and when the train pulled up at a huge station we were ordered out to the platform. It was an intensely cold night of hard frost and a number of our comrades had to be helped to the station exit.

Once outside we found ourselves in a large square and on the station entrance was the name ZARAGOZA in large concrete letters. So here we were at the 'hell prison' of Spain. The entrance to the prison was on the opposite side of the square and when we reached it the enormous steel gates opened automatically to allow us in and closed again behind us. We were finally herded into a large cell containing about one hundred and fifty men of every known nationality. Most of them had fought against Franco's army while others had been picked up in Spain and imprisoned because they had no identification papers.

Right from the start the treatment meted out by the guards at Zaragoza was very much worse than we ever imagined. In an effort to reduce the numbers of Republicans held in custody, Franco's army encouraged some of these prisoners to volunteer as guards for the policing of the hundreds of different nation-alities imprisoned there. In return they were promised that their prison sentences would be reviewed if they performed satisfactorily. These volunteers were not favourably disposed towards the British contingent and if one of us stepped six inches out of line in the food queue we were clobbered over the head with a heavy club. A more serious breach saw us reported to one of Franco's supervisors, who attacked us with the dog whip carried by all supervisors.

A few days later we had a second visit from the British Military Attaché. This time he arrived with more cigarettes and one pound of raisins per man. He informed us that another batch of British troops were presently in prison at Huesca and no doubt would be joining us at an early date. This proved correct and, having known all the newcomers as internees at Marseilles, we now shared our straw with them and swapped stories of our experiences since we left Fort St Jean. Conditions in Huesca, if anything, were worse than those we had experi-enced and they were badly infested by lice and scabies.

In spite of this they remained cheerful and full of life. One lance corporal in particular was the life and soul of the party. He hailed from West Lothian and had for ten years been employed in the regimental tailor shop of a well-known Highland regiment. He had spent half of his service in India and was known to everyone as 'Darzi'.* Apart from the army his only interest in life was greyhound racing or as he described it, 'the dugs'. His only conversation was of Powderhall, Carntyne and the White City, where he appeared to have spent all of his army leaves.

After a few days we became acquainted with trebles and accumulators and what to look for in a good 'dug'. He appeared to have something on his mind and he was seen to take a louse from under his arm and, after examination, return it. I was a non-smoker and had half-a-dozen cigarettes left from our last distribution. Darzi begged me to give him three, which he

---

* Hindu word for tailor

passed to one of the guards who supplied him with a sheet of brown paper the following day. When the next meal of beans and potatoes had been issued Darzi turned the empty pail upside down and drew a large ring on the paper. A small round rubber band was placed in the centre of the ring and the betting-shop was complete. In true army fashion he then issued his orders.

'I will preside at all race meetings and due to lack of room only five punters can take part at one time, but the remainder will all get a turn. Each punter will place one raisin in my paper bag and will then select a runner from his body which he will place carefully within the small rubber ring. When that has been done, I will raise the rubber ring and each owner must carefully watch his runner. To the owner of the first louse crossing the outer ring I will pay the first prize of two raisins and the runner-up, one raisin. The raisin bank will receive the remaining two, which will be used by me to subsidise the entertainment!'

Darzi did not claim to be the originator of this pastime and agreed that it had been used in the trenches of the First World War. Nevertheless, it helped to pass the long afternoons and the even longer evenings. It was only when the raisins became unrecognisable that enthusiasm waned.

However, the days went slowly by and we longed for a move to the concentration camp at Mirando de Ebro where, according to all reports, we would be able to work and exercise within the barbed wire enclosure. To make conditions even more difficult, there was quite a scare when an outbreak of typhus was confirmed by a number of medical officers sent from Madrid by the Spanish government. About twenty political prisoners died in ten days but there were no cases among UK troops – probably because of inoculations received during war-time service.

A number of the last UK prisoners to join us at Zaragoza had been wounded prior to the fall of France; when they were sufficiently recovered the French hospital nurses risked their lives by planning their escape. Safe houses were established in many parts of France and Resistance agents kept in touch with the larger hospitals and were on hand when the nurses smuggled the soldiers out.

One of them, a Private Park from the Glasgow area, was not really fit to attempt the mountain crossing but eventually made it to Figueras and ended up with us in Zaragoza. On his first night there we were visited by a high-ranking Spanish bishop who presided at a religious service. I suggested that we should fall in with their wishes and take the line of least resistance and the remainder agreed – all except Park who had lived all his life in a Rangers/Celtic atmosphere and refused to kiss the babe symbol.* Three guards immediately attacked him with rifle butts and then dragged him down the stairs with blood pouring from his nose and mouth. We tried to rescue him but the remainder of the guard arrived with fixed bayonets and we were reluctantly shepherded back to the main prison. We did not expect to see Park again, but he was made of good stuff and reappeared three days later, a mere shadow of his former self.

The Concentration Camp

A few days later we were roused about 5 a.m. and mustered at the main gate, where we were told we were bound for the concentration camp at Miranda de Ebro, some two thousand metres up in the foothills of the Pyrenees. We were taken in a closed truck to the railway station where we entrained in the now familiar wagon, accompanied by six civil guards who chained us up in pairs. Our ration for the day, one small tin of sardines per man, was put in charge of the guard, and about 9 a.m. we set out for Miranda.

There are no towns of any importance between Zaragoza and Miranda de Ebro, and the train covered the one hundred and forty miles in roughly eight hours. We were met at the station and escorted to the camp by five Spanish officers, twenty senior NCOs and sixty Spanish militiamen. The latter appeared to be about eighteen years of age and wore a similar uniform to the

* It is not clear whether the author meant 'papal' or whether the reference is to some depiction of the infant Jesus on the bishop's ring.

sentries at Lerida and Zaragoza. Left to their own devices, I believe these youths would have treated us reasonably well but the senior NCOs encouraged them to use their rifle butts to club us for no apparent reason. They were all proud of the reputation Miranda had acquired and were there to see it lived up to its name.

I'm quite sure few concentration camps ever received such an intake of filthy, repulsive and disreputable individuals as comprised the newly-arrived British contingent. All our personal belongings had been taken from us at Lerida and we had had no opportunity to wash, shave or have a haircut for over a month so we were in a dreadful state when we arrived at Miranda.

However, the Spanish guards let it be known that we would get an issue of clean gear when we were inside the wire. The light was beginning to fade when we entered the gates but the guards marched the whole forty of us to the barber's hut where staff used clippers to shear a two-inch parting from the back of the neck to the forehead. We were then told by an English-speaking Spaniard that we were required to report first thing in the morning to have our haircut completed. This resulted in us becoming, as a Cockney soldier said, the first of the skinheads. We were then escorted to the parade ground, where we were issued with a tin plate and a spoon and given a small portion of boiled potatoes and beans. Two of the troops asked for more but were threatened with punishment for asking.

Although it was now dark we were marched to the camp stores and issued with a cheap cotton tunic, cotton trousers, a cotton skull cap and a pair of light plimsolls. On the pocket of our tunic a large black 'P' confirmed the fact that we were prisoners, while each skull cap carried the same embellishment. The barbed wire surrounding the entire camp was floodlit and was patrolled by sentries during the hours of darkness. By this time the British contingent were utterly exhausted but in spite of our condition we were mustered on the flood-lit parade ground. The Franco flag was raised and lowered as a very out-of-tune military band played the Franco anthem. We were then instructed in the Fascist salute and all had to shout in unison, '*Franco! – Una grande! – Libre! – Arriba Espana! Viva Espana!*'

The parade ground was covered in three inches of slush and our worn-out footwear meant that our feet were completely without feeling. When the parade was dismissed the prisoners were marched back to the camp clothing store where an issue was made of one filthy blanket between two. We were then shown to our sleeping quarters and were each given a small bundle of straw, which we spread on the concrete floor. Ted and I shared the blanket and, despite the usual vermin, we slept very soundly.

Life at Miranda began with the Spanish bugles sounding at 6.30 every morning. Two minutes later hut doors were thrown open and a dozen militiamen armed with clubs burst into the building. Anyone who was still in bed was beaten over the head until they staggered to their feet. A senior NCO carrying a dog-whip gave the militiamen every encouragement. We dressed as quickly as possible and were then allowed ten minutes to visit latrines in a huge ramshackle wooden building erected on piles over a backwater on the river Ebro. Breakfast, consisting of a tin plate of hot water coloured brown to resemble coffee and about 200 grammes of black bread, was served and once more we paraded to give the Fascist salute. After the half-hour parade we were dismissed and allowed two hours for exercise.

As we had no opportunity of exercising during the six weeks spent in Lerida and Zaragoza, our move to the concentration camp with its open spaces and fresh air seemed wonderful. Despite the many disadvantages the fact that we could use our legs again to walk about far outweighed all these. We learned from a Canadian prisoner that there were five hundred Spanish Republican prisoners, three hundred Poles, fifty British servicemen, seventy Belgians, forty Frenchmen, two dozen German deserters and an assortment of Yugoslavs, Armenians, Algerians, Hungarians, Czechs, Greeks, Rumanians and even two Chinese occupying the forty huts in the enclosure. In fact, apart from the Scandinavian countries, I think every state in Europe was represented.

The Miranda camp was approximately three hundred yards long by one hundred and fifty yards and covered about eight acres of ground. It was bounded by high wire on three sides and the river Ebro on the fourth. The river was frozen over on our arrival and sentry posts lined the far bank. The UK prisoners were housed in two huts with any vacant spaces allotted to various nationals picked up in other prisons. A very pro-British Hungarian, who had once owned a hotel in Majorca, was responsible for law and order in our two huts and everything ran very smoothly. He was known as 'The Cabot' and confessed he could see no future for himself if Germany won the war.

There was no lighting of any kind in the huts but the prison canteen staff used to drain the oil from sardine tins and barter it for some cigarettes if any were available. We used to tear a strip of shirt or jacket lining and soak it in the oil before lighting it, which as a rule gave us a glimmer of light for about two hours.

When darkness fell the camp took on the aspect of a very active Black Market. It always amazed me how everyone managed to acquire such an assortment of valuables, despite the fact that all their belongings had been confiscated by the guards at Zaragoza. In the ensuing six weeks all our party had by some means accumulated a personal treasure trove by buying, bartering or stealing and were now engaged in flogging it at an inflationary price. It was never safe to allow a stranger near your single blanket for your belongings could disappear and be disposed of at the other end of the camp in a matter of minutes.

It was very fortunate that I did not smoke and could save my cigarette rations for Black Market transactions. For ten cigarettes I managed to get a pair of Spanish Army boots from one of the guards – I'm not sure whether he stole them from the camp stores or took them from a dead man.

Those not engaged in Black Market activities displayed unexpected accomplishments, ranging from wood-carving to metal work. An artist who was fortunate enough to occupy a corner of the hut had procured an extra blanket, which he used to form a private cubicle. He had decorated the walls with very attractive pastel drawings. Each evening a violinist could be heard playing to a silent audience of music lovers while a large group of Poles took English lessons every night. They were still hoping to get to the UK and join the free armies of the world.

A week after our arrival at Miranda another contingent of UK troops arrived from Figueras. There were only ten in the batch but they included an anti-aircraft gunner who was gifted with a wonderful baritone voice. As he stood 6 foot 7 inches he was known to everyone as 'Tiny' and was in great demand – especially as he always started his recitals with *Jerusalem* and *Marta*. Five minutes after he started to sing a detachment of Poles would arrive at our hut, followed by a group of Spanish Republican prisoners and then a mixture of every nationality from Europe and Asia. Finally, the militiamen of the guard would arrive to investigate the gathering but they too would forget their duties and wait at the entrance to worship Tiny. He was completely unassuming and was altogether a very attractive personality. When I asked him if he was a professional entertainer he modestly and truthfully replied that he was 'a coalman from the London East End'.

In a previous chapter I related how Clr/Sgt Leiper and I were made responsible for taking particulars of all internees consigned to the Fort St Jean by the Vichy police. One of these internees was an Argyll who was an estate worker and hailed from the Inverness-shire/Argyll border. He explained to me that he had worked in the forestry during the spring and summer but, during the shooting season, he was a pony-man who conveyed the grouse in panniers to the nearest road, where the bag was transferred to a van. During the stalking season he did the same with the deer. He spoke very enthusiastically of his employment and it was plain to see how much he enjoyed it. When I asked him if he could gralloch a stag he replied with a smile, 'None better'.

I had often wondered how he had fared in his escape over the mountains and was very relieved to see him in the latest party from Figueras. He was now engaged in the pastime of louse extermination and had his vest and shirt spread along a low wall while his hands were covered in blood as he cracked the vermin between his thumb nails. As I passed him I remarked, 'A good bag, Maclean?'

He looked up and smiled, 'Six hundred and twenty seven and a half brace and I'm no' finished yet!' This was by no means an exceptional bag, for it was not unusual to kill a thousand one day and twelve hundred the next, such was the population of vermin living and breeding in great profusion on the warmest parts of our bodies.

By this time every prisoner in the camp was suffering from lice infestation and scabies. At night we scratched our bodies without being aware of doing so and any broken skin resulted in further lice attacks and eventually scabies. Those who were badly affected were isolated in a 'leper's hut' where they were not allowed visitors. When they were discharged they looked like skeletons and it was only with great difficulty that they managed to walk back to their original hut.

To complete our misery, practically every one of the thousand prisoners went down with a serious outbreak of dysentery. It originally started amongst the Republican prisoners and spread like wildfire through the entire camp. To make matters even worse the latrines on the River Ebro were three hundred yards from our huts and to reach them we had a long journey through snow and slush. When we did arrive we found accommodation for only six hundred, so there was always a very impatient party waiting for a place at the steps leading to the makeshift toilets. On average we had to visit them at least four times nightly so there was a continual line of men coming and going.

Brutal Treatment

At this stage I must mention how proud I was of the British soldier. At times the Spanish officers would hint that no further UK soldiers would be repatriated unless Gibraltar was returned to Spain and I'm sure some of our boys were beginning to have doubts they would be released before the end of the war.

Despite disgusting conditions of cold, filth, sickness and, most of all, starvation, their morale was incredibly high and their ability to sing, laugh and crack jokes when things were at their very worst was quite beyond the understanding of the other nationalities in the same circumstances. At the same time I was impressed by the bearing and dignity shown by the Poles, who had probably received worse treatment at the hands of the Germans, the Russians and now the Spaniards than any other displaced persons.

Not far from the camp there was a huge stone quarry with a light railway connected to the main railway network. Two or three days each week we were shackled in pairs and conveyed to the rock-face, where we broke stones for re-metalling roads. We then had to carry the broken stone in baskets to a railway truck, which had to be completely filled before we were allowed back to camp.

On the days we were not breaking metal we spent six hours in the potato hut peeling potatoes for the whole camp. One day some of our fellow prisoners collected some small pieces of driftwood washed up by the river and, as I was going on potato fatigue, I volunteered to bring back a few slices of potato. The senior NCO did not normally search prisoners coming off potato peeling but this was my unlucky day and they found six slices of potato in my pocket. I was marched to the prison cell where the NCO instructed the guards to fill a sack of stones. This they tied to my shoulders and forced me to walk five times around the camp. As the sack weighed about seventy pounds I made sure I was never again caught stealing potatoes.

At this time the treatment meted out by the guards to the prisoners was becoming worse day by day. For the slightest breach of discipline they used their rifle butts to club the offenders while the senior NCOs applied the finishing touches by use of their whips. It was not unusual to be roused from our beds at 3 a.m. by the sound of the camp hooter. Three minutes later, we were expected to be on parade in the square to pay tribute to Spain and General Franco with the Fascist salute. No matter what the weather was like we were not allowed to use a blanket for our protection. One stormy night an old Pole emerged from his hut with a blanket over his head and was immediately attacked and left unconscious face down in the slush. Two of us recognised the old man and stopped to help but were immediately attacked by a Spanish sergeant. In the resultant mêlée the sergeant was knocked down and lay on the ground shouting for the guard to come to his assistance.

My companion managed to rejoin the parade but I was captured by the guard and marched to the prison cell. By this time the parade was over and the British troops congregated round the prison – with the Cabot acting as interpreter – demanding that I should be released. The sergeant had by this time contacted the camp commandant demanding I should be flogged for assaulting him, but when the cabot explained that the British prisoners were prepared to tear the place apart if his demand was not rescinded the commandant left his house and made his way to the prison. I think the sight of thirty Poles taking their place alongside the British troops made him think again; the order was rescinded and I was allowed back to my hut. The next day the old Pole passed away and his British fellow-prisoners were very bitter about the whole affair.

The sergeant with whom we had fallen out had been wounded in the Civil War and walked with a limp. Perhaps it was for this reason that he resented the British internees and recommended that they should be punished, sometimes for no apparent reason. The day following the assult on the old Pole he was in charge of us on all our fatigues and I had the feeling that he paid special attention to me.

The next day we were detailed to work in the stone quarry and again he was in charge of the working party. When we left the camp he personally shackled me to a filthy Belgian, with whom I had to work for the full day. In the evening the whole party, still shackled in pairs, were returned to the camp in an ancient truck. On our arrival, the shackles were removed but the key required to unlock the chains which attached me to the Belgian was 'missing' and we were marched back to the prison cell.

When the sergeant opened the prison door to allow us both to enter, locked it behind him and then unlocked the shackles, I knew I was going to be the victim. One of the militiamen gave me an order which I did not understand so he clubbed me with his rifle butt. That was the signal for the sergeant and three guards to attack me and when I fell to the ground they proceeded to kick me to the far end of the building, a distance of about thirty yards. I was conscious of them kicking me on the head, face, shoulders and the ribs before I mercifully blacked out.

I was then left on the floor with severe head, mouth and face wounds. The prison building was about twelve feet high with what I can only describe as a half-floored loft, which normally housed half-a-dozen long-term prisoners. At the time it held one Frenchman, two Chinamen and a Puerto Rican. The latter had a good view of the proceedings and when the guards left the cell he carried me up the ladder running from the hut floor to the loft. My newfound friend had only two words of English, which he repeated continually. Later on I was glad to learn he had used them to describe the prison staff!

The following day I regained consciousness and learnt from the Frenchman that I had been a full day blacked-out. When I did regain my senses I had no sight and for a dreadful minute I wondered if they had blinded me. With the help of the Puerto Rican we discovered the kicking I received had opened the head wound I had sustained at St Valery and that the congealed blood had effectually sealed my eyes. I found it extremely difficult to breathe and suspected my ribs had been damaged, while I could not move my right shoulder without extreme pain in the region of my collar bone.

After a very uncomfortable night I was returned under escort to my hut. A miserable day and night followed, but on the next forenoon the British Military Attaché arrived at the camp with the very welcome news that a detachment of twenty-eight UK internees were due to be released within the next two days. This included the whole batch who arrived with Ted and me from Zaragoza and the rejoicing in the camp was hilarious. The

Military Attaché was furious on seeing my injuries and declared his intention of taking the matter up with the Spanish authorities on his return to Madrid.

Gibraltar

The following morning a 30-cwt truck arrived from Madrid and with the permission of the commandant twenty-eight deliriously happy British soldiers climbed aboard and started on our final leg to Blighty. Hidden by a covering tarpaulin, we began a dangerous journey over snow-covered roads until we reached the town of Burgos, where two or three cups of steaming hot coffee were provided. With the help of the Embassy courier I attempted to buy a ration of bread at a nearby café but was told there was none to spare. I was shown the daily ration for a civilian – it was about the size of a Swan Vestas matchbox.

We then re-boarded our truck and our next stop was the British Embassy at Madrid, where we arrived late in the evening. I think the ambassador, Sir Samuel Hoare, was on a visit to the British Consul at Valencia at the time. Nevertheless, we received a very warm welcome from his deputy, who congratulated us on our escape. We then sat down to our first knife and fork meal for over four months. It consisted mostly of seafood – prawns, mussels, squid and crabs – but after months of watery potatoes and beans it tasted wonderful.

After our meal we were taken to the Embassy baths, but found the water was only lukewarm. We would all have preferred to soak in a hot bath for hours but were allowed a very limited period as a Spanish mob were demonstrating outside the Embassy, demanding that Gibraltar be returned to the Spanish nation.

The following morning our filthy prison clothes were taken away for burning and we were outfitted in second-hand civilian clothes. After a good breakfast we were conveyed by truck to the main railway station, where four compartments had been reserved for us in a train travelling south. We were in the charge of a British Embassy courier, who smoothed things out when Spanish railway employees attempted to put us off the train at Aranjuez.

At this juncture it was obvious that the British were not the most popular travellers on Spanish railways. The courier was in charge of rations taken from Madrid, which he distributed without favour to twenty-eight hungry men. At the next stop, Valdepenas, he attempted to buy some oranges at a railway fruit stall but was refused. However, we arrived at Cordoba just as darkness was falling and the staff of a station food stall were packing up for the night so the courier purchased all the remaining foodstuff, which was enough to see us safely to Malaga. Here we were held up for five hours while some bomb damage to a railway bridge was repaired. The next morning, in brilliant sunshine, we travelled down the Costa del Sol to La Linea and finally to the magic goal of Gibraltar.

Our first impressions of Gibraltar were of the amount of bright lights everywhere and the huge army of Spanish civilians on their way to work in the town on contracts from the British Services. Someone remarked that La Linea was the only prosperous town they had seen in Spain. On the last leg of the journey the men were strangely quiet; I think that they all wanted to be alone with their thoughts of home. However, when they reached the frontier there was a moment to gladden the hearts of the Scots in the detachment – for the troops furnishing the guard were men of the Gordon Highlanders. As one Jock remarked, 'It was great to see the old balmorals again.'

It was now dark so we fully appreciated the bright lights all over the town as we were conveyed to the Spanish Pavilion, occupied by a battalion of the King's Regiment. They had hot baths ready for all of us and an hour later, feeling considerably cleaner, we had a talk from their Medical Officer, who advised us to go easy on the first two or three meals.

'It's likely to be sausage and eggs for tea, so I would advise you to limit it to twelve sausages and six eggs to start with!'

In my case, although I felt very hungry, I was unable to eat much as the pain from my ribs and shoulder made eating very uncomfortable. I had a word with the medical officer and he agreed to examine me at the Military Hospital immediately after tea. When I arrived there I found he had also asked the MO of the Canadian Hard Rock Tunnellers to be present, as the latter had very extensive experience of industrial injuries. After a thorough examination they agreed I was suffering from a cracked rib, a broken rib and a broken collarbone but, after being strapped up with plaster, I felt much improved. I was kept in hospital that night and the following day was discharged. When I left I was given my measurements – 5 feet 5½ inches and 88 lbs (40 kgs).

During our stay at Gibralter we had, on average, three sulphur baths each day in an effort to rid ourselves of the vermin picked up in the Spanish jails and camps. They proved to be very tenacious and there were numerous occasions when we believed we had finally got rid of them, only to find on the following morning that they had returned overnight. In fact, it was almost two months before they finally disappeared for good.

It was a wonderful feeling to walk the clean, bright streets of Gibraltar, able to buy whatever one fancied in the shops. By this time we had been outfitted in new battle dress and forage caps but, as the latter were not the proper head dress for a Scottish soldier, we spent an afternoon searching for the Headquarters of the 6th Black Watch, who kindly supplied us with new balmorals. At the end of ten days we were advised we would be repatriated to the United Kingdom by the next suitable convoy. As soon as we arrived in Gibraltar I posted a letter home to say I was on my way and hoped to be there in a matter of two or three weeks.

There was great excitement when we were informed that we were due to leave for the UK in the Polish cruiser *Sobieski*. She had taken part in the action against the Vichy French forces at Senegal and the entire ship had been badly scarred by small arms fire. The crew, with the exception of the senior officers, were mostly Polish and were delighted to be fighting on the Allied side against the Germans.

Going Home

Our journey home took exactly one week. Off the Azores we joined a convoy comprising a New Zealand cruiser, five or six destroyers, three tankers and half-a-dozen merchantmen and sailed due north until we cleared the British Isles before turning east. Our first sight of land was the west coast of Lewis and Harris. In this area the convoy was attacked by U-boats, but our escort took care of that and we docked safely at Gourock.

In addition to the UK party there were about a dozen other nationals who became attached to us at Madrid and Gibraltar. We were all regarded as security risks so a number of Intelligence personnel were present when the *Sobieski* docked at Gourock and escorted us to Glasgow. Here we were housed and fed at a military establishment near the Central Station and the following morning caught the London train.

On the journey the security was very strict and on reaching London we were conveyed direct to Whitehall where we were housed in an empty hotel. In the morning we were addressed by a team of brigadiers and colonels and in the afternoon were presented with pens and unlimited writing paper to set down in our own words what had happened since our last connection with British forces.

By the time we had completed our reports it was the afternoon of our third day at Whitehall and once they were handed in we felt much relieved. The following day we were still regarded as security risks and spent much of our time resting in our rooms. On the fifth day we were questioned by Intelligence officers who had already gone over our reports and for the whole of the afternoon we answered questions on what we had seen and heard during our travels. I was hoping to be released in time to catch the midnight train to Inverness but three of us were advised that further questioning was necessary and we would be required to remain another two days.

The following morning I was ushered into the presence of a civilian, who I was later told was one of the top Intelligence men. He was very pleasant and easy to speak to and told me right away that he was interested in my account of our watch on the derelict Hotel Britannique in Marseilles and the arrival of coaches there, thought to be transporting men of the Afrika Korps to Marseilles docks.

I mentioned to him the part the Scottish officer, John Garrow, had taken and he said he could get through to someone who would get Garrow to confirm my report. He then switched to the subject of Sergeant André Varnier, who had accompanied us on part of our journey down through France, informing me that his father was a Frenchman employed by the French Embassy in Berlin between the wars. He had married a German girl employed in a government office. It appeared that two persons purporting to be André Varnier had applied to join the Free French forces in Britain. I confirmed that the one we knew was a footballer who played left back in the Côte du Midi league team and should readily be recognised by many Free French servicemen at present in Britain. I also quoted Private McGowan in his description of a 'one-footed' football player and he laughed heartily.

I then asked if he knew anything of the fate of Donald Caskie, the Church of Scotland minister. He replied that he was aware he was in enemy hands but did not yet know whether he was being held in Germany or Switzerland. He agreed that Donald had done wonderful work in feeding and clothing escaped prisoners and passing them to Resistance couriers who finally saw them over the Pyrenees. He mentioned that Donald was attempting to find a new escape road by Luchon when he was picked up by the Gestapo. I replied that I could confirm that, as Donald had sent two of us to find if the Luchon road was passable in winter time and that I had sent him a letter to Rue de Forbin advising that it was impossible until late in the spring. I said I doubted if that letter would ever be delivered.

That evening we were given tickets and passes to Inverness and the following morning I reported to the Cameron Barracks. We were home.

Back with the Army

On my arrival at the Cameron Barracks the scene was one of unbelievable confusion, with what seemed to be hundreds of soldiers and civilians milling around the square. The latter appeared to be an intake of new recruits who by the end of the day would certainly all be in battledress. There was a parade of new ATS being drilled on the square, with a young officer looking somewhat self-conscious as she introduced her squad to the intricacy of the 'about turn'.

I was spoken to by the adjutant; he took me to the CO, who asked where I had come from. When I replied, 'Gibraltar, sir,' he said, 'Good heavens, I didn't know we had any of the Regiment in Gib.'

He did not appear interested in how I got there but then suddenly spotted that I had no rifle and pointed out that a soldier without a rifle was worse than useless. He made me feel that I had committed a major crime and when I saluted and turned to leave the room he remarked, 'Remember, Colour Sergeant, there is no excuse for not having your rifle with you at all times!'

Later that morning I returned to the Orderly Room to collect my pass for seven days leave and my return ticket to my home at Killin, Perthshire. When I arrived there I learned from my parents that John McGlynn, my original companion, had spent a weekend with them soon after he arrived in the UK at the end of 1940 – so they knew of all the happenings at St Valery and afterwards.

Before my leave expired I requested a further week to allow me to visit the homes of a number of Harris soldiers who were still reported missing. I later requested a further three days leave to visit some Skye homes, but this was refused. I then reported back to the Depot and spent a very boring ten days there. The only bright spots in that period were an evening out with McGlynn when we remembered all the good times we had and an afternoon when I checked the kits of two cadets who were on their way to OCTU. One gave his name as L/Cpl

Fitzroy Maclean but this meant nothing to me until some years after the war when I read his book *Eastern Approaches* dealing with his adventures with the Yugoslav partisans.

At the end of a fortnight I was delighted to receive a posting to the 5th Camerons of the new 51st Highland Division, who were stationed under canvas at Turiff. With the exception of the senior NCOs, the Battalion was composed of territorials from Kingussie, Fort William, Nairn and Inverness and was a very competent and happy unit. I found I was the senior colour sergeant and, being supernumerary, was posted as acting sergeant major of the 152 Brigade Signals School at Banchory for a two-month period.

In the meantime the 5th Camerons were secretly moved to Balmoral. As His Majesty the King was Colonel-in-Chief of the Cameron Highlanders, it was assumed they would be furnishing the guard during the king's grouse shooting holiday. This is exactly what happened and a few days later the CO, Lieutenant Colonel Alexander Cattanach, was invited to dinner with the royal party. In the course of conversation the subject of the surrender of the 51st Division at St Valery was discussed and the CO mentioned that he had a colour sergeant recently posted to his Battalion who had been taken prisoner there and who had escaped from Germany. His Majesty expressed an interest in my escape and suggested to Colonel Cattanach that he might arrange that Colour Sergeant MacDonald be detailed as one of his personal guards at a shoot on Invercauld estate in two days time. The following day I was recalled from Banchory and instructed to draw a complete new uniform from the regimental stores.

Next morning we left Abergeldie Lodge at 7.30 a.m. and our party of seven sergeants was joined by the king's detective, a Scotsman by the name of Cameron. On our arrival at Invercauld Estate a Sergeant Groat and I were placed in position overlooking the butts to be occupied by the king during the forenoon individual drives and we spent time admiring His Majesty's marksmanship. After lunch on the hill the detective approached and advised me to accompany him to the king's presence. On the way I asked him how I should address the king and, after consideration, he replied, 'As he is Colonel-in-Chief of your regiment it will be sufficient to address him as "Sir", as you would any senior officer.'

I found His Majesty to be very interested and very easy to speak to. After congratulating me on my escape, he asked if I had come down through the centre of France and if I had gone near Paris. He asked how many miles I had covered on foot and I replied, 'About fifteen hundred.'

It was obvious that he had interviewed others who had come out through Spain for he asked how I found life in the Miranda de Ebro concentration camp. Before the interview finished the queen came across to ask if I would be sent back to the front. I replied that I hoped so and she warned, 'Don't let them catch you again.'

Two days later I was summoned to appear before the CO, who informed me that the king had requested a written account of my experiences and I would be given two days to prepare this. This was duly done and after the orderly room staff had made a typed copy it was despatched to Balmoral Castle.

At the end of a week I was again instructed to appear before the CO, where I was handed an acknowledgement and asked if I had ever considered applying for a commission. I replied that I was very happy in the ranks and my ambition was to become a company sergeant major, but then he suggested that I should think it over for a matter of ten days. At the end of that time he again had me up for interview and informed me that he had entered my name for a War Office Selection Board interview at Inverness in two weeks time. I was duly informed that I had passed the required grade and three weeks later I was posted to 164 Officer Cadet Training Unit at the Royal Military College, Sandhurst.

Gregor Grant MacDonald had a distinguished war. He was mentioned in dispatches for the courage and initiative he had shown during his escape. In August 1942 he was commissioned into the Camerons and won the Military Cross in Italy with the 2nd Battalion, fighting their way from Cassino to San Marino. After further service in Greece he was finally demobbed in November 1945 after six years and three months in the army.

Long after the war he was contacted by a Colonel of the Camerons in Inverness who told him a Croix de Guerre had arrived for No. 2931666 Colour Sergeant MacDonald. Gregor's number was 2931066 so he modestly assumed that the award could not be for him.

Despite the number confusion, the colonel was pretty certain that he was the only MacDonald who fitted the bill – especially after hearing of the incident with the French colonel at the Oisement railway line (see p. 54). He said he would do some checking to make sure.

Unfortunately the colonel was taken ill and Gregor heard no more. However, the medal eventually arrived at the depot but there was no special presentation. Because the confusion had never properly been cleared up, Gregor was reluctant to wear the medal and did not mention it to anyone – not even in his book.*

In January 1946 he returned to the Bank of Scotland counter at Tarbert but, like many of his companions, found it very difficult to settle down. In common with many others, he missed the comradeship and so was very pleased to rejoin the Territorial Army immediately it was re-started. He served with the 4th/5th Camerons till 1962. In 1950, when the memorial to the 51st Highland Division was erected on the cliffs above St Valery, he was very proud to be appointed second-in-command of the Guards of Honour selected from the five Highland Regiments.

He retired from the bank in 1972, having completed forty years service – latterly as manager in Grantown-on-Spey.

Gregor died on 15 March 1994 and is buried in his beloved Harris.

* This information was taken from his interview with D. Ferguson of the Bank of Scotland in 1987.

Under the Shadow of the Swastika

DONALD JOHN MACDONALD

Do na gillean uile, mar theisteanas air misneach, fad-fhulangas is uaisle ri aodann geur-leanmhain.

To all the lads, in testimony to courage, long-suffering and nobility in the face of adversity.

MacDonald's dedication in the original book

Donald John MacDonald, born in Peninerine, South Uist, was a member of C company of the 4th Battalion, Cameron Highlanders.

This account of the wartime experiences that were to change his life forever was first published (in Gaelic only) as Fo Sgàil a' Swastika *by Club Leabhar in 1974. A new edition in parallel translation (Acair 2000) first introduced this riveting account of the POW experience to a non-Gaelic readership.*

The tale illustrates vividly how an irrepressible spirit and sense of humour helped MacDonald withstand the pressures and deprivation of captivity. That it is told with all the verve and immediacy of a natural raconteur should not surprise us – for he was born into a family of storytellers and bards. His father, Duncan MacDonald, was a traditional storyteller of legendary repertoire, while his mother Margaret was a sister of Donald Macintyre, the Paisley bard.

Despite being steeped in Gaelic oral culture from infancy, Donald John was a reluctant conventional scholar, desperate to leave school at fourteen. South Uist in the 1930s was a land of poverty where crofters wrested a bare living from a hostile environment, using manual methods long since abandoned on the more prosperous mainland. Alternative employment was virtually impossible to find and such luxuries as holidays unheard of. Small wonder that the annual fortnight's camp of the Territorials was seen by the young men as a welcome and even glamorous break from the unremitting grind of work on the land.

When war was declared in 1939 it seemed to promise a heady mix of excitement and adventure. 'At last!' the twenty year old Donald John exclaimed to his sister, Ann. Spirits were high as the Uist Territorials left to join the Cameron Highlanders, although the older generation who had suffered in the carnage of the First World War must have watched them go with wiser eyes and heavy hearts.

When the 4th Camerons moved to the Aldershot area, his army contemporaries report that Donald John seems to have found the army training methods of the time somewhat intimidating. Although he had been a high-spirited and mischievous teenager, his reaction was to display an apparent under-confidence and shyness. Military instructors of the period famously believed that bullying tactics turned boys into disciplined men, so his diffidence singled him out for more than his fair share of latrine cleaning and potato peeling duties. This account makes clear that his natural qualities of spirit and courage soon re-asserted themselves – particularly in defiance of his captors.

This rebelliousness manifested itself in the several ill-starred attempts at escape which he describes. The reader may consider them to be impulsive and reckless to the point of foolhardiness but, as the writer explains, they were his way of demonstrating to the Germans that the love of freedom of an independent spirit could not be crushed by captivity.

MacDonald was one of the beneficiaries when men of the 51st were allowed to go on leave in early May 1940. To their great surprise, they were not recalled when the offensive began. In fact, when MacDonald returned from leave he found himself in a holding camp near Le Havre and was only reunited with the Camerons when he volunteered to take the place of another man.

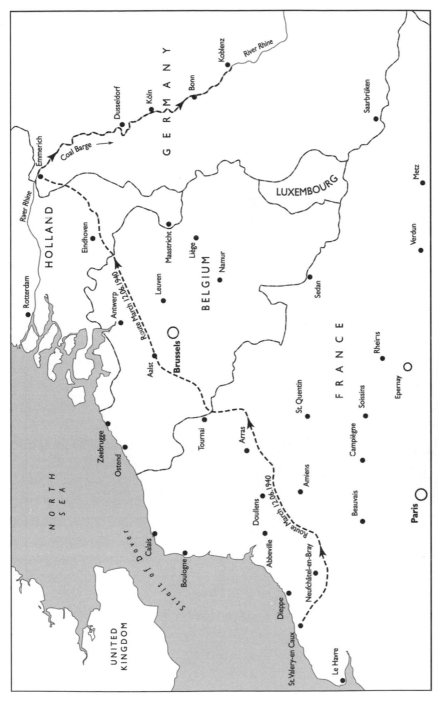

Map 5: Approximate route of march from St Valery to the Rhine, June 1940

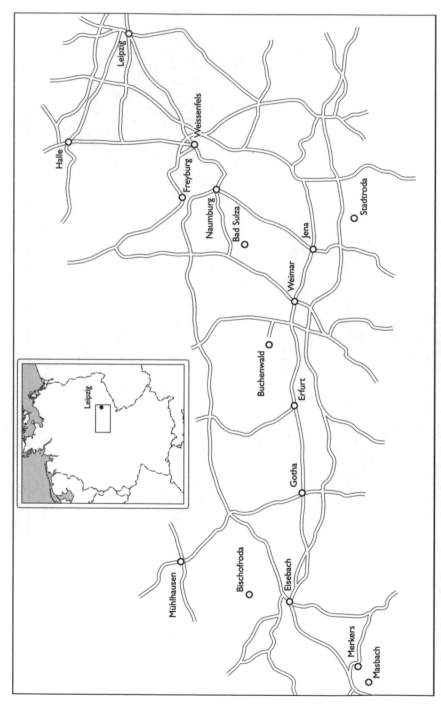

Map 6: Sketch map of the Thuringia region of Germany, showing places mentioned in D.J. MacDonald's account

St Valery

St Valery was loud with
Shots and thunder of war;
We left many young men
Lifeless, dead on the shore.

Translated from MacDonald's *Eilean Beag a' Chuain*

The ships of the British Navy lay about three-quarters of a mile
from land. The sea shone like silver in the bright sunlight, for
the day was very hot with not the tiniest cloud to mar the deep
blue of the sky. Birds sang in the trees around, their song being
the only sound to disturb the peace and quiet of this lovely
summer day.

But as the old saying goes, 'there is another side to the hill'
and we had certainly experienced plenty of proof of that other
side in the preceding two weeks. We were sitting on a high green
wooded hill above Dieppe in Northern France on that special
summer day, and the year was 1940.

The defeat and victory of Dunkirk was over and the Highland Division had been driven back from the Somme to
the shores of the Channel. So there we were on this hill
looking out to sea at the ships of our country which could
not venture any closer to the beaches; so near to us and yet so
very far away.

The powers above had expected that the Highland Division
could be rescued by ferrying them from the port of Dieppe but
Rommel's powerful forces had been swifter. In the afternoon of
that beautiful summer day, the blessed peace we had so briefly
enjoyed was shattered by the roar and thunder of artillery and
we were ordered to prepare to move on.

The trucks came – large trucks of the RASC which could each
carry about thirty men – and we were on the road again. We
travelled quite a few miles in these trucks and then halted. We
had little or no knowledge of what exactly was happening, but

we were not long left in that state. We were lined up and one of
the officers, Major Hill, came to talk to us.* The Major was a
fine big man – erect, mature, well-proportioned, grey-haired. I
think he had fought in the Kaiser's war. He told us that
Rommel's army had broken through to the coast and, if we
were to be saved, it would be necessary to make for a little town
further east of Dieppe, which also lay on the Channel coast.
This was St Valery-en-Caux, the town where hope was
shattered and many a strong, sturdy lad in the fresh springtime
of youth was laid cold and stiff in alien soil.

We came into St Valery on the Monday night. Tuesday
morning we had orders to make ready to go into battle array.
We had to attack and drive the Germans back from a high hill
outside the town. We set off, but a little way from the town we
were made to lie low in a large field of corn. We were ordered to
remain still and silent and on no account to reveal our position
to the enemy. We never heard what went wrong, nor were we
given any reason for being left lying for a whole long summer's
day in a great field of corn with bullets cutting ears from the
stalks above our heads.

What lovely corn that was; although it was only the middle
month of summer it was already starting to ripen. I often
wonder if it was ever harvested. The man who ploughed, sowed
and harrowed it in the spring little thought that it would
be flattened under the boots and wheels of the German
Wehrmacht by the autumn.

But who knows? The fact that so many of the French
themselves collaborated with the Germans was the prime reason
that France did not hold out longer. But I have to say that the
majority of the French army was as loyal and steadfast as
limpets on a rock. There is no country or nation that does
not have more than one Quisling in it.

With the onset of dusk and the darkness of night, we were
able to get to our feet again and return to St Valery. Then the
battle started to defend the town. By one or two in the morning,

* Major Stanley 'Daddy' Hill from Inverness was second-in-command of the
battalion.

much of it was in flames and the Germans were pouring a continuous stream of firepower in amongst us. It was obvious that there was no way out of the trap we were in other than to drive the enemy back. The town was surrounded.

With one or two others I was having a breather inside a big long building which looked like a storehouse. We noticed a large hogshead on a stand at the other end of the room. One of the boys went up to it and discovered that it contained beer. Well! War or no war, we would have our share. We loosened the mugs that hung from our kit and at that very moment came the explosion! We all flung ourselves to the ground, hands over our heads. When we realised we were still alive, we rose. We could barely see each other through the smoke and dust throughout the building. When the dust settled there was no sign of the other end of the house – or of the hogshead. The floor where it had been was not even wet.

'Well', said one fine lad in the company, 'they can destroy the houses, but they might have left the beer alone!'

About nine o'clock in the morning there came a lull in the storm. We and the French were still firing our .303 rifles – the only weapon we had against the huge armoured tanks of the other side. The mouse fighting the lion, I could say!

Major Hill appeared again and asked us all to line up. We were on a low road that had been cut into a high hill on the outskirts of the town. The steep slopes on either side of the road made an excellent shield against shrapnel. The Major started to speak and tears were running down his cheeks.

'The order has come from High Command,' he said, 'that the surviving members of the Division should surrender to avoid a massacre.'

None of those present could comprehend fully the implications of these words. Not a man standing there had considered in his heart such an eventuality. No one had any inkling or insight that most of the British army was already in England, having been evacuated from Dunkirk. So, therefore, surprise was the first emotion that affected our minds. But, as the major continued to speak, the facts began to sink in and we realised the situation was not just dangerous but completely without hope. The enemy that surrounded us had vastly superior numbers and firepower and there was no way that a boat could get within a mile of the shore. The battle had been fought and the battle had been lost.

The order 'Ground Arms!' was given. The men looked at one another, but each one still kept a death-grip on his rifle. Usually in the army, if an order was disobeyed it was a serious offence and the guilty would be dealt with accordingly, but this was a different matter.

The order was given a second time and it was explained to us at the same time that the enemy was ready to destroy the town and kill everyone in it unless the soldiers surrendered. Two or three dropped their weapons. The rest looked at each other again. It has to be understood what a difficult dilemma this was. If you gave up your weapon, it was as if you were naked without your support. You regarded your rifle as your only basic protection when amongst deadly enemies. No wonder then that, despite the order, we should be reluctant to part with the one thing that could make the difference between life and death.

A burst of machine-gun fire over our heads gave convincing demonstration that the threats were not vain. After that, the arms were dropped. An armoured truck came down the road with a lot of heavily-armed Germans standing in it. After them came more and more.

The castles built in the air by the young were now in ruins on the ground, and among the rubble lay the bodies of many a young man who had helped to build those very castles.

The Great March

The sun was so hot. I myself was parched with thirst and there was not a drop left in my water-bottle. We were all tired. Lack of food, lack of sleep and in particular the situation we found ourselves in were the main causes of the heaviness of mind and body on our journey.

We were in a large grassy field a short way out of the town where we had been assembled when the fighting ceased. Beside me sat another man from Uist, Alan Mackay* from Lochboisdale, and I asked him for a drink. Alan handed over his own water-bottle and I tipped it up and drank. I was so dry that I could not stop and certainly I left little in it. But when I paused I hiccupped. It was cognac that Alan had in his bottle and I had drunk nearly three-quarters of a pint of it! I stretched out on the grass and very shortly was sound asleep.

This was about half past ten in the morning and it was four in the afternoon when I was awakened. There were hundreds of French and British gathered in this field as well as Moroccan French – black men. They did not believe in surrender; their tradition was to fight to the death. After the cease-fire had been called that morning I had seen one of them leap on a German soldier and stick a long thin knife in his throat. Next moment the black man was killed by a hail of bullets from an armoured car.

That afternoon started the march which was to last longer than three weeks. It seemed to me that the line of men walking the road was more than a mile long – perhaps closer to two. This mass of men was guarded by armed soldiers walking on each side with others in vehicles and on motor-bikes. Before we left the coast of France our path took us along by the sea and we saw a big ship lying a little distance out from the shore. The German tanks turned their guns out to sea and fired on her and we saw the splashes where the shells struck very near to her.

Next minute, fire was returned from the ship herself. This was worse than ever. Better to be killed by enemy guns than those of our own countrymen – but we were ever moving away from the shore and so we got clear of the shells from the ship.

There was nothing for it now but walking. We covered a distance of about thirty kilometres each day. In the evening we would be camped in a field or some such suitable place with our

* Alan Mackay survived the war and died in Uist in the mid 1980s.

greatcoats for blankets. A French loaf or German ryebread would be distributed to six men – or eight if bread was scarce. Each man's share was very little.

But often as we marched through towns there would be a chance to forage here and there. One day we were passing through a pretty little town on the road to Belgium. Some men had a little money left while others had none at all. One or two went into a shop as we passed by to find something to eat – the nearest guard being some way off. But before the shoppers could get their hands on their purchases, about twenty of us burst into the shop. There was no time to pay before the guard would be in after us, nor was there time enough for an assistant to serve us. It was every man for himself with the weakest getting the least. It was 'self-service'! Much of the shop's goods were strewn on the floor or on the street outside, but we had a goodly part of it in our pockets or stuffed into our uniform blouses. This sort of thing was a common occurrence when we passed through towns and even though many shots were fired no one that I knew was hit. However, I heard later that some men were badly wounded while raiding shops.

There was also good plunder to be had in the potato fields, though this too had to be out of sight of a guard. If four or five plants could be pulled, the pockets of trousers and blouses would be full of potatoes. At the end of the day when we halted for the night, the potatoes would be cooked on fires made from wood splinters and anything else that might burn. You can bet that there were many feasts on potatoes boiled in their jackets or sometimes roasted.

But think of the effect of forty or sixty men descending on a little field of potatoes, even for three minutes. Five hundred yards behind there would be just as many in another field. By the time ten thousand men had passed, you can understand there would not be many potatoes left in the ground. Apparently news of the potato looting spread throughout the country, so that before we reached the Belgian border the French would be standing at the end of their fields with guns and sticks to protect their crop from the raiders.

I could not blame them for that. Their world had been completely disrupted and they knew not what the next day or week might bring. The even tenor of the life they had led for the previous twenty years had been turned upside down and, though they knew that we were hungry, they had to preserve the food they had planted for themselves. It had certainly not been planted for us or the Germans.

But much kindness was also shown – especially in Belgium. The day the prisoners were to pass would be known beforehand and women would stand here and there with great pails of soup. Our mess-tins would be filled if we should happen to be close to the pail and that was a rare treat. At other times a loaf would be thrown but often the one who caught it had the least of it in the end. I saw one man catching a loaf like this. About ten pairs of hands grabbed at it and all that he was left with was what was trapped in his ten finger nails!

Always the men walked. All day in the full heat of the sun with a stop in the evening where the guards saw fit. If the heat was difficult to endure during the day, the cold of the night was worse. By now very few still had their greatcoats – they had been abandoned to save weight – so there was nothing for it but to sleep on bare ground without any kind of cover. It was a somewhat restless sleep, but after the fatigue of the day's march, sleep nevertheless.

Feet started to give out. Great water blisters would form on soles and before feet could be put back in the boots, these had to be burst to release the fluid. That was when the real pain started. It was no good sitting down by the side of the road. A heavy blow from a guard's rifle butt would impel you quickly upright and the prodding of a bayonet would force you to walk, however painful your feet.

One day, on the way through Belgium, a little car came along pulling a trailer. There were five or six of us in a little group trailing about a mile after the rest – having fallen behind with sore feet. Every man leapt at the car. The trailer filled but it would only take six so that it was full before I could get in. But I was not to be beaten! I jumped on the back of the car between it and the trailer and grabbed onto the spare wheel tied to the back. The car went off at a goodly rate. With the weight in the trailer behind, the car was snaking from side to side and I kept slipping down between the two vehicles. The wind blast was close to blowing me off but I kept a death-grip on the spare wheel although it was a struggle to breathe. A guard stopped the car after about two or three miles of this and I was very thankful to get my feet back on the ground, hunched and lame though I was. My head was spinning like a windmill.

Many a man gave up. Through hunger and fatigue many became exhausted and fell by the wayside. What happened to them all I cannot be sure. Undoubtedly some were transported in trucks, but I think many were simply eliminated. Human life was not worth much then – it was just like crushing a fly that landed on your nose. A black time indeed.

Thirst and lack of water were the worst of our sufferings. A shower of rain was a great blessing – particularly close to houses – for a man could rush across and catch the water draining from the roof in a jar or mess-tin. A mouthful of water collected in this way was sweeter and tastier than the most expensive wine in France.

As I have already mentioned, we were shown much kindness on our way through Belgium. It was obvious too that the people of Belgium were more antagonistic than the French to the Germans. When the women came out with pots of soup, a guard would kick them over if he came near. Every drop would be spilt on the ground but he would be reviled in language not fit to repeat here – and I even saw one attacked and heartily kicked by some women.

When we reached the soil of Holland, some men were put in vehicles and some in little railway trucks which ran on tracks through the streets and some highways. I well remember that I received a heavy blow on the head when I reached out from the side of the truck to grab a loaf which a woman offered us in passing. I did not see the great pole by the side of the road until it met my head. But though my world went black after the first white flash, I did not lose my grip on the bread!

It will be easily understood that after three weeks of this sort of life, without much food and sleeping in our clothes, that a man would be plagued with lice. Often when we stopped in the evening, men could be seen here and there with shirts about their shoulders, killing lice. But, however many you killed, the bugs multiplied sevenfold so that your clothes could almost walk off your back. This was the state in which we reached a busy harbour in Holland, a destination which meant the end of the marching but the beginning of more hunger, thirst and suffering for four days sailing up the River Rhine.

The Barges

There were seven or eight barges at these wharves. The Rhine is a busy waterway in peacetime with every kind of boat sailing up and down the river, but this time it was to carry an unusual load – three or four barges full of prisoners of war on their wretched journey into Hitler's yoke of bondage. To anyone who has an eye for wonderful scenery and takes pleasure in the beauty of nature, unforgettable scenes are revealed little by little while sailing up the Rhine. This is especially so between Bonn and Bingen. Even though we did not get that far south on this occasion, there were some scenes delightful to the eye – but only to the eye of freedom and not the downcast eye of the prisoner, who can get no pleasure from beauty even at its fairest.

We were given a little round loaf of bread each and we were put on board the barges. If we had known beforehand that we were to be four days aboard we would not have eaten most of the loaf that first afternoon. But we still had a little of the potatoes and carrots of Belgium in our pockets.

I missed my watch. I had bought it in Inverness at the beginning of the war after we received our first pay. As far as I remember it cost fifteen shillings. I had sold it to a Belgian the week before for ten cigarettes and a bit of bread.

But the lack of a watch was the least of our problems now compared to the lack of food. We were packed below in the hold of the barge like sardines; you had only your own length and breadth. The deck above was just as crowded. As well as the heat of the sun during the day, the suffocating warmth of the men's breath made you heavy and sleepy. The only opening was at the top of a ladder so there was only room for one at a time to stand there.

The barges made very little speed upstream; theirs was a slow and tedious journey. By the second day we had finished what was left of the bread and were now dependent on a few scraps of potatoes and carrots – legacies of the foraging in Belgium and France. There was only one stove on the barge, so that only rarely could a man get a chance to cook anything like potatoes – for everyone had some.

Though we were troubled by hunger, the craving for a smoke was powerful too. The cigarettes I got for my watch lasted only a day. Donald John Morrison from Uist* went up one day to the stove to boil a little pan of potatoes. A Frenchman was cooking something before him and what did my boy do but return instead with ten cigarettes. But we had more potatoes and, despite the hunger, we had a good smoke!

A boy from Paisley took a bit of bread out of the breast of his jacket; all that was left of the loaf he was given on the first day. The scrap of bread was alive with lice. For anyone who has never known or suffered hunger in his life it might be hard to believe that all he did was scrape the lice off with his fingers and eat the bread. In this kind of state, each man clings to life and cares only for himself. If you yield to weakness of any sort, you are lost. There was not one of us but would have done the same, if only we had had the bread.

Although the hunger was bad, thirst was the greatest ordeal. Some lowered tins tied to strings into the river. They would haul the tin up by the string and drink the water. You do not need too much imagination to realise what kind of water runs in the Rhine, or in any river that flows through cities and industrial areas. So it is no wonder that those men were left

* Donald John Morrison lived by Loch Roag in Snishival – very near to MacDonald's home in Peninerine. He survived the war but was killed in a collision while riding his motor-bike in South Uist in 1956.

miserable and sick with diarrhoea after drinking the water. As they had no food in their bellies, it was mostly blood they were passing.

One day I saw Duncan MacCormick from Daliburgh eating potatoes.*

'How did you cook them?' I asked.

'I didn't cook them at all,' he said, 'there were others before me at the stove, so I just started to eat them raw as they were. Try it and you'll see how good it is.'

Duncan was cutting them up in thin slices and dipping them in some salt he got from a Frenchman. I tried Duncan's way myself and I have to admit it was very tasty. We ate raw potato till we were full. There is no doubt that hunger makes anything taste good but I certainly would not eat raw potato now. Many suffered a lot of stomach trouble afterwards in Germany, myself included. Some even died because of it. Doctors said that poor food, eaten raw on an empty stomach, brought this situation about.

One dream was a particularly bad nightmare for me every time I slept and it is just as vivid before my eyes today as it was on the barge. I would see buckets full of water sailing on the wind before me, but every time I tried to grab one with my tongue reaching out for the water, the bucket would move away from me. My heart was desperate for a drop of it; my lips and tongue were as dry as embers of fire, but the more I pursued the bucket the farther away it went. I think that this harrowing dream was even worse than the thirst itself, so that it was a relief to wake up.

But there is nothing, good or bad, that does not end eventually. The barges drew into a quay and tied up. At the time we had no inkling of where exactly we were. After some time we were brought out. We then saw that this was the town of Emmerich† and realised that we were on enemy soil. We stood on the earth of Germany. We were then taken to large halls on

* Duncan MacCormick survived the war but died suddenly in South Uist in 1959 at the early age of 39.
† Emmerich was the first railway town on the Rhine inside the German border.

the outskirts of the town. I am not sure what buildings they were – schools or town halls perhaps – but it was there we had the first taste of the cruelty of our oppressors.

The First Camp

When I got to my feet, my head felt dizzy. The light of day darkened for me and I had to grab the nearest support or I would have fallen to the ground. Lack of food was the major reason for this sorry state, but chronic fatigue – together with more than three weeks of broken sleep – had a lot to do with it as well. Most of us were in the same state.

We were gathered in the great hall which I have already mentioned. We were all as naked as the day we were born, our clothing having been taken from us for much-needed cleaning. Now two or three of us at a time would be taken out to another room, but for what reason we did not yet know. A black-uniformed German stood at the door and anyone who did not pass him quickly enough would be lashed across the back with a slim black whip he held in his hand. I escaped the whip when my turn came but there was many another poor fellow who had a huge red weal across his shoulders where the whip had curled with full force of arm.

When my two companions and I reached the other room, clippers were passed over our hair till our heads were as bald as though they had been shaved. In the same way our chests and groins were sheared and we were then returned to the first room until our clothes were cleaned and ready. Once or twice the one with the whip passed among us with a blow here and there but I managed to avoid being struck by keeping a sharp eye lest I be caught unawares.

We were given a bowl of some white stuff like porridge. We did not pause to question the taste of it but gulped it down regardless of whether it might be poison. Whatever it was, it was warm and filled the empty hole in our stomachs.

After that we were crammed on top of one another into cattle trucks. There was a scattering of straw on the floor – bedding for the cattle that had used them last, I believe. But this litter was now to serve as our bedding for more than twenty-four hours without food or water on our journey across the alien land of Germany.

This train halted at last at a station and the cattle-truck was opened. We were taken out and saw the name Bad Sulza. We had reached our destination: the headquarters of Stalag IXc in the very middle of Germany.*

Here we were each given a little plate with individual numbers written on it. From now on I was Prisoner of War 1197 in the eyes of the German High Command. I have to admit they were well organised. Everything had been prepared beforehand. Four or five men sat at desks taking your name, regiment and home area of Britain. It was a stern-faced blonde man who questioned me. He looked like the very devil and I was certainly relieved to get past him. When I answered his questions he then asked, 'Do you speak Gaelic?'

'Yes,' said I.

'Sit over there then,' he said, pointing with his finger to the upper end of the room. His English was good.

I went where he had directed and found four or five Uist boys there before me. It was not long before more arrived. Apparently they were asking the Gaelic question of every one from northern Scotland and all those they found who spoke it were being put together. So we Gaelic speakers, together with a few Lowlanders, were separated out to go to Work Camp 323, a stone quarry in the town of Freyburg.

It was a bright, sunny day when we reached Freyburg station. We were accompanied by three guards, Wehrmacht soldiers. The Wehrmacht was the main army of Germany; quite separate from the SS. The SS were the real Hitlerites, closely involved in the Nazi party. Even the soldiers of the Wehrmacht were somewhat apprehensive of them.

The country was ruled by fear. A German workman would tell me things about the government of the country that he

---

* *Stalag* (abbr. of *Stammlager*) – a POW camp for non-commissioned officers and men. *Oflag* was the equivalent camp for officers.

would be too frightened to say to one of his fellow countrymen. Freedom of speech was stifled in their throats for fear of the midnight knock at their doors; a knock which would have only one outcome – disappearance without trace.

This sort of disappearance was common enough in Hitler's Germany. When all the criminals, scum and worst of mankind in a country are brought together, given authority and granted great power, the state of that country can be imagined. It was from that class of people that most of the Gestapo had been recruited. (Gestapo was short for *Geheime Staatspolizei* – Secret State Police).

I only met the Gestapo face to face on one occasion – for they had no authority over us as prisoners of war – but that occasion was quite enough. I will touch on that meeting in another chapter. The Gestapo's responsibility was for political prisoners. There was no international law of any kind to protect such prisoners. They were subjected to the cruel brutality of this group, who had not the slightest drop of pity within their icy hearts.

Freyburg was a small, pretty town, surrounded by large vineyards spread out on the slopes of the high hills facing the sun. Much wine was made in the town and there were underground cellars containing hundreds of gallons of it. But we were not destined to work in the vineyards, but in the quarry about four miles out of town.

Our living quarters in the town were quite good: a large building with lots of windows, with a dormitory and living room and other small rooms for the guards. However, the first winter in Freyburg was hard indeed. We had no decent clothing except for the rags of the uniform we had been wearing when captured. Shirts and socks had worn away and, through work in the quarry, boots and trousers were full of holes, while the cold was such as our country has never known. There is no doubt that the effects of the cold were aggravated through lack of proper food and decent clothing, but that did not make it any easier to bear.

We were turned out of our beds at five o'clock in the morning.

It took three quarters of an hour to march to the top of the hill where the quarry was. We worked from seven in the morning till six at night. Whether the day was good or bad we had to turn out, though if their own workers had to give up, we also could return to the camp. But the site had to be completely snowbound for them to admit defeat.

Red Cross parcels had yet to arrive that winter, so we had only the meagre rations which they allocated to us. That was not much in relation to the work, but it kept body and soul together. To make matters worse, we were without cigarettes. Some of the Germans were very kind about smoking. I was working with a man called Otto Billing and when his cigarette was half finished he would leave it on a rock. I would finish the rest of it. These workers were much like ourselves. They were prisoners in a different sense to us, but prisoners nevertheless.

There was plenty of Gaelic in this camp. There were about seventeen of us from North and South Uist, with a few mainlanders amongst us. But more and more were arriving and, as happened in Scotland itself, English soon gained the upper hand.

About the beginning of 1941, some of the crew of the ship *Vandyke* arrived. She had been sunk near Norway and there were six or seven of them. There was one old fellow from Wales by the name of Johnny. I cannot remember his surname, but he was over sixty years old. Welsh was Johnny's native tongue and his English was a bit rocky so some made fun of him.

A fifteen-year-old German boy called Heinz, an attendant in the quarry, was always annoying Johnny. His pipe never left Johnny's mouth, even though there was not a shred of tobacco in it. He would just suck at it as it was.

One day Heinz had a packet of tobacco and he would puff away, walking up and down in front of Johnny. Eventually the old man could stand it no longer, with his own pipe empty. He leapt at Heinz and grabbed him by the throat.

'You bugger,' he cried, 'give us a fill of tobacco!'

Heinz got such a fright that he gave the old man half his packet. Poor Johnny – that way of life did not suit him at all. I hope he got back to England among the old and sick in 1942.

There were French prisoners working in the wine cellars who lived in the same block as us, though separated from us. The French would cook and eat snails, which they find especially tasty as food. But even if I was dying with hunger, I could not bear to sample them. Often the French would offer them cooked to us. One lad did try them and recommended them strongly, saying they were tasty, juicy – just like winkles of the seashore.

As I mentioned before, the stone quarry was on top of a lump of a hill. Down at the foot of the hill there ran a railway with a little station alongside. Open trucks came into the station to be filled with rock. The stone was carried down in little barrows suspended from overhead cables. The weight of the full barrows pulled the empty ones up and so the transfer went on all day without stopping. The rock had to be extracted and broken with hammers and loaded into the barrows and the trucks had to be filled before the day's work was done. The work was hard on so little food, but much worse was to befall me later in the *Straflager* (Punishment Camp) – another rock quarry in Masbach where I was sentenced to three months hard labour as punishment for escaping from the Freyburg quarry. But more of that later.

My socks shrank so much from washing that eventually the mouth of the sock would not cover my heel. They were not much use like that, so the Germans gave us strips of thin cloth to wind about our feet inside the boots. This was a substitute for stockings which they themselves had to employ as well. They called them *Fuss-lappen*.

It was towards the end of spring 1941 that parcels from the Red Cross started to arrive. The hunger was not quite so bad now. We would get a parcel a week each and a few British cigarettes. We also got a change of clothing, but with this new apparel many of us looked more like the scarecrows you might see in the middle of a field of oats than British soldiers. It was clothing the Germans had looted from the countries they had overrun and so we had French jackets and Belgian knee-breeches. In any case, fashion counted for nothing with us; we were happy enough covered in any kind of rags that would keep out the cold.

I remember New Year's Eve 1940 better than any other Hogmanay since. There were still only three or four Lowlanders amongst us in the camp, the majority being boys from North and South Uist. Someone got a bottle of beer from a friendly guard and I do not know where the cigarette came from. We all sat around in the dormitory at midnight. Each one had a mouthful from the bottle; the cigarette was lit and each man had one puff of it. By the time it reached the last man it was burning his fingers, but he managed one draw before the ash burnt through the paper into his mouth. That night you can be sure that we drank to the health of Britain and bad luck to Germany.

About the middle of summer 1942, I was suffering terrible stomach trouble. I was forced to work every day but when I took food, the pain was so bad that I could hardly see at times. Once I had vomited what I had eaten I would feel much better and could work till evening. But I was growing ever weaker and the German doctor took no notice of me. One day when he was testing me, I pretended that the pain was in my lower right abdomen and when he prodded me there I would let out a cry. I was ordered immediately to hospital in the town of Stadtroda with appendicitis.

I myself was pretty sure that was not the problem so when I reached the hospital and saw the stretchers inside the door, I took fright. I told the doctor, who was British, the method by which I had been admitted and he was greatly amused.

'You did quite right to get yourself admitted through lies,' he said, 'but we will put you right.'

Major Lauste was the Englishman's name and he was a real gentleman. They kept me in nine weeks and I was in good shape when I left.

There was one lad in the hospital who had lost his legs. He had only about six inches of stumps left of his thighs but he could move about on his bed as briskly as an oyster-catcher on the shore and there was no one there as happy as he.

The winter of 1942 passed in the same routine; breaking rocks all day, returning in the evening to the camp where, thanks to the Red Cross, we now had books to read.

Concerts were put on. Any man who could sing, dance or recite would be picked out and he could demonstrate his talent on the night of the concert.

Gavin Macleod from Edinburgh was an accomplished dancer; he had won all the highest awards in the 1st Camerons. He taught four of us to dance and we often appeared on stage. Donald Macintyre and Finlay MacDonald from North Boisdale, William Duffy from Stirling and myself were accomplished dancers by the time Gavin had finished with us. We could do the Sword Dance, the Flings, Lochaber Broadswords and the Scotch Reel itself. But we had tired, aching feet as a result of Gavin's lessons!*

Escape

There was but one thing uppermost in my own mind and as time passed it was ever strengthening in my thoughts. This was the idea of escape. I knew there was not much chance of getting across the boundaries of Germany for we were at least three hundred miles from the border with Switzerland, which was the nearest free country. But it would break the monotony which ruled our lives and, even if I did not make it home, I would at least get to a different part of Germany itself. Norman Maclean and 'Big' Archie Macphee from South Uist were the first two to escape from this camp. We heard they had been caught but then heard no more about them.†

After that, Donald John Morrison and I decided to escape and, as it would not be easy from the camp, we would make a run from the quarry. Donald John was also from South Uist, a neighbour of my own at home. Unfortunately, he was killed in an accident in Uist in 1956.

We did not let anything on to anyone else. We put a little food and chocolate aside and on the day of the escape we took this

* Donald John marked his suffering while learning to dance in a ruefully humorous song, *Oran Danns a' Chlaidheimh*, The Song of the Sword Dance, which can be found in parallel translation in his collected works, *Chì Mi* (Birlinn 2001).
† See Archie Macphee's story p. 207

with us in our bags along with the usual bits of bread. It was in our favour that there were no guards with us at work; the only supervision was by the gaffer.

When we took our food at the midday break, we sidled across to a little shed at the edge of the quarry. There was thick forest in front of us, but there was about a quarter of a mile of open ground between us and it where we could be easily spotted. But nothing ventured, nothing gained. The Germans were eating in the shed and this was the moment. We had an hour before we would be missed when work resumed after dinner. We made for the wood. We ran and ran till we were amongst the trees but did not stop there. On we went through to the other side. Now there was open country before us with not a house or village in sight. This was good. We had no wish to meet anyone till we had put a goodly distance between us and the quarry.

We reached another wood, which we penetrated deeply and then stopped. It would not be safe to carry on in daylight so we would wait for night. We had a bite to eat and lit a cigarette. We were free.

When night fell, we set off. We came upon a major road but did not walk on it. Then we reached a river. The water flowed quiet but deep without a bridge in sight, but we had to find a way across. We followed its course for a little way until we came upon cables strung about ten feet above the river, suspended from two iron poles, one on each bank. There was a little boat on the other side which could be brought across by the cables. The boat had a high mast, the tip of which engaged a roller on one of the cables but, as we did not know how to work the mechanism, there was only one course open to us.

We would cross hand over hand on the cable suspended ten feet above the river.*

That was what we did. But we had a few anxious moments above that dark, deep water, fearful that the strength of our hands would fail with our lives depending on them. We got across safely but our hands were shaking from the effort of supporting the body.

* This river would be the Saale, a tributary of the Elbe.

On we went. It was now raining, a soft penetrating drizzle without a breath of wind. Very soon we were soaked to the skin and consequently cold. We were now nearing a town. If we could find the train station we might be able to hide in a truck which would take us somewhere. The town was still sleeping – it was about four o'clock in the morning and our boots clattered on the hard cobbles of the street. That is what betrayed us. A policeman appeared from a doorway and came to meet us. He stretched out his hand,

'Identification papers?' We said nothing.

'*Kommen sie mit*,'* he said, urging us before him through the door. There was another man sitting at the desk. He pointed to the clothes we wore.

'*Engländer*?'

He had recognised the army uniform.

There was no point in denying it and we gave the name of the camp we had escaped from. Having spoken into the phone, he said that guards would come for us about midday but meantime we could sleep. We were given a blanket each and put in a small cell in the prison. Wrapped in the blanket with soaking wet clothes, we slept till ten in the morning. When we woke our clothes had dried on us.

This was the town of Weissenfels and the policeman was a really fine fellow. So far we had avoided the dread of every escapee – the Gestapo.

The guard arrived and we were taken to Mühlhausen, the holding camp which supplied prisoners to the *Arbeitskommando* (work-camps). We were given our sentence there: three months hard labour in Masbach† *Straflager* – another rock quarry but twenty times worse than the one we had escaped from.

Masbach quarry was also on the top of a hill. The rock was harder and the barrows were bigger. We had to produce four-teen barrows each every day. We were given little plates with individual numbers each morning. My number was eight and I was given fourteen plates each with that number. A plate had to

* 'Come with me.'
† Masbach lies about 50km south-west of Eisenach.

be hung on each barrow that went out and until my fourteen plates went out on fourteen barrows, I would not be allowed off, even if it was pitch dark.

Every trick was tried to get into hospital. The work was so hard and our hands had painful hacks open to the shafts of the hammers. When we complained the gaffer said, 'Piss on them.' We tried that and it was better than any other treatment that I had ever found for hacks!

There was a lad from Australia who came to me one day in the quarry.

'Will you take off a bit of my little finger with the hammer?' he asked.

'Very well,' said I, 'if you can stand it.'

'I can,' he replied, 'if you have the courage to do it.'

One end of the hammers had a sharp edge. He placed his hand on a rock. I raised the hammer above my head with the sharp end facing down. But at the last moment my courage failed. I lowered the hammer slowly to the ground.

'I can't do it,' I said. Joe Hay from Arisaig was standing nearby.

'I'll cut it off for you,' said he.

He raised the hammer and brought it down with all his strength on the Australian's little finger. The man put his hand between his knees.

'Thanks a million, pal,' he said.

He was taken to hospital and we saw him no more. He had lost his little finger but he was free from the hell of Masbach.

Donald John Morrison also got himself out of Masbach. He put a sock on his foot and poured a kettle of boiling water over it. By the time he removed the sock, his foot was a red sore. In a day or two the scald had deepened and Donald John was taken to hospital. I did not see him again till I met him after the war in Uist.

The quarry was on top of a hill and the hill was about 500 feet high. There was no way of getting out by stealth and there was only one road. But two men did manage to escape!

'China' MacDonald never remained long in any camp. He

used to call everyone 'China', so that was the nickname given to himself. China and another English lad escaped from Masbach quarry by descending over fifty feet of cliff face where they could scarcely find a foothold. They were recaptured and their interrogators did not believe that it was Masbach they had escaped from.

The three months passed. There was no footballer or boxer ever as fit as we were leaving Masbach. Our muscles were like rubber balls and our chests and arms so dark with the sun that one might mistake us for Indians. I think we would have won the longest race at the Olympics without breaking breath!

Fifteen of us left Masbach for a seed factory in Erfurt, but that did not weaken the workforce. Escapees were continually being sentenced and there was no shortage of stone-breakers for the rocks of Masbach.

The Seed Factory

In my opinion, Erfurt was as pretty a town as I ever saw. Its streets were broad and level with rows of trees lining some of them. The streets were always clean with no rubbish allowed to lie for long and the country round about was as green and fertile as any I have ever seen. With a belt of such rich soil surrounding it, it is easy to understand why Erfurt was one of the top towns in Germany for market gardening and seed production. Fields more than a mile long and broad stretched out from the outskirts of the town with every kind of planting coming into bloom there.

The market gardens belonged to the company Zeiglers, which had a large factory in the town. This was the factory in which we worked. The camp was on the outskirts of the town with the usual twelve-foot-high fence of barbed wire surrounding it. This was a very pleasant change after the mud and mire of Masbach.

I worked with four others at tables laden with packets of every kind of seed. Thousands of orders came in from every corner of the country. We would make a circuit of the table with the order in a little box and the packets required would be placed in the box with the order. At the end of the table the whole thing would be packaged and the parcel would travel out on a conveyor belt through the wall of the factory to be loaded onto a delivery truck. Thousands of parcels went out in this way – but that year the purchasers received some very strange parcels. The one who wanted only a packet or two of turnip or carrot seed for a patch of garden would get three or four kilograms of peas or beans and nine or ten packets of celery or leeks. The one who had sent in a large order would get a packet of carrot seed and a lot of brown paper. I would have liked to have seen their faces when the orders arrived that year.

Men were so scarce in the country – they were in the army, but for a few – that it was a woman who was in charge on our floor. There was one redhead we called Ginger. She was a bit scared of us. Quite often, when we grew bored with work, a battle would start with the packets. Without any warning you would get a kilogram of beans or peas in the side of the head. The floor would be thick with all kinds of seed.

Ginger stuck her head inside the door one day and got a kilogram of peas fair in the face. She fell unconscious. We ran to her aid and poured water on her face. When she came round, we each gave her a bar of chocolate and that would have bought her silence even if we had half-killed her. She swept the floor with us and the incident went no further.

We were searched every evening lest anything should be taken. Beans were a very good food and they knew they were disappearing, but they only ever searched our bags and pockets. We would tie string round the legs of our underpants and four or five packets of beans would fit in between our legs. We were never caught. The beans made a great feast, cooked along with ham from the parcels.

In the spring we were out in the fields planting. Whole carrots, just as they might be bought in a shop, were put in holes in the ground. Rows of holes had been drilled beforehand and carrots had to be placed, one in each hole, with the upper end above. The hole would be closed with soil and the plant would run to seed.

We left the Zeiglers factory before we saw the fruits of our labour at that year's planting but I strongly suspect that the harvest was but a poor one. Most of the carrots had been planted upside down! I wonder if they ever grew?

'Tich' Cowper from England and I decided to escape. We noticed that the check on our numbers leaving the factory in the evening was not very meticulous as our guard was not too strict. We thought we would stay in hiding in the factory when the rest left. We could then leave by the window or some other way.

So one evening we hid among sacks of seed in a loft on the second storey and let the rest leave. There was no count made as the others departed and thus we passed the first hurdle.

Now we had to get out under cover of the darkness of the night. There would be no *Appel* (rollcall) in the camp till bedtime and so we would be safe from pursuit till then.

When it grew dark we moved down below and looked around. There was a night-guard sitting in a little office with a pistol lying on the table in front of him. We were sure the pistol was loaded and that he would not hesitate to fire if he saw us. This was not so good.

We heard a commotion outside. There was a clank of the locks and then a loud knocking. We leapt underneath a pile of empty sacks that lay nearby. The guard went to the door and called out who was there.

'*Polizei.*'

He opened the door. Two men entered. They stood inside the door looking at the guard. We saw out through the sacks that these were no ordinary policemen; they did not wear police uniform and we trembled with horror. There were only two or three empty sacks between us and the Gestapo.

We had never been in really hot water till now. If we were discovered while they were there, God knows what might happen to us. By rights, they had no authority to have anything to do with prisoners of war but no law – international or any other kind – counted with these brutes. Even if they half-killed us, what body in Germany had the power to punish the Gestapo?

The guard's face was pale as he looked hither and thither. One of them spoke. He asked about one Heinrich Müller. Did the guard know him? What kind of man was he and so on. The guard replied that he knew him but we did not pay too much attention. We were in a really tight spot. The one who had not spoken walked about and stood beside the sacks.

I was afraid to draw breath. We could see his boots and part of his trousers two yards away. The thumping of my heart was so loud that I feared he must hear it. About half an hour passed – the longest half-hour I had ever known. Then they went and the guard closed the door. He stood for a while, hand on chin. Then he went into the office.

We moved out from among the sacks and, as if he had heard the sound, he came out and saw us. I think his head was still in a muddle and panic showed in his eyes. First the Gestapo and now two British prisoners. But he pulled himself together and asked what we were doing there.

'We had finished at the table,' said I, 'and we went upstairs and slept. We did not hear the others leaving and we woke only ten minutes ago. We have to get back to the camp.'

He swallowed these lies and he himself took us back to the camp. Nothing happened to us but the escape attempt was frustrated before it had barely begun.

Shortly after that we went to another camp – a shoe factory, still in Erfurt but on the other side of town. Four of us were sent to this camp. It was just a small place with only sixteen men there before us, but they had been very busy before we arrived. They had nearly completed a tunnel out of the camp. As we were escapers we were let into this secret – six of them were going to make a break for it at the end of the week.

Very good! If they could get safely away then we would follow them before the guards found the tunnel. But unfortunately, the day before the six were due to escape, the guards discovered the tunnel. It could not be helped. Two days after that the four of us and five of the others were sent to Mühlhausen, the holding camp. We did not know why but we had a pretty shrewd suspicion. The work was too easy for escapers like us and we were certain we would not stay very long in Mühlhausen. This surmise turned out to be quite correct. This time it was not a rock quarry we could look forward to but sites more difficult to escape from.

'Alabama'

Anyone who saw the Cameron Barracks in Inverness as they used to be will understand better my description of our living quarters in Mühlhausen. The buildings were taller – five or six storeys – and they formed four sides of a square paved with cobblestones. I think they must have been military barracks, though they were now quarters for prisoners of war. There was one great iron gate for entry and exit and, as was to be expected, there were two German soldiers on guard day and night just outside the gate. We had a reasonable degree of comfort there with good beds – triple bunks. The food was not so plentiful but we had the Red Cross parcels so, to some extent, we were less dependent on it.

As always happens when a lot of men are gathered together, there will be one amongst them who stands out as different from the rest in some special way. The man we called 'Alabama' was one of those and I would like to say something about him especially in this account.

Alabama was from America and, as you might expect, he had been born in the state of that name in the US. His real name was Tom Jones but even if you called him by that name no-one would know who was referred to unless you said 'Alabama'. If any man or creature of any kind gave the Germans headaches and problems then that was Alabama. Although he would often make a fool and idiot of himself, he was quick-witted and street-wise and I never saw another who could get the better of him.

Alabama had been in the US Marines at first. He escaped from that famous unit a year or two before the war and crossed the border into Canada. He then enlisted in the Canadian army and it was with them that he came over at the outbreak of war and was captured at Dieppe.

He and I got on very well together but our conversations were not on foolish things, for Alabama had above average knowledge and intelligence. He would say to me, 'If you want to play the fool, Mac, you must play him to perfection,' and certainly he could do that. He could give the impression that he was a complete idiot.

He was going off to a work camp from Mühlhausen with a group of others. At the gate what did my brave fellow do but start weeping and wailing, wanting to turn back to kiss and take farewell of the Kommandant! One of the guards returned with him, scratching his head, and Alabama went up to the Kommandant, kissing and embracing him and pleading to stay where he might see him every day! They could not cope with him and so he was left behind.

Alabama was with us too in the Masbach *Straflager*. He was working next to me filling barrows with stone and one day he came over to me.

'Now, Mac,' he said, 'you must play this one with me. I'm going to throw a fit. I'll make it look very realistic, foaming at the mouth accompanied by violent convulsions. You will rush over to me and call for help.'

'All right,' said I.

Whenever the gaffer walked near us, I kept a keen eye on Alabama to see when the 'fit' was going to strike him. I heard a scream and saw Alabama fling himself into the mud and mire beside the barrow. I ran across and shouted for the gaffer to come and help me. He came.

There was a white froth about Alabama's lips as he writhed in the mud. The gaffer was horrified. He had not the slightest idea that Alabama had put a piece of soap in his mouth and it was that which was producing the white foam which bubbled from his mouth. I called on one or two others who were working nearby and said to the gaffer we would have to take Alabama back to camp. First we took him to the little hut where we ate our bread and laid him on a table. It took him half an hour before he decided to come round and then he did not know – or so he said – where he was. Another man and I went with him back to the camp and then we did not have to turn out any more that afternoon.

Another morning in Masbach he complained that he was suffering terribly with piles and demanded to see the doctor. He got no sympathy from the Germans and was sent on his way to the quarry with us. But Alabama walked with his two feet as far apart as they could be and when the guard saw him and his method of progress he fell about laughing and returned Alabama back inside.

It was he who invented the trick of beating your knee with a little bag full of salt. By doing this every now and then during the night before you went to the doctor, there would be a great swelling in your knee in the morning and you could get a day or two off work till the swelling went down. A man could keep the swelling going in the knee as long as he wished. Perhaps it was all the blows my knees received from bags of salt that left them so painful today!

He showed us another way of tricking the doctors, which was to chew a little lump of silver paper in your mouth and then to swallow the little lump, or maybe two of them, before you were X-rayed. This would show up on the plate, indicating that you had stomach ulcers.

Alabama had nothing to learn. He was once sent out of Mühlhausen to a salt mine. He refused to go down below without his sleeping companion – his guitar. He would start to play for the Germans and, naturally enough, this was not unpleasant for the workers – listening to American hillbilly songs – but was not popular with the gaffers. When Alabama's guitar was banned he would just cry in the mine all day and eventually it was less trouble and distraction to return Alabama and his guitar from whence they had come – to Mühlhausen.

Mühlhausen

A very good concert band was founded in Mühlhausen. An Englishman, Dick Tanner, and a Scottish boy, Jimmy Macfarlane, were the two principal leaders. Most of the instruments were obtained through the Red Cross, while others were bought in Germany itself. There were up to six men in the band, each with his own instrument, and you can bet there were plenty in the audience when Dick Tanner's Band struck up.

As Mühlhausen was not a work camp, it was only to be expected that the food was not so good in quality or quantity. Thus the life of each one was dependent on the parcels of the Red Cross, mixed with the little local food that was shared out amongst us. But a lad from Norfolk, 'Tich' Ellis, and I found a way to improve our rations a great deal. When we were sent out in working parties round the town – something that happened now and then if any company in the town needed workers – we also asked men here and there if they would barter anything for a tin of coffee or chocolate or things of that kind. In this way we made contact with one German whom we used as an intermediary between ourselves and a highly productive market: the Black Market. I would get a dozen eggs for a tin of coffee and a loaf of rye bread for a bar or two of chocolate.

The German himself might have been able to get two dozen for the tin of coffee although we got only the one, but we were satisfied enough. He was as entitled to make a little profit on the transaction as ourselves. He was under the greater danger if the matter was discovered. We would be given some minor punishment, but he risked losing his life.

But human nature can never be completely curbed. Despite this mortal danger for the people of the country oppressed under the iron fist of Nazi rule, there would be some here or there who would break the law if they could make some profit, great or small, out of it. It was ever thus and always will be so long as people have to earn their daily bread by the sweat of their brows.

As I mentioned earlier, Mühlhausen was a primary holding camp for the Stalags so no work was done there. If there was anything to be done in the surrounding area, working parties would be sent out for the day. This happened one time after some heavy bombing by American planes on the railway station. When the raid started all the passengers went down into the underground shelters beside the station. A bomb fell right in the middle of one of the shelters and exploded. When the planes had gone, I was one of a working party which was sent from the camp to clear up a little of the destruction that had been wrought.

Words alone could never adequately depict the dreadful scene that greeted us that day: parts of heads and arms and legs scattered hither and thither; scraps of clothing even hanging on the overhead electric wires; pieces of human flesh lying about in the street and the cobblestones around them red with the blood which had flowed before it froze. There was not one complete human being to be seen of all those who had been inside the shelter. There were only fragments.

There were ten in our party and the first thing we did was to sit down and be sick. The sight was as horrific as any that I have ever seen. Furthermore, many of the people of the town turned out and, when they saw us, they went berserk. They made for us to tear us apart and we had need of our guards that day. They kept the people away by training their guns on them but one or two of us received blows. One man was knocked unconscious by a stone to the head.

In the clean-up we found a girl's leg. It was complete to the thigh with a cotton or lisle stocking but that is all there was. We were back there again three days later and the girl's mother – we were told – came to collect the leg. How it was identified we never found out, but the poor woman took the leg away in a pram. The guards hid us while she was there and they were quite right. I can believe that the British were the last people on earth she would have wanted to see that day.

The bombing now went on night and day: the Yanks by day, the RAF by night. The Flying Fortresses appeared one day from the west, formation after formation of them. The first squadron had disappeared in the east before the last one was in sight. In the evening smoke rose and the sky reddened to the east of us. Another German town was ablaze.

Escape from the Salt Mine

Spring 1944. We had spent six weeks at Mühlhausen and we were well content. We did not have to work and help Germany. This did not last. One day my name came up in orders together with another two. We had to leave on the morrow for the salt mines at Merkers.* George Skead from Leith and William Thomson from Inverness were the other two.

This was not so good. We held a council of war that evening and swore that we would escape at the first opportunity, for we had no wish to work in a salt mine. We had no wish to do any work but this was worst of all.

'We'll be back in a day or two.' And so it proved.

We reached Merkers in the evening and got settled in. The next day we worked from six in the morning till six in the evening. The three of us worked on the surface but we were sure that would not last too long. Any day we might be sent down below and escape would then be more difficult. We resolved to escape the next day.

This escape did not mean that we had any better chance of getting across the German border than on my previous attempts. It was more that we were rebelling against the authority of our enemies over us, a power that threatened to crush the spirit of freedom in hearts and minds unless a man resisted it strongly. By escaping you demonstrated that you were not content with your lot.

You showed by escaping that the spirit of freedom was more precious than anything else on earth. By escaping you were, above all else, proving to yourself that you were not resigned to being content in captivity, however comfortable; that you were enough of a man to suffer cruelty and hardship for the sake of justice.

On the next day we went to work again at six in the morning. We were fortunate that there was a fairly thick mist, which was greatly in our favour. At the first opportunity, the three of us

* Merkers lies about 30km south-west of Eisenach.

moved slowly behind an old cattle truck that was stopped on the railway line. We were now out of sight of the guards.

Without further delay, we took off into the mist and in a few minutes were on the edge of a wood about half a mile from the workplace. We went deep into the wood for it would not be safe to leave its cover and shelter till darkness fell. So we settled ourselves down to await nightfall. We had no food except for a little chocolate – and by evening we did not even have that. The wood gave excellent shade from the sun, for it was very hot once the mist dispersed.

In the dusk of the night we moved off. The hunt would now be on for us, but we had the shades of night as a shield from prying eyes. Once or twice we heard dogs barking nearby and we assumed it must be the hunt. If so, they did not find us but we had a few fairly anxious moments until they drew away from us.

We carried on walking all night. We kept to the road, which made for easier walking, but when we heard a car or bicycle approaching we hid in the roadside ditch till it passed. About five in the morning we came to a little village in a low-lying country valley. The village was asleep and, like thieves in the night, we moved quietly and carefully through it unseen and emerged on the other side.

But shortly after that we heard the roar of a motor-bike. Before we could hide, he was upon us. He gave us a very suspicious stare but carried on. Very good. He must have thought we were French or Poles going to work – *Ausländers* as they called them. But shortly after passing us, he stopped. He stood looking back for a while and then he returned. At first he went on into the village but after five minutes he came back.

He asked in German where we were going. We said nothing.

He ordered us to walk into the village and that he would follow but not to try any tricks for there were two or three guns trained on us.

We could see a little group of men on a corner at the outskirts of the village and we were certain they were armed. He would not have attempted to take the three of us by himself.

A group of Highlanders, English and Australians in Work Camp 323, Stalag IXc in December 1941, after receiving new uniforms (Donald J. MacDonald is fifth from the right, second back row)

Camerons from South Uist in the group above.
Back Donald J. MacDonald, Roderick MacDonald, Neil MacInnes , Roderick Mackintosh, Finlay MacDonald
Front Piper Donald Macintyre, Donald J. Morrison, Cpl. Norman Mackinnon, Duncan MacCormick, Neil Walker

Eighty-six-year-old General Sir Derek Lang (seated centre) with some of the 51st veterans attending the 60th anniversary parade at St Valery in June 2000 (© Bill Innes)

The standards are lowered as Pipe Major Donald J. Macintyre plays a lament. His father, Piper Donald Macintyre, was captured at St Valery and is one of the Uist men shown in the plates from Stalag IXc. (© Bill Innes)

June 2000.
Above. Sir Derek Lang takes part with French civic and military dignitaries in a wreath-laying ceremony at the ex-naval gun which serves as the war memorial for Veules-les-Roses (© Bill Innes)

Below. Services were held at churches in the area where the simple military headstones of the 51st stand among local graves. The group on the right includes Sir Derek and Pipe Major D.J. Macintyre. (© Bill Innes)

June 2000 in St Valery.
Above. The band of the Queen's Own Highlanders Association (Pipe Major Macintyre) playing in front of the Town Hall. (© Bill Innes)

Below. A service in the immaculately tended war cemetery which holds both Scottish and French dead (© Bill Innes)

Gestapo

We were taken into a large room in the village, a bit like a café with tables and chairs all around. There were five men seated on one side with Italian rifles trained on us. Another man came through a door with a smile on his face and you could almost read 'Gestapo' in his eyes. We were told afterwards that he was indeed one of them who happened to be in this area seeking information on parachutists. They had suspected at first that we might be some of those. We also noticed the badge on the breast of the jacket of the dark-clad one who had captured us. We knew for sure that there would be no mercy or compassion shown by one who wore the Nazi emblem nor certainly by a member of the Gestapo.

'Is this the end?' we asked ourselves. We realised that it was time to set aside pretend-ignorance and asked that a message be sent to the nearest senior army officer. We knew that if a soldier came that they would not be allowed to touch us but meantime we could see that we were in the hands of the real Nazis, without the protection of the German army.

In other words, we were in mortal danger. Our situation struck a lot of fear into us, but we were not going to let them see that we had any weakness. We heard the dark one speaking on the phone and that gave us some hope, but how alive would we be before a guard could come? That was the question.

We said we were British prisoners of war who had escaped from Merkers camp.

The dark one spoke to the other in a low voice. We did not catch his reply but heard the word *Strafe*. We understood that to mean there would be physical punishment, but if any guard or soldier arrived we had a chance of escaping with our lives. In the hands of those brutes, it was only a slim chance.

'*Englische Schweinehunden*,'* said the dark one, coming over to us with a piece of rope in his hand. He tied George's hands in front of him and then my hands and William's hands. He said he

* 'English bastards' (slang).

was going to tie us to the back of a car and drag us all the way back to the camp. He then turned round with a double-tongued rubber whip in his hand and beat me about the head with it. It was fortunate that my hands were in front of me even though they were tied, for I could at least protect my face and my eyes from the strokes. The whip curled round my head and ears and, my word, those strokes hurt but I did not utter a sound. I just kept my two hands, bound as they were, in front of my face.

When he had spent some time on me, he turned on William. With the first stroke he caught William unawares before he had time to protect his face with his hands. The double tongue on the tip of the whip curled round his eye. You would scarcely believe how fast the eye swelled up out of his head as it streamed with blood. He managed to protect himself from the other strokes but the eye looked in a sorry state.

After giving William his share of the blows, he came to George. At the first blow he received, George dropped to the floor, feigning unconsciousness. That did not work for one of the others was called for to hold George up by his hair until he had received his share. While all this was going on, the other one watched us with a treacherous smile on his face. It was obvious to see and understand that we were but a hairsbreadth from death if soldiers from the camp guard did not soon arrive.

But another reason for fear and terror entered our thoughts. The dark man was on his way towards us again, the look of a real murderer in his eyes, but this time with a slim sharp knife in his hand. Just then the door opened and two soldiers from the camp arrived. Never before or after were we so thankful to God as we were at that moment for the appearance of two German soldiers. We had realised that this venture would end in an agony of torment and that no mercy would be shown.

One of the soldiers shouted at the dark man to stop immediately and release us. This was done and the soldier warned him of the dangers of interfering with British prisoners of war who were, as laid down in the Geneva convention, under the protection of the German army. The black-garbed man maintained that once we had escaped we were no longer prisoners but British soldiers and thus enemies of Germany.

The false smile on the face of the other one turned to a grimace of hate but he said nothing. He walked out without a word of defence for his colleague, even though we were all certain that he was the one who had incited the other to torture.

At first we were taken back to Merkers, but, instead of being allowed inside, we had to stand outside for two hours. We were weak and faint from lack of sleep and food – and especially from the ill-treatment we had received – but we were not allowed to sit. The other boys would pass cups of coffee to us through the wire but I remember well that it was only after the sixteenth cup that my thirst was satisfied.*

That evening we were back in Mühlhausen, and the boys were greatly surprised to see us back so soon. It was a Uist man, Kenny Mackenzie† from Lochboisdale, who was first to welcome us inside the gates. He felt our heads, which had lumps the size of hens' eggs from the strokes of the rubber whip. William was taken to hospital and fortunately did not lose the sight of his eye.

We had made our point and, although we had nearly paid very dearly for it, that danger would not deter us another time. We rose and slept under threat every day and danger was so close-woven into our lives that we sometimes thought of it as a friend.

Solitary Confinement

We knew that there would be further penalties to pay for this escape so we reported to the doctor complaining that we were suffering badly from dizziness as a result of the beating we had received. We claimed also to be suffering from every other sort

---

* Thirst is a common reaction to the adrenalin surge caused by any traumatic experience. Normally coffee, which is a diuretic, would make matters worse. However, much of the coffee available in Germany during the war was ersatz – made from unsatisfactory substitutes as acorns.

† Kenny Mackenzie lived to the goodly age of 91, dying in South Uist, February 1999.

of complaint we could dream up so the doctor put us on light work. This meant that they could not send us to Masbach *Straflager* on this occasion. Instead we would spend twenty-one days in prison cells on bread and water in solitary confinement.

If I had been as wise going there as I was on my return, I would have preferred three months in Masbach to the three weeks on bread and water, however arduous the rock quarry.

We were searched three times going into prison, but despite that I got into my cell with ten cigarettes and nearly half a box of matches! I unpicked the collar of my jacket where the material was stitched double. This opened up the collar all round like a purse. I laid the cigarettes one after another all round the collar. I cut the matches to half size, put them in among the cigarettes and sewed up the collar again. I pressed it together as much as possible less a suspicious eye noticed it looked rather bulky and so proceeded to the first search. They opened our mouths and even probed our navels but never touched the collars of our jackets. Despite German efficiency, they still had much to learn. The other two searches were passed in the same way and I got into my cell with my smokes intact.

The little cell was about ten feet long by eight feet wide. I remember it well, for I measured it many times during the three weeks for the sake of something to do. There was a hard wooden bed on one side with a single blanket. The one window was so high in the wall that I could not see out and it was fitted with four iron bars from top to bottom. They left me a little prayer book which I had in my pocket and this was all I had to read for the whole period. I almost knew it by heart before the time was up.

We would be given our bread ration every day about noon. There was not much – I would say about six ounces – and that was it till the next day. Sometimes I would leave a little for the evening but more often I would eat it all together and still feel hungry. We could have as much water as we wanted. Every three days we had some warm food; a cup of broth as thin as water, but it was warm and that itself was a treat. I had no watch but after a while I could make a fair attempt at guessing the time and not be far wrong.

Every evening we were allowed out for half an hour, walking round one after another in the prison square. Talking was forbidden. The guards stood nearby and we had no great faith in the restraint of their trigger-fingers.

For one who has never experienced it, it is difficult to comprehend the depressing effect of lack of companionship on the human mind. By lack of companionship it is not just the lack of human company that I mean. There are many kinds of companionship: birds singing in the trees; cattle and sheep grazing in the fields; the mountains; the sound of the sea – even the noise of planes and bombs exploding. Each one of those things is some kind of accompaniment. You are amongst them and they play a part in your life. Although you do not speak to them, your mind is engaged in silent dialogue with them and they with you.

In this miserable little hole you had only four black walls around you. The monotony of the day today promised only more of the same tomorrow. The dawning of the twenty-second day was the only chink of light I could look forward to in the darkness, but many days and nights had still to pass before I reached that light. There was only waiting, waiting, waiting . . .

You were always waiting. Waiting for the bread; waiting for the evening; waiting for night and the time to sleep. Sleeping and waking all through the night and, in the morning, waiting again. Is there any wonder that I said I would prefer the rocks of Masbach to this kind of punishment again?

I would spend some time walking back and forward and some time reading the prayer book. Eventually I could read it with my eyes shut. The cigarettes lasted only about two days so I did not even have that pastime. But the days passed, tedious thought they were, and the sentence came to an end. Tomorrow we would be free. Free but still captive? Yes, but free from this spirit-crushing bondage.

The next morning the cell doors were opened. We got a Red Cross parcel each and fifty cigarettes. The train did not leave till midday and the other two joined me till it was time to go. When the guard came to the door to fetch us, he could not see us for smoke!

In the train we were going to have a great feast from the

parcels, but after a bite or two of rich food we were all sick. All that afternoon, food was the last thing on our minds. We had not a wink of sleep that night because of having so little food but in a day or two we were hungry enough.

The Second Salt Mine

Sixth of June 1944. We rose that morning as usual. About ten o'clock in the morning, the news spread that British and American forces had landed in France that morning. There was great excitement throughout the camp. What would happen? Would it just be like the Dieppe raid?*

That evening we heard a broadcast on German radio. The speaker was explaining how this invasion would be halted in about twenty-four hours but, instead, within twenty-four hours the Allied forces had reinforced strong positions ashore and were ever pressing forward. Everyone's spirits lifted as every day brought fresh news on the second front in France. Although there had been plenty of fighting in Italy for some time, we all knew very well that relief would not come from that direction. France was the lock that had to be opened and the key had now been firmly inserted and was being continually turned in the grip of powerful fingers.

But, right in the middle of this joy of spirit, a thunderbolt struck which dragged me down from the cloud I was on back to the cold, alien earth of Germany. I was to be sent the next day to another salt mine in the town of Bischofroda.† There was no alternative, but I swore as usual that I would not stay there. I did not know then what lay before me or that my escaping days were over, but where there is still life, there is hope. I had great confidence going off to Bischofroda but if it had not been for the timely arrival of the Yanks, I would have had a very slim chance of escaping the deep trouble I found myself in there.

---

* The reference is to the unsucessful commando raid on Dieppe in August 1942 in which Canadian regiments in particular suffered heavy losses and nearly 2,000 men were captured.
† Bischofroda lies about 8km north of Eisenach.

In time of peace the salt mine at Bischofroda was a huge workplace. Apart from the mine, there was a factory above where the salt was milled and granulated, depending on the use to which it was to be put. The work went on night and day and hundreds of tons were produced every twenty-four hours.

I reached Bischofroda one lovely autumn afternoon after a four-hour journey by train. I was taken first to the office of the Kommandant and that is where my hopes of escape suffered their first blow. Who should the Kommandant be but the very one who had been in charge of Masbach *Straflager* while I was there. In the very moment that I recognised him, he recognised me. He issued strict orders that I was to go down below in the mine the very next morning.

'No-one yet has escaped from Bischofroda since I arrived,' he said, 'and you will not get the opportunity to be the first.' Well it could not be helped, but I still had some hope.

The work in the mine was not too bad. Going below, we wore only trousers and jacket of thin denim and, on coming up again, we went into the showers before donning our own clothes. Below, there was about a mile to walk to the face where the salt was extracted. The *Steigers* (pit foremen) travelled about on bicycles. The tools used were mostly scrapers so the work was not so arduous. But your hands and lips were always salty. The cigarette in your mouth and the bread that you ate tasted salty. However, there was one blessing about being underground that winter; we did not have to suffer the cold.*

A little while before Christmas 1944, an English lad was leaving the camp for Mühlhausen and I saw nothing better than to send a letter with him to Monty Banks from Dundee, whom I had left in Mühlhausen. Monty had also been in Masbach so he too had good knowledge – or bad knowledge perhaps – of the Kommandant.

In the letter to Monty I did not spare writing some strong language about the one I had found before me as Kommandant. It would be relevant here to set down the exact words I wrote

---

* See Appendix 2 for another account of life in the salt mines.

about him for it was because of these very words that I put myself in danger of losing my life: 'When I arrived, who was Kommandant here but that swine-faced bastard, our old friend from Masbach.'

Having told how he had ordered me down the mine and everything, I carried on: 'May his rotten German bones roast in Hell. If I'm still here when the Yanks arrive, I'll tear him apart myself with my bare hands.'

The English lad put the letter inside his boot but, unfortunately, he was searched and they found the letter. Unfortunately too for me, I had put the figures 1197 at the bottom of the letter. This was my prison number and Monty would have understood very well who it was. The Germans understood it even better! If I had signed my name, it could not have been easier for them.

Shortly after New Year, I was summoned to Bad Zulza along with three others who had beaten up a guard. The letter was placed before me. 'Did you write that?' asked a thickset fair-haired man in good English.

I read the letter. I realised that I was in hot water. There was not much point in denying it; I was betrayed by the number 1197, but why should I confess while I could still oppose them.

'I did not write that,' said I.

'Write part of the letter on that paper,' he ordered, handing me a blank sheet. I wrote the first part of the letter but I used a different writing.

'That is not your usual handwriting,' he said. 'Sign your name.' I signed my name in the same false way.

He handed me the last letter I had written home. They had held it back to compare the two letters and the writing in both was the same. The style in which I had just written was totally different.

'Do you know,' he asked, 'what the sentence is for anyone who libels a German officer?'

I said nothing. He handed me a paper.

'Sign that,' he said.

Written on the paper in German and English were the words: 'I confess that it was me that wrote the letter and that I libelled a German officer.'

'I will not sign that,' said I. He rose from the table and came round. I did not feel the blow that struck me in the ear till I found myself lying on the floor.

'Now sign it,' he said.

'I will not sign,' I replied, 'but I want to see the British Commandant immediately.' Sergeant Major Townsley was the Commandant in Bad Sulza.

In response he ground the lit cigarette in his hand into my cheek. I was close to the door, which I knew was not locked. I leapt and opened it and was out through it in about a quarter of a minute. I walked down the narrow passage and the two guards met me. He did not come out after me. I told the guards that I was finished and that the blonde man had told me to go out. I said nothing about what had happened. The guard took me back into the blonde man's office and asked if I was cleared to go.

'Yes,' he said, 'his trial will be in the town of Halle next month.' To me he added, 'You may as well make your last testament.'

He said nothing to the guards of what had happened between us before; he knew himself he had no right to go so far. The trial of the other boys was to be at the same time.

The train was about to leave when the planes arrived. The bombing started. One plane crashed in flames about half a mile away. We let out a great shout of triumph when we saw the black crosses on it.

That night on our way back, we had to leave the train and walk about three miles around a little village because the railway lines had been damaged that afternoon by the bombers.

A month went by and though we heard nothing about a court, we certainly heard much more of other things. The sound and rumble of the guns never stopped, day or night. The railways were all wrecked and salt was not leaving the factory for want of transport. The farmers round about had a heyday in this situation, taking away all the salt they wanted with their carts.

The mine and factory were cut back to eight hours working out of twenty-four by lack of electricity. One day a plane came over very low and we all ran out, waving towels and shirts. It made three orbits above our heads to show that we had been seen and then set off to the west again.

On the Move

'Deutschland Kaputt!'
They would not dispute this now but they could scarcely believe what was happening. War had not been waged on their own soil since the time of Napoleon; it was a totally new situation for them.

The workers questioned us about the Yanks. What would they do and what sort of men were they? Would they spare their lives?

Eventually the guards told us we were to leave the next day.
'Where are we going?'
'We have our orders. The prisoners have to be taken to a place of safety away from the barrage of the guns.'
'We do not want to leave.'
'We have to take you away.'

On the morning of the next day, three of us hid under the floor, thinking that the rest would go without us. But the guards searched the place from top to bottom and we had to follow the others. The Americans were about fifteen miles west of us, approaching ever nearer, and it seemed a great pity for us to be moving further away from them. But we reasoned that we could not be taken too far east or we would meet the Russians and the guards would rather be in the claws of the devil than in the clutches of the 'Russkies.'

These guards were very good to us. The officer whose character I had given in the letter had left a month before this; I expect he feared for his own safety. There was not a man in the camp who would not have taken a gun to him at the first opportunity.

After three days walking, we came to a town and we stayed that night and the next day in a factory on the outskirts. That evening we were told that we were going no further; that the army in the town were not going to resist and the Yanks were about a mile outside. But shortly afterwards a large force of the SS came in and preparations were begun to defend the town.

Our guards (there were ten of them with us) said we must leave; there was no knowing what the SS might do. So we were on the road again. Our numbers were ever increasing, group after group falling in with us and joining up with us. Every sort of nationality was there: French, Belgians, Poles, Italians and Russians – all prisoners before this but now going with the flow, each one following the other. National boundaries were set aside and we were all like one family, whether Russian, British or Italian. Each one was just a member of the human race, colleagues in the same misfortune. We all shared a common language, even though it was German.

That night we were in a farmhouse about five miles east of the town we had left. Tanks and armoured cars streamed past, retreating from the army which was overrunning them. Those manning them were just young boys about seventeen, exhausted by fatigue and lack of sleep. Even though they were Germans, we felt sorry for them, but at the same time when we thought of Poland, of France, of Holland and all the other European countries they stamped under their boots, we said, 'Serves them right.'

Before morning came, American shells were bursting all round us. A regiment of German tanks arrived where we were and so we had to be moved on again. Another two miles of walking and we could get no further. We were surrounded. Another farmhouse, but the last move.

Liberation

Food was getting scare. It was every man for himself, the German guards just as much as ourselves.

'We have to hand you over safely to the Americans,' they would say, 'and see that you put in a good word for us.'

That was easy enough to do for they were fine men. But where was the little officer of the letter now? His character would have been read to the Yanks if he had been with us there. Where was the blonde man who ground his cigarette into my cheek and knocked me unconscious with a fist in the ear? Where was the big black-clad man of the rubber whip? Unfortunately none of them was present and neither I nor anybody else could have said a bad word about those who were.

We saw a deer on the edge of the wood above us. One of the guards got out his rifle and raised it to take aim. He set the range at about three hundred metres. He fired the bullet and immediately the deer fell. It had been shot in the head but was still alive. Without delay, he and ten prisoners were on to it and finished it off. It was dragged down by rope, skinned, and within a quarter of an hour the whole carcass was inside a great cauldron by the side of the house with a blazing wood fire underneath boiling it.

Lips were being licked listening to the sounds of the deer being cooked, with every man imagining a chunk of venison in front of him, when there was a burst of machine-gun fire over our heads. The bullets struck sparks from the high rocks facing the house. Everyone dived for shelter. This went on for about half an hour and then stopped. When the lull came, we ventured out but there was nothing to be seen.

A Belgian and I were standing near the gate in front of the house; the main road ran on the other side of it. The Belgian pointed his finger up the road. '*Wer ist das*?' (Who is that?) he asked.

I looked. There was a little open car moving slowly and carefully down the road towards the house. It had only one man in it. He was standing inside it. This was not a German vehicle and, in addition, the soldier's helmet and uniform were not German.

'Americana!' shouted the Belgian. 'The Yanks!' I yelled at the top of my voice. Eighty men rushed down to the gate with the guards shouting at us to slow down. Before the man in the car reached the gate, a dozen or more of us were outside it.

The soldier was standing in the jeep with a cocked Tommy-gun trained on us. '*Kamerad?*' said he.*

---

* *Kamerad* – Literally 'comrade'. Because it was called out by German soldiers surrendering, there was an assumption by many during the war that it meant 'surrender'. (cf. 'Friend' as answer to a sentry's challenge, 'Who goes there?')

We shouted that we certainly were; we were prisoners of war.

'Not you, but these other guys,' he responded.

'They are surrendering.'

'If they are,' he said, 'tell them to stack their weapons by the wall.'

We translated this and the Germans did as he ordered. Without a moment's delay, the guards' weapons were in the prisoners' hands, and I was one of those with a loaded rifle in my grasp. It made me feel really powerful to be an armed soldier again. It was nearly five years since I had had to lay down my rifle at St Valery – five years in which I had experienced the epitome of the noblest of human nature but also brutality and the lowest depths of evil in man's mistreatment of his fellow creatures.

Five years in which Europe had been locked in a vice of steel; a grip which at times seemed impossible to break. The satanic powers which had kept poor countries in a yoke of slavery for years were losing their strength and force but they had not yet surrendered. Though their sins were graver than any previous crimes which had blackened the name of mankind, they would not yield even though the forces of justice were at their doors. The main stem of the powers of darkness which had flourished in the centre of Europe had to be torn up by the roots before every branch that drew nourishment from it would wither.

By my way of it, now I had a gun in my hand, I was going to spread-eagle Germany face down. There were another nine with me experiencing the same emotions now that they had guns and German bullets. But then one of the guards was noticed, pushing through the mob of men to the jeep, putting his hand at the back of the leather belt about his middle. In a twinkling of the eye he had been grabbed by three or four and the pistol in the holster at his back had been removed. He was handed over to the American without pistol or belt or jacket.

There were many questions being put to the Yank. Where were the others? Were they far away from us? Did he have any smokes or chocolate? He did have some of those two luxuries and he threw out some packets of cigarettes and chocolate. But, understandably, he did not have enough to satisfy more than eighty men. I was beside the jeep and I took one cigarette from a packet and shared out the rest. I asked the Yank for an autograph and he gave it to me and one or two others. I still had my army pay-book in my pocket and he wrote on a blank page his name and address in New York city. I still have that page carefully preserved.*

He was so proud – and just as excited as ourselves – at having single-handedly liberated over eighty prisoners from enemy hands. He lined the Germans up on the road and he himself followed behind them back to where his compatriots were – about a quarter of a mile up the road. He invited us to follow along after them as we wished. We were only too eager to do that. We met more Americans on the way and each one asked if these Germans had mistreated us for, if so, they would deal with them. But we could not say that they had. The guards were taken away and we did not see them again.

Freedom

The Americans had plenty of food and smokes. White bread was a great treat and it seemed to me I had never seen any whiter. A Russian camp had been liberated that same day so there were a lot of mouths to feed. The Russians had not been as fortunate as us for their country was not party to international conventions and therefore the Red Cross had no responsibility for them. So they had only the food that they received from the Germans and at the same time they had suffered cruel treatment at the hands of the enemy. To a great degree this was the main reason that, when liberated, they turned on the Germans like wildcats.

The Americans had to use us as policemen to protect the local people – many of them women and children – from the Russians wreaking revenge. They would walk down the streets with great wooden poles and leave not a window in any house or shop

---

* Sadly, the pay book was not found amongst the author's papers.

unbroken. Every man or woman they met was in mortal danger. One day five of us had to burst into a shop where two Russians were trying to strangle the young girl behind the counter.

The Yanks had liberated their camp on the one day. Next morning they went down the mine as usual and hanged all the *Steigers* and anyone else that had not had a chance to flee. They tore down a banner with a life-size portrait of Hitler and left not a shred of it intact. They even ripped at it with their teeth.

We spent a fortnight with the Yanks and we had no shortage of food or smokes.

A boy from Aberdeen and I were sitting one day on a hill above a nearby village. Two children – a boy and girl – came to us and we gave them chocolate. They would then come every day for more bars. We asked them one day whether they had any drink at home and, if so, to bring some the next day. They returned in the afternoon.

'Our mother says, if you want a drink you will have to go for it yourselves,' said the girl.

Very well; we accompanied them and reached the house. There was only their mother, who was about thirty, and an old man in bed in the other end of the house. She was a really nice woman and she set plates and knives and spoons on the table so that we expected a great feast. But all that came to the table was a thin slice or two of black rye bread with a small piece of sausage and black coffee made from acorns. She had offered us all the food she had, however little it was.

She brought down a bottle of pale stuff as clear as water. The liquor was hardly as strong as many a water I have drunk so we left it to her. But we came back again that evening with a load of tins of meat and milk with chocolate for the little ones – not forgetting the old man. We brought him five packets of German tobacco we had looted from an army store. The feast in that little house that evening had not its like in any house in the land.

The little girl would rush in, lifting her arm and shouting, '*Heil Hitler*.' Her mother leapt at her and shook her.

'You mustn't say that any more!'

The little one had no idea what the words meant nor why she

should not say them any more, but her mother knew very well. Although Hitler had still not surrendered, it was another country from the other side of the world which now ruled her home town and, according to what she said to us, if things did not improve there was no way that they could be any worse.

We would have great ceilidhs along with the Poles. They were still in the camp where they had worked till liberation but, like ourselves, they were now supported by the Americans. They had a kind of alcohol they had made from potato peelings and other ingredients, but it was really strong and we had some very heavy drinking sessions. There was one American who joined the Aberdonian and myself in a tour of the village in search of drink before visiting the Polish drinking den. We used to call him 'Yankee Doodle'.

Yankee Doodle would go around with his rifle on his shoulder and his steel helmet on his head and could not be parted from either one. He visited the Poles with us one night and I was never at such a ceilidh. Songs were sung in Polish, American, Gaelic, English and Russian and toasts were drunk to every country under the sun – except for Germany alone!

According to what I was told later, the three of us were escorted back to our own camp by two Poles. At any rate, when I woke in the morning, Yankee Doodle was lying behind me sound asleep – but still clad in his steel helmet and rifle!

Freedom was a very novel way of life for us. It was difficult to comprehend that we could go as we liked at any time to any place that was not too far away. We were under the care of the Americans so, although they were not our guards in the way the Germans had been, they had authority over us as our military superiors and certainly we had no objection to any of that.

We were often in and out of German houses. The only people left were women and children and the very old, but they were all as grateful as us that the war was nearly over. They were in a bad way. They had no food or work or money and even those who had a little money found it useless for there was nothing to buy with it. They would admit that Nazi rule had only ruined the country and that the common people had suffered shortages before the war had even started when all the best went to the army – as was evident from the Nazi slogan, 'Guns before butter.'

After passing a week there, the British and Canadians amongst us were taken to the town of Magdeburg, where we were to find the planes which would carry us back to England. It was here that we first heard from the Americans about the brutal camps like Belsen and Buchenwald. Some of them had liberated Buchenwald and it was difficult to believe that the dramatic accounts they gave us were true. I had seen inmates from Buchenwald a year or two before working under guard in the station at Erfurt and they had looked no worse than any of ourselves. But apparently the ones I saw were either in their first couple of weeks or were some who were in favour. At the same time I did see one or two of them receiving some painful blows from rifle butts.

The history of those evil camps has been known to the entire world long before today but at that time, newly heard from the very men who had liberated Buchenwald, the tale seemed unbelievable to us and, I can say with certainty, to a large proportion of the ordinary German people. They knew there were some such camps for political prisoners, but the majority of the workforce that we came into close contact with had not heard anything of the gas-chambers where more than six million Jews were put to death.

It was only now that I understood clearly the sort of country in which I had passed five years of my life and realised how fortunate I had been. If I had had that knowledge all the time I might not have been so insolent and bold in many confrontations with people I did not know.

I now realised for certain that if the business with the letter had happened a year or two earlier, when the whole of Europe was locked in the iron grip of the Nazis, that my life would have been at stake. There were many ways in which death could strike you in that country in those days, especially if you were in a *Straflager* – as I would undoubtedly have been according to the charges I was facing. There were many fancy names for

murder in those camps and, apart from that, it would not have
been to the likes of Masbach *Straflager* that I would have been
sent on that occasion.

The Way Home

We spent more than a week at Magdeburg aerodrome, sleeping
in the aircraft hangars. We had now been separated from all the
other nationalities; there being only British and Canadians in
our group. I remember how sad the Poles were when we left.

'You are lucky,' they said, 'you have a country awaiting your
return, but we are stateless and homeless.'

This was true. Many of them had no loved ones there to
welcome them back and they knew not what awaited them if
they did return. The Russians were in their country now and,
according to the Poles, they were no better than the Germans.
They were not the only ones. Most of the countries of eastern
Europe were in the same state, although their situation was not
quite as bleak as the Poles.

We were divided into groups, twenty-five men in each. Each
group was numbered from one upwards and I was in Group 10.
That meant that our group would travel in the tenth plane.
There were days when only one plane would arrive and some
days none at all, for they were ferrying from other places and,
besides, the war was still going on.

We were mixing with plenty of the people here, the ordinary
folk of the country, and it would be appropriate to record their
opinions when we asked them about how things had turned out.
Most of them, to a degree, thought that Hitler should definitely
have surrendered when the enemy crossed the River Rhine,
before the Russians started the great push which took them across
Poland to Berlin. If he had done that there would not have been
such great destruction of the country or of people's lives.*

They admitted it had been obvious to anyone that the war was
lost once the enemy had set foot on German soil. He knew it as

* Thuringia, the region of Germany that Donald John spent his war in became part
of Eastern Germany – under Russian control until the fall of the Berlin Wall.

well, they said, but as his own fall was obvious to him, he determined to take the country down with him. More than one said to me that it was a great pity that he had not been finished off in the attempt on his life in July the year before.

'But it was yourselves that elected him,' I said to more than one of them.

'He got the majority of the votes in this area,' said one man, 'but I certainly did not vote for him.'

Not one German would admit to me that he had voted for Hitler in 1933, but it was my considered opinion that many of them had turned their coats in the twelve years since then.

Our plane arrived at last on a Sunday morning at about nine o'clock. When Group 10 were called for, half of us did not wait to pick up coats or haversacks or berets but ran across to the plane as we were, except that I stuffed razor, soap and brush in my pockets. Three planes were departing that day and there was great excitement round the aerodrome for this was the first time that many of the boys had been on a flight.

I myself had never before been inside a plane – even on the ground. But we had experienced more than the events of a complete ordinary lifetime in about five years of our lives, so flying to us was just another of the novel, strange experiences that were an inevitable consequence of our way of life during that time. So we looked on the journey before us as a fresh leap into the unknown, just as Scott must have regarded his journey to the South Pole or Columbus his voyage across the Atlantic.

The plane left the ground with its usual roar and before long was accelerating smoothly on its course to the west. It was a beautiful morning – especially lovely for us as we left the country of so many hardships behind and sped on our way back to our home country.

The pilot showed us the River Rhine, the river on which I had sailed in the barge in 1940. The section below us now was much farther south than the bit on which I had sailed for we could see Cologne quite clearly, apparently with hardly a stone left standing except for the walls and spires of the cathedral. Crossing the border into France, the plane ran into a snowstorm and we were tossed about like a ship in heavy seas. The pilot climbed to twenty-five thousand feet to try and get above the snow but the weather was just as turbulent at that height.* He then descended so low that we could see the tops of the trees swaying in the wind and apparently almost touching the underside of the plane. But still the storm did not abate and the outside of the plane was thick with ice. Then we found a clear patch and he said he would land at Metz aerodrome. That he did and the other planes were there before us. We had a meal there and passed a couple of hours waiting for the weather to improve. I had been in Metz before, in April 1940, before we were hurriedly transported to the Belgian border when the Germans invaded that country. It had been partly destroyed now – a legacy of the gunfire – but a small price to pay for freedom.

We left Metz when the weather improved and halfway across France we had a bright, sunny day. The river Seine lay below us like a great silver serpent in the sunshine until eventually it broadened so much it that it became the sea. We were above Le Havre, the port where I had landed in January 1940, totally innocent of the turbulent ways of the world. But now, five years on, I knew and had experienced every kind of evil and inhumanity that the mind and heart of man can devise while wading through the blood of his fellow creatures to higher status in this world.

It was eight in the evening, eleven hours since we left Magdeburg. We were now in Le Havre with nothing between us and England but the Channel. But this time there was not a single person trying to stop us from crossing the Channel as had happened the last time we were there. Rather, everyone was doing their utmost to get us across with as little delay as possible. The plane which brought us from Germany was going no further, but returning to that country. We asked the pilot to carry on across the Channel before landing.

---

* The planes used were usually the ubiquitous but unpressurised C47 Dakotas, which would not have been capable of climbing to such a height. Although POWs were also ferried in Lancaster bombers (sometimes even in the bomb-bays!) every one would need to be on oxygen at that level.

'I wish,' he replied 'that I was allowed to do that.'

Other planes were coming to fetch us from England, but they were not expected for two days. We would have to while away that time still in Le Havre.

Epilogue

Had the five years just passed merely damaged our lives, or did they have any positive aspects? Speaking for myself, I would say that I had not suffered any great harm, except for a measure of ill-health. On the other hand, I had broadened my mind and gained more understanding and experience in that time than I would have in eighty years of uneventful ordinary life.

As I said in a previous chapter of this book, I had experienced the noblest of human nature in the hardship of distress. I had experienced close fellowship and love of justice in hearts that would withstand without flinching the agonies of suffering – yes, even brutal death – for the sake of their companions and country.

On the other hand, I had also experienced the black depths that the hearts and minds of some people can descend to when they abandon human kindness and Christian compassion, degrading themselves in form and deed to the level of the demons of darkness.

There is no doubt, therefore, that the five years under the shadow of the Swastika had some beneficial effect on me. Despite that, if I was twenty again now, I would certainly not wish to go through the like again. I sometimes wonder if it was a judgement that came upon the world then, just like Noah's flood or the destruction of Sodom and Gomorrah.

Destruction there was without any doubt, and destruction which cost millions their lives but whether or not such a thing was ordained only God Himself can tell. At other times I say that it was the Great Destroyer who got completely free and controlled and directed the war machine of Central Europe.

One thing is certain: that it was the forces of evil and iniquity and that they were defeated by the power of justice. According to the reasoning of philosophy, that is the moral outcome that should be expected in such circumstances.

The English Channel was shimmering bright below and we were all keeping a sharp lookout to see who would be first to spot the coastline of England on the horizon. Everyone on the plane was silent; not a word was being uttered. This was a pregnant moment and no pen could ever describe the feelings in the hearts of all the boys, each one with eyes alert, looking ahead for the first sign of the land of his birth. When the white cliffs of Dover appeared out of the sea, each living soul on board let out the same triumphant yell and those with bonnets chucked them up in the air.

A minute or two later, swimmers wading in the surf were waving and shouting to us and we were answering, though they could not hear us.

We had come home.

Donald John MacDonald's story ends here with the return to Britain – but for many of the men the period of readjustment to normal life at home was painful and prolonged. Undoubtedly the strong bonds of companionship forged in the face of oppression had been a powerful sustaining force. Donald John's pre-war close friend, Donald Bowie, could not settle anywhere after his years in Stalag XXb and spent the rest of his active life wandering from job to job around New Zealand and Australia. Many others found it impossible even to talk about their experiences for many years. In a radio interview in the 1970s, Donald John spoke of the feelings of loss and loneliness he experienced on his return home – feelings which often surfaced in his poetry.

> Gur tric a bhios mi smaointeachadh
> An caochladh thàinig oirnn:
> Na companaich bha gaolach leam,
> 'S bu chaomh leam bhith nan còir,
> An-diugh gu sgapte, sgaoilte
> 'S iad a' saoithreachadh an lòin,

The cuid dhiubh dh'fhàg an saoghal seo,
Air raoin a dh'aom an deò.

How often I think upon
The changes we have seen:
Those comrades that I loved,
Whose company I enjoyed,
Today dispersed and scattered
As they earn a livelihood;
And all those now departed –
On the field who breathed their last.

He had started to compose songs in his native Gaelic as a teenager and the wartime experience not only added another perspective but gave him time for reflection. Understandably, his wartime songs are imbued with nostalgia for home and the vanishing simple way of life of his childhood.

It was a great poem started in the Stalag which won him the Bardic Crown at the National Mod in Glasgow in 1948. He died in 1986 at the relatively young age of 67, but it was not until his poetry was published in parallel translation that his importance as a major Gaelic poet was at last recognised by a wider audience. The translations of the two poems in the next pages are taken from that work – Chì Mi (Birlinn 2001).

The Boys That Are No More

The original Gaelic song, Na Gillean nach Maireann, *in tribute to those who fell in the assault on 4 June 1940, was composed on the way to Stalag IXc in June 1940 but not written down till after the war.*

Horo boys, hao o boys
Horo boys who were splendid –
Sad for us to leave you
Lying there at Abbeville.

Morning had barely dawned,
Just before the sun arose,
When we were given orders
To do battle with the foe.

Explosions came on every side,
Guns spreading death there,
Whistle of lead and powder smoke,
Bangs and thunder everywhere.

Before the sun had set that evening,
Many a brave, strong young man
Was lying amongst the corn,
His blood reddening the ground.

Though we forced them back a little,
That attack was not successful –
The Division was all alone;
They had nine with armour.

There fell from Uist noble lads –
From North and South the numbers –
Fine men in first flush of youth,
Some never found alive or dead.

Camerons from the land of mountains
And from the Lowlands, splendid lads –
Sad for me that you are lying
Far from the land which gave you birth.

Far away from the land of peaks,
That land your bones belong to –
Many's the night we passed there
Together singing Gaelic songs.

I think of you at this time –
How you were left in France –
While we are in enemy hands
On the Rhine confined in barges.

The War Memorial

This translation of An Carragh–Cuimhne Cogaidh, *composed long after the war, reflects MacDonald's sadness that succeeding generations had forgotten the sacrifices of two world wars.*

Freedom! Dear was it bought,
Blood spilt in gallons;
Freedom! Cheap is our passage
Through the young men's sacrifice.

Noble red blood of the Islands
Enriching Europe's earth;
Foreign turf concealing
White bones without flesh.

Far from Island shores
In alien land without kin,
Precious dust of heroes
Enriching that foreign soil.

Tread lightly with care
On the fresh earth of Europe,
For this soil was once
The still eyes of young men.

The memorial stands on the brae,
I myself sit nearby –
Does every name here survive
In the minds of today?

Is every name remembered
With gratitude eternal,
Or has this new generation
Forgotten their sacrifice?

That blood was spilt
On the fields of Europe
To save us from bondage,
From the pitiless yoke.

Did I hear a voice cry
From a grave deep in France
'Is our sacrifice scorned now,
The people uncaring?'

'We delivered to your hands
The splendid chalice of freedom –
Is the sun of our memory eclipsed
By the world's fleshly pleasures?'

★   ★   ★

You that come by Kildonan
Ere you descend into Bornish,★
Bow your head in respect
At the young men's memorial.

Tender great gratitude
To every name on this cairn –
It's thanks to them that you
Can walk free in this land.

★ The South Uist War memorial stands on Ben Corary between the two villages
mentioned. It bears the names of 123 who died in the First and 46 in the Second
World War from an island with a population of about 2,000.

Big Archie Macphee's Story

In his prime Archie Macphee from Garrynamonie in South Uist stood six feet two inches tall and weighed sixteen stone, so it is little wonder that he was known in Uist as Eàrdsaidh Mòr Mac a Phì, *'Big' Archie Macphee. When I interviewed him in 1999 he was still an impressive figure of a man at the age of eight-nine. His memories of the war remained vivid, although recollection of dates and names inevitably had become vague after a lapse of sixty years. Aged nearly thirty at the outbreak of war, he was more mature than most of his companions joining the 51st.*

In the nineteen twenties life was hard in Uist. 'Absolute poverty,' *he said,* 'just what you could get out of the land or the sea.'

So at nineteen he joined the Metropolitan Police for the princely salary of £3 a week. Compared to the impressive technical backup and equipment available to the modern policeman, there was little then in the way of resources to fall back on.

'Only a whistle – and God help you if you had to blow it – for there would be nobody there!'

But he never settled to London life and his request for a transfer to a more rural station was refused; so he returned to Uist. After some odd jobs, including driving for Polachar Inn, he followed the example of other young men and joined the TA. For many islanders that meant the horse-mounted Lovat Scouts. They were expected to provide their own horses and those who did not have one for the heavy work of the croft would borrow from a neighbour for the annual fortnight's camp. The reward for man and horse was £12, which was a significant sum in those days.

He remembered his early TA camps in places like Boat of Garten and Beauly in 1933 or 1934 but eventually transferred to the Camerons. As a regular heavy events competitor at the South Uist Highland Games, he was soon involved in brigade athletic competitions such as tossing the caber. He was a member of the very successful tug-of-war team.

After six to eight weeks' training at Bordon in Hampshire he sailed for France in November, eventually arriving in Bolbec village near Le Havre. Because of his maturity and driving skills he was by then a corporal in Motor Transport.

This transcript of the interview is in his own words. The capricious cruelty of war is illustrated by one particularly traumatic incident which he recalled.

I was allocated a job to take some ammunition up to the front line (near Arras). The company sergeant major had given me a Geordie to go with me. You had to go before daybreak. You weren't allowed to use any lights at all or anything like that. It was a dodgy old run – from the second line of defence to the front line would be about twenty or twenty-five miles – just track it was. I had about five tons behind me – ammo – all sorts – grenades, bullets and shells and what-have-you.

As I was about to leave, one of the islanders came – in fact he was a relative of my wife – a chap from Daliburgh called John Macleod. Poor lad – he was young you see – only nineteen. He knew me, you see, so he came to plead to go with me.

'Well,' I said, 'as much as I would like to take you, I don't want to take you – because anything can happen. The place is full of snipers,' I said, 'and a barrage might start any minute. We've got a dangerous load here and it's not a very healthy trip – so I would advise you not to push your luck at all. Even if I wanted to take you, I'd have to get permission from the company sergeant major.'

'Oh,' he said, 'I'll have a word with him.'

Against my better judgement, I let him go and he came back to say the CSM had given him permission. The Geordie was clapping his hands!

Off we went and on the way there were craters – shell craters and bomb craters and what have you. We went about ten miles along this rugged track and all of a sudden all hell broke loose – the German barrage started.

I said to John, 'We're in a serious spot here – if we can make it to the next bomb crater we'll jump and get clear of this truck – because,' I said, 'just one bit of shrapnel would do it and the whole lot will go up.'

'Oh,' he said, 'we could go under the truck!'

'There's no answer to that!' I said, 'but you watch me. The next bomb crater I'm going to jump and you jump too.'

It was February time and I had a greatcoat on. I made the crater – it was as big as this kitchen here. There was this huge explosion and I knew the truck had gone. The barrage only lasted just three or four minutes and when it finished I never had a scratch – but the bottom of my greatcoat was cut round by a piece of shrapnel as though by scissors!

But when I looked for John, there was no sign of him – he wasn't there. I went out and found his glengarry – that was all that was left. He must have been caught in the blast when the truck went up. I had to crawl my way back to the second line of defence – no truck or anything.

The funny part of that episode, you know – my future wife Mary Kate* – I think she was a cousin of his – dreamt about all that. She told me after the war that she dreamt that night. In her dream, she said, 'I couldn't see John – all I could find was his hat.'

It was fifty-nine years after the event when I met Archie at his home in Wales but the memory of that fateful 12 June was still painful.

At St Valery, we were in a cornfield there and we were being strafed day and night by the Heinkels and the Stukas. You couldn't put your head up.

---

* After the war, Archie married Mary Kate MacDonald, who was a sister of one of South Uist's most famous bards, Donald Alan MacDonald.

The officer said, 'We're surrounded by a ring of steel. You have to lay down your arms.'

Believe me, that was the worst sentence I heard in all my life. We had to obey the order – but it was the saddest day of my life.

He confirmed the other stories of desperate scrounging for food on the long march into captivity and the hellish conditions on the Rhine coal barges. Like Donald John MacDonald, he ended up in Stalag IXc.

If we came across a field of potatoes, it was all green when we got there and when we left it was all black. You had no water or anything. They gave us the odd bit of black bread . . .

The trip in the barge on the Rhine was awful, man. We were packed in like sardines in a bloody can . . .

Winter weather could be much more bitter than the men were accustomed to, particularly as clothing was often inadequate.

It was so cold where we were in the Black Forest that when you went out in the morning there seemed to be no oxygen in the air. The frost went three metres in to the soil. If you took hold of anything iron your fingers stuck to it.

Like Donald John Macdonald he also served his time in the Freyburg quarry.

Before you went to the quarry all you got in the morning was a cup of ersatz coffee and to this day I don't know what they made it from. At nine we had *fruhstuck* – some black bread with nothing on it – with coffee. For lunch we had some *kartoffel suppe* – potato soup. In the evening it was more black bread and ersatz coffee. The coffee was made in a big cauldron with an aperture underneath it for fire, for which we had some dross to burn. One night it was my turn to fire the boiler and so I filled a shovel but instead of putting it on the fire, without thinking, I dumped it in the open cauldron. I daren't tell anyone what I'd done or we wouldn't have had anything to drink – so we drank it anyway. I didn't admit it till afterwards!

Archie went on to relate the story of the escape attempt mentioned by Donald John MacDonald on page 166

The billet we were in was like a big chateau – the bottom half was occupied by German soldiers and twenty-five of us were locked up in the top half. I was about thirty then – a mature man – and I was a tough old bugger, mind! There was a sergeant from Iochdar, South Uist – Norman Maclean, *Tormod Sheonaidh Ghobha* – in the same billet. Norman was a little younger than me and we put our heads together. The windows had three bars of solid iron but we thought that if we could find a bit of hack-saw we might be able to get through them.

I said, 'One of us will have to find a way to stay here to cut these bars.' Days went by and, as it happened, I did find a bit of hack-saw in the quarry and hid it in my boot. I remember well – it was on a Sunday – and I thought something has to be done.

You might not believe this but when you are in a desperate situation, you do desperate things. I must have been off my trolley to have done this. There was a big stair and I threw myself down. It's amazing I didn't kill myself but all I did was put my ankle out. That was what I wanted to do and, funnily enough, that was what happened. The boys went to tell the guards and two of them came and put me in a wheelbarrow to wheel me down to the local doctor. He told me there was nothing broken but he dressed the sprain. Then they wheeled me back to the lager and the officer in charge put me off work – which was just what I wanted. They usually issued us with clogs at night but as I couldn't get them on because of the swelling, I was allowed to keep my boots. During that week I was off I worked on the bars. I had to be careful – filling the gap each time I left it.

I said to Norman, 'It's getting near Hitler's birthday – 20 April. The guards will be celebrating and that will be our chance.'

It got to the stage where I could take one of these bars out and I said to Norman, 'Tonight!'

So when the guards locked us up and started their carousing

downstairs, I ripped that bar out of its socket. We were about fifteen feet from the ground so I had to tie about four or five blankets together. Norman went out first then I followed – and off we went.

By the time our absence was discovered the next morning we had a head start of about eight hours to get clear. But the thing we hadn't taken into consideration was that we had no compass and we were literally going round in circles. To make matters worse, Norman developed a cough. We were travelling at night – God knows where we were going! We had to pack it in before day-break and usually hid in a barn. This morning we were shacked up in a hayloft and when day broke I saw two soldiers out in the yard and I realised they were French. Norman had a smattering of French so he said he would go and talk to them to see whether they would give us a drop of water and a bit of bread.

'No', I said, 'don't do it – I don't trust them at all.'

Against my better judgement I let him go. I saw them chattering away and then the Frenchmen left and came back with a bottle of water and some black bread and went off again. Before we had finished the water and bread there were two German guards outside with fixed bayonets. The Frenchmen had gone straight off and reported us.

When the guards got us out of the hayloft I said to them, 'I'd like to say goodbye to my French friends.'

'*Verboten!*' he said – he knew me and he knew what was behind it. I would have killed one of them.

Norman was sent off to another camp and I was put in solitary confinement on bread and water for about a week. Then I was back in the quarry again. Once you put a foot wrong you were a marked man then. Mind you, the Wehrmacht, the German army, to give them their due, they weren't too bad. If you were involved with the others – the SS or the Gestapo – look out then. One of them used to come in every morning to check up on me.

Anyway, things died down after a bit but then I had a run-in with one of the foremen in the stone quarry. The stone had to be loaded onto bogies at the top of the hill and they ran on cables down to the bottom. The trolley system depended on the loaded bogies bringing the empty ones up. Hermann was the old German in charge of about six of us. The foreman was an eighteen-stone pig of a man who didn't like us.

Hermann warned us, 'Keep clear of the foreman. So long as you do your work he won't bother you.' I said to Hermann, 'According to the Geneva Convention, prisoners should only do half of the work of a German, so therefore, that's how it will be with you and me. You put two stones in and I'll put one in.'

'You can't do that', he said, 'you'll get into trouble.'

'That doesn't matter', I said, 'when it comes to the crunch it's him or me.'

As you might expect the gantry stopped. Up came the foreman. In his hands he had one of the long-handled five-pronged forks like I had for picking up the rubble. He started shouting – calling me an English swine and so on – and I was goading him on. I was hoping he would have a go at me with the fork for I would have had him first. He realised that and didn't come any closer. As sure as anything I would have stuck it in him.

The next day Hermann said, 'You've upset him now – he's a dangerous man.'

'Be that as it may,' I said, 'we're going to do the same again – I'll put in one stone for your two.'

Of course the gantry stopped again. Up he came again. He didn't have the fork this time but he was waving his arms about. He kept coming near me cursing in German. My fuse has always been very short all my life. He prodded me in the chest with his finger and so I hit him then – smack between the eyes. He went down like a log and there was blood everywhere – he'd cut his head on the rail.

The guards came and took me away and I was locked up till there was a court martial, which was set up with German and British POW officers. I got away with it by the skin of my teeth – mainly because another foreman from the sugar-beet factory spoke up against the quarry man. If there had been any Gestapo involved in the court I would have been shot.

I shouldn't have done it – I knew the moment I hit him that I'd done the wrong thing – but it didn't matter to me then if they had shot me. Perhaps you won't understand this – I was in that frame of mind – I had made my stand and if they shot me – so be it. As luck would have it I got away with it but after that I was a marked man.

Towards the end of the war Archie made another escape attempt which was to have a better outcome.

In 1945 the Germans started to get a bit jittery – things were getting a bit tight, you know. They knew the Americans were advancing and the Russians advancing from the other side. They kept us moving about. So I thought to myself then, 'Now I'm going to escape again.'

The chap that went with me this time – I think he was from Ross-shire – can't think of his name now. I had a word with him and I said to him, 'Now, I'm going to escape tonight if you want to come with me – because the Germans will be moving us again.

'Yes,' he said, 'I'll go with you.'

So before they moved we scrambled away from the camp. The Germans then were getting a bit careless – they were getting a bit fed up with it all. We laid low in a culvert somewhere till the camp left. Then we set off when it got dark and landed outside a German farmer's house. There was a tool shed and we scrambled in there. And then bloody shells started falling here and there. The Germans were sending a barrage up and the Americans were sending another and we were in a dodgy spot there. This was in Regensberg in Bavaria now so we had travelled a bit, see.

We were holed up there and I said to my mate, 'This is all very well but we have nothing to eat and there's a farm house here. I'm going to ask them for some food.'

'Oh,' he said, 'don't do that – they might bloody kill you.'

'They might,' I said, 'but if they haven't anything to shoot with they won't kill me! I'm going to take a chance on it, otherwise we'll starve here.'

So off I went down to this farmhouse and knocked on the door. A woman came to the door and looked at me – I looked a picture, mind – I had a beard and looked quite rough.

'*Gefangenen?*' ('Prisoner?') she asked.

'Yes,' I said.

'*Englander*?'

'*Ja.*'

Then she shouted to her husband. He came through – he'd be about forty-five or fifty – and asked if I had escaped.

'Yes.'

'Oh,' he said, '*Ist gefährlich*' [dangerous].

'*Gefährlich* or not,' I said, 'we need something to eat.'

This old lady said, 'You go back to the hut and I'll send my sister up with something.'

When it got a bit dark she came with some coffee and bread. We were holed up there for about a week or so and they kept us in coffee and that. Mind you, we were in Bavaria and a lot of the Bavarians were against Hitler – although that's where he started and that's where he had his hideout.

We were very lucky – they could have shot me – but I've been always rather lucky through life. Anyway we thought that either the Americans or the Russians would come through at any time. Bugger me, one morning we heard a rumble and I saw this tank coming with the Stars and Stripes on it. I ran out with my hands up – I looked a picture, mind – but the tank commander stopped.

'You English?' He asked.

'No,' I said, 'I'm a Scot.'

'What Division were you in?'

'51st – Cameron Highlanders.'

'Have you got any proof of that?' he asked.

'Not a great lot,' I said. 'If you can't take my word for it, I can't help you. I have a tattoo on my arm here you could look at!'*

'What's your army number?' he asked.

You never forget that: '403196,' I said.

'That's a cavalry number,' he said. He knew, you see.

'It is,' I said. 'We transferred from the cavalry to a mechanized unit.'

'What part of Scotland are you from?'

'The Islands.'

---

* Archie's tattoo was of a kilted Highland soldier.

'Yes,' he said, 'there's one more thing I want you to tell me. There's a famous golf course in Scotland – what's it called?

'St Andrews.'

'OK,' he said, 'you'll do!'

So he took me in the tank and gave me a tin of bully beef. I was bloody ravenous! Then he saw the farm and he started to turn the bloody turret round. 'I'm going to blow that house up,' he said.

'No,' I said, 'don't do that – for these people have saved our lives. But for them my mate and I would have starved.' I don't know whether he believed me but, 'Right,' he said, 'you'll take me down to them.'

So we went to the house. I could speak pretty good German then, you see, so I had a chat to the farmer and told him what was what – that these were Americans. They had been terrified the Russians would come through and I explained they would be all right now – the war was practically over.

So we went back to the American base – they gave me an American jacket to wear and with a good wash and a shave. I was a different man. I was with the Americans for a couple of months till I was repatriated back to Blighty again from Brussels in a Lancaster bomber – twenty-five of us. Then we were sent to Cirencester for a six-week rehabilitation course to update us how the world was going. We were sent out to various jobs to give us an inkling of how things went. Six of us went as security guards to a Maintenance Unit near Gloucester – a little village called Quetchley. There was a lot of lease-lend equipment which had to be destroyed. Motor-bikes, blankets, God knows what there.

After demobilisation, Archie applied to join the prison service but then he heard that they were looking for ambulance drivers. Undecided, he tossed a coin and so spent thirty years as an ambulance driver. He married his Mary Kate but never went back to Uist except on holiday. But he did keep in touch with the German family who had been so kind to him at the end of the war – in sharp contrast to the behaviour of his one-time Allies in the previous attempt.

He died in Wales in 2000.

Suathadh ri Iomadh Rubha

Touching On Many Points

ANGUS CAMPBELL

Angus Campbell was born in Swainbost, in the Ness area of Lewis, the third of six children. The island protocol of naming children after relatives resulted in him having a younger brother also called Angus so the Lewis tradition of giving nicknames was particularly useful. Angus senior became better known by his nickname Am Puilean *while his younger sibling was called* Am Bocsair. *They were both poets.*

This graphic account is a translation of chapters dealing with his experiences in the Second World War in his auto-biographical Suathadh ri Iomadh Rubha *(Touching on Many Points), published by Gairm in 1973. Given that he received no formal education in his native language at school, the literate quality of the original Gaelic is remarkable. Like his fellow-poet, Donald John MacDonald, he was determined to leave school at fourteen so his education owed more to the oral culture of the Gael and wide reading.*

When he was thirteen the family moved to Berneray, Harris, where his father was the Free Church missionary. Angus acquired expertise in the work of the croft and the handling of sailing boats. In 1924 he became a steward on a luxury racing yacht. This period of sailing round the Mediterranean as well as the usual British venues he was to look back on as one of the happiest times of his life.

Other work was hard to come by, so the following year he enlisted in the Seaforth Highlanders for seven years. Most of that was spent in India keeping the peace on the Northwest Frontier. He became a supremely fit athlete but, having decided the army life was not for him, refused any promotion. He carried this attitude into the Second World War for otherwise his experience would surely have been capitalised upon. However, the annual bounty of £20 was sufficient incentive for him to remain in the reserves until the outbreak of war.

After leaving the army in 1932 he returned to Swainbost as a shopkeeper and in 1933 married Mary Mackay, with whom he had seven children. The custom of the house ceilidh which had been the cultural forum of the Gael was dying out, so he was a prime mover in setting up the first bothan (meeting hut) in Ness. The original intention was just to have a meeting place where young men could meet and swap songs and stories of the oral tradition. The idea soon spread but it was a matter of considerable regret to Angus that the bothans became just drinking dens.

Times became particularly hard for the small shopkeeper with the arrival of mobile van competition so he worked for a while in Fairfield's shipyard in Glasgow.

As a reservist Angus was recalled to his old regiment on the outbreak of war in 1939. The 2nd Battalion of the Seaforths was a regular unit and so formed part of the original BEF sent to France within a few weeks. In March 1940 it replaced the reserve 6th Battalion as part of the exercise in strengthening the 51st. His subsequent capture at St Valery was doubly unfortunate for, had Angus got away at Dunkirk, he would have been deemed to be too old for further active service in view of his age of thirty-seven.

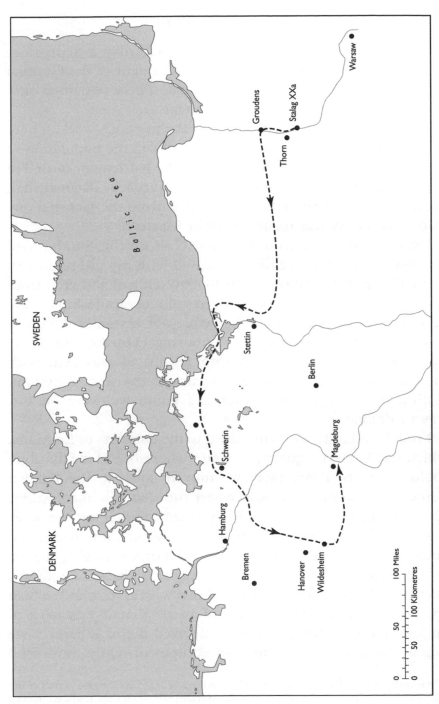

Map 7: Route of the long march from Stalag XXa, 9 January to 11 April 1945

The Phoney War

The anxious waiting ended at last. On Saturday 2 September 1939, we heard on the radio that the full might of the German army had launched an attack on Poland. There remained only one course of action open to Parliament.

The navy men had been called up the previous week. There were so many of them that it greatly reduced the population of Lewis. After the war we often heard of the bafflement caused to English clerks by place names such as Arivruach, Balantrushal, PortnaGuran and Skigerta – quite apart from the fact that one man in every six was named Donald Macleod!

I was one of three who left from Ness on the Sunday – in my case to Fort George to be reunited with my old regiment. More than a thousand reservists like myself had gathered from all corners of the country. Many old comradeships were renewed – although neither the venue nor certainly the occasion would have been of my choosing. During our short stay there, we were divided into groups. I was sent with the majority to Aldershot to reinforce the 2nd Battalion. Within three weeks of my leaving home we were on our way to France.

From Cherbourg we went inland to the outskirts of Le Mans, which had been designated as a site where the 51st Division* could form up. From there we moved north to the Belgian border. This was the very area where the bloodiest and costliest battles of the Great War had been fought. Hill 60 on the other side of the border was out of bounds to us but Vimy Ridge had been preserved as it was for the eyes of tourists. In some places the opposing trenches were only thirty yards apart. The surface of every field and hillock was so riddled with craters and so torn apart by the awesome mayhem of battle that it was hard to understand how men could have survived there. Wherever we dug we came upon old arms and equipment. Only those who

* In fact the 2nd Seaforths were originally allocated to the 15th Division as part of the BEF and did not join up with the 51st until March 1940 when they replaced the 6th Battalion.

had taken part could possibly comprehend the misery and suffering of that kind of warfare.

This was the period known as the Phoney War. Along with the French, we were digging in along the border but, apart from no-man's-land between the French Maginot line and the German Siegfried line, there was not an enemy to be seen.

That winter was unusually cold. During the day we had to dig trenches and revetments (walled pits) to act as tank traps. Most of our senior officers had seen service in the Great War. Though you might think that subsequent developments in land and air weaponry might dictate different tactics, they were still steeped in the attitudes and practices of that time. At any rate, when it came to the fight, all our work was to prove fruitless.

Most of our accommodation was wretched, dirty and worthy of condemnation. Such was the cold and lack of comfort that it was impossible to pass the evening till bedtime there. The only other option was the café and what a scene that was of laughter and noise! The times and circumstances encouraged behaviour in the majority completely out of normal character. How could you cope with hardship and discomfort without a little resort to the drink that makes the mind merry and dispels the gloom of apprehension!

There was one old barn we stayed in which was alive with rats. They were of various colours as well as being rapacious, bold, without fear of man. But of course we had heard from the soldiers of the First War that the three things which caused them the most misery in France were the louse, the mud and the rat!

By the beginning of April 1940 the 51st Highland Division was at full strength, having been reinforced by a battalion from home.* We were sent to the town of Metz in Alsace Lorraine. From there we moved up to take over a section of the Line of Contact from the French so that at last we were at the battle front. But, apart from sporadic artillery barrages from alternate sides, little happened during the day. Once darkness fell, however, night parties were out on each side – some setting ambushes

* Several regular battalions replaced TA battalions on March 6th.

and others involved in hit-and-run operations. This firing and fracas was a nightly occurrence. While not as deadly as the heavy fighting that lay ahead, it kept us alert and on guard.

Empty tin cans were strung on the barbed wire in front of us to give audible warning of any enemy approach during the night. A raiding party came on one occasion and the clanking of the tins gave the alarm before they could throw their grenades. They were fired on as they tried to make their escape. The light of dawn revealed three of them lying about fifty yards away and a group went out to check whether any were still alive. On seeing us approaching, one young officer rose on his elbow, took a picture of a girl from his pocket and kissed it. Then he took his pistol from its holster and shouted at us, '*Englander Schweinhund!*'* He put the gun to his head and before he fired shouted, '*Heil Hitler!*'

It is hard to understand how fanaticism and hatred could so twist the mind, but he was no different from many other young Germans who were in a ferment of mindless adoration for the evil figure of the Führer.

The German Onslaught

At the beginning of May 1940, the fighting became more intensive; when we heard that the German army had attacked the borders at full strength we realised that the real war had begun. In terms of armament and firepower on land and in the air the enemy had substantial superiority but, in spite of that, we stood our ground steadfastly. However, the news that he had broken through to the west of the Maginot Line and that we were in danger of being caught in a trap from the rear forced us to make a quick retreat. The strife was bitter and the noise of battle deafening. In particular a battalion of the Black Watch took heavy casualties.

Very quickly the main British Expeditionary Force found itself in a situation in which it was impossible to regroup into a

* Slang equivalent – 'English bastard!'

viable battle order. The fortified walls of the supposedly impenetrable Maginot Line caused the enemy little hindrance. Instead of laying siege they simply bypassed it, breaking through the French army with the destructive spearhead of the *Blitzkrieg*. The BEF suffered a similar fate. Instead of remaining behind the defences they had taken so long to prepare, they entered Belgium. Within a few days they were surrounded and could only retreat towards the coast in a half-circle that was constantly being reduced and squeezed by external enemy pressure.

That, then, was the forlorn and confused situation that both we and the French found ourselves in in the latter half of May, when our division had to retreat from the jaws of a swift-moving, formidable battle formation we were ill-equipped to resist. We were put on trains at Metz and, because of the chaos and disruption of all that was happening, we had to detour round to the south of Paris. Then we were hastily deployed up north to the Somme near Abbeville – an area which had seen carnage in the First World War. Weygand, the commander of the French Army, was trying everything in his power to close up and secure the breaches the invading enemy had made. While the rest of our army was hemmed in around the beaches of Dunkirk we were assigned to the French IXth Corps.

It was obvious to all that, in terms of strength, power and mobility of equipment, the Germans had the upper hand. As far as we could see, the Luftwaffe had the freedom of the skies to do as they wished. In addition, there was not a single attack on us without tanks to act as a bulwark, opening the way for the infantry. In all the time I was in France I saw British aircraft on only two occasions and the few tanks we had were old and obsolete. The French army was even less well-prepared and, whereas we maintained a stubborn resolve to do our duty as trained soldiers in battle conditions, they were in a bad way – short of food and less well-equipped. Many of them gave the impression that their morale had collapsed and defeat was accepted as inevitable.

Day after day, we were involved in hard fighting in an attempt to stem the enemy advance. When darkness fell, the order to withdraw would be given. Often we were told we were far in advance of the French – which was the reason our left flank was exposed and defenceless. We had to hurry to make the next position before the break of dawn – for trenches had to be dug anew each morning before the bombers came. Sleep was dependent on the little time between settling in and the appearance of the enemy – and often that interval was very short. It was distressing to see the lads with their eyes swollen and blinking from lack of sleep. Sometimes they could not keep awake even when their lives depended on it.

The 4 June 1940 was different. Headquarters decided that, instead of retreating, we would attempt to mount a major counter-attack. About 3.00 a.m. we were in battle order waiting for French tanks that were going to lead the way for us. They came – and what monsters! I saw eight of them come through the field where our battalion stood and we advanced behind them. The first light of day revealed us to the Germans and in an instant all hell broke loose. We took up firing positions on the edge of a wood but it was not long before a swarm of the Luftwaffe were attacking us like bees whose hive had been raided. As far as I know none of the French tanks returned and, without cover in front or overhead, we were in a tight spot, from which there could be no escape without heavy losses.*

Who could describe in words the horror of such a time? Your companions cut down alongside you; some blown to pieces, the wounded crying out in pain, trees torn out of the ground by the roots, the destructive thunder of the big guns, the terrifying explosions of the bombs – and yet the courage of soldiers clinging to hope in a desperate situation.

The French came to help us disengage from the one-sided struggle and those of us who survived managed to withdraw. We talked among ourselves about the reason for sending so many souls to their deaths. The superior strength of the enemy was not unknown when we were sent to face such unwarranted

---

* The French Char B1 tanks weighed 32 tons and though regarded as extremely formidable in 1939 they were much slower than the lighter and more manoeuvrable Panzers. Most of the ones taking part in this particular assault were destroyed in an unplotted minefield.

slaughter. Perhaps they wanted to add another battle credit to the gory annals of the 51st.

By 9 June fatigue and exhaustion from lack of sleep had taken their toll of us. We were in the heat of battle in a small town. Close to our platoon on the right stood a large oil refinery. In the middle of the uproar they fired a full barrage from all the big guns and scored a direct hit on the factory. You would have thought we would have been roasted alive from the great inferno that arose. The shock was so powerful that those of us standing in the trench were thrown on top of each other. One of the lads went clean off his head; he started to cry, threw away his gun and his kit and disappeared from sight.

We had to withdraw hurriedly and take up new firing positions behind the stone wall of a little church with a steeple. Luftwaffe fighters soon found us and made many attacks, swarm after swarm of them diving on us from behind. We had to lie prostrate on the ground but strangely, though they struck sparks from the wall above, we all survived.

When dusk came, our platoon was ordered to provide cover for half an hour while the rest withdrew in the usual nightly fashion. In a quiet moment what should we hear but a cry in French from a family pleading to be allowed through as they fled from the Germans. They were seven – an old couple, their daughter, whose husband was in the army, and her four children. In their flight they had been caught in the perilous crossfire of no-man's-land. The poor souls were exhausted with fear and terror. We took them to the church where there was an underground crypt, gave them some food and advised them to return home once the tide of war had swept past.

Who should we find crouching in the crypt but the lad who fled when the refinery exploded? Like many others reduced to this sorry state by the horrors of war, he was sobbing and trembling – especially his hands. We were able to take him with us.

The next night we were given sudden orders to withdraw without a moment's delay for we were in a bottleneck and in imminent danger of being surrounded. We were warned to avoid roads and proceed as quietly as possible. We had retreated about a mile and were travelling along the side of a hill planted with young trees when we were suddenly fired upon from the top of the hill. Total confusion reigned with all the officers and NCOs issuing different conflicting orders. But, 'cometh the hour; cometh the man.' It was an ordinary soldier who shouted loudly, 'Who the hell is shooting up there?'

Immediately the firing ceased and there came a return shout asking who we were. It was our own A Company. Like ourselves, they were on the alert and nervous about withdrawing safely. When they heard the noise below they had assumed we were the enemy. One man's common sense saved us from inflicting mortal injury on each other.

St Valery

On 10 June we awaited the usual enemy assault but, from dawn to dusk, we were left untroubled. We certainly needed the respite, having had fourteen days with little rest from strife or any chance to sleep except for such hurried naps as we could snatch. The next day was the same, with headquarters staff wondering what the enemy might be up to during this untypical hold-up. It was High Command in England that shed light on the situation.

The Panzer divisions which had reached the coast south of Le Havre had now turned north along the shoreline. Meanwhile, naval and other vessels were on their way to the little fishing port of St Valery. We were required to make our way there without delay so that we could be taken off before we were encircled and caught in a trap from which there could be no escape. Anything we could not take with us was to be destroyed and burnt and then we set off in trucks. The little spark of hope alive in the mind of each of us burned brighter the closer we came to a destination offering relief and refuge. Hence the disappointment when it came was all the harder to bear.

Night had fallen and we were only about a mile out of the town when a sudden shout halted us and we were ordered out of the trucks. In the do-or-die race for safety, the Germans had won. We were caught in his trap and the one escape route open to us had been slammed shut. It became obvious why the pursuit had halted for the last two days. The enemy had waited to give the spearhead of Rommel's Panzers time to advance along the coast from the south so as to spring the trap.

Though we could not see them, we were told that rescue ships were off St Valery and there would be no surrender without a fight. About 3 a.m. our battalion was moved about three miles away from the town and spread out in an arc. Later on, we learned that we were to act as a rearguard to hold off the enemy while the rest escaped. If fortune failed we were to be left behind – a sad remnant.*

Dawn came – bearing little favour on its wings. We heard the thunderous roar of every kind of weapon while smoke and fire completely obliterated the town from view. Swarms of bombers flew overhead every now and then, aiming at the navy ships, but as far as I know without hitting any of them.† Marines with guns were put ashore north of the town. We listened to the roar of battle without the least idea of what was going on.

About 11 a.m. all went quiet, without us knowing whether this meant cause for celebration or otherwise. We sent messengers to find out what was happening but not one returned. We had time to cook and eat some food. About 3 p.m. a German spotter-plane flew over us in leisurely fashion and we realised that, like the vulture, its appearance did not bode well.

It was not long before our fears were confirmed. About fifty tanks emerged from the wood about a quarter of a mile away. Immediately their guns roared and, as the plane had given them our exact position, they were right on target.

My platoon was in a farmer's apple orchard and, because of the trees, I could see only three of the others. The garden was bounded by a hedge with aspen trees growing here and there amongst it. One of these had been cut down about a foot above ground so the platoon sergeant and I cut a hole in the stump and set up our anti-tank gun on top. I had picked out a tank and

---

* The 2nd Seaforths position was the village of Le Tot to the west of St Valery.
† In fact, such ships as did venture close inshore took heavy punishment from Stuka dive bombers and Rommel's guns on the cliffs and were forced to withdraw.

fired on it when the sergeant asked to take over. He had only just done so when a mortar bomb exploded over to my left where the other two were. One was killed outright and the other had a death rattle in his throat. I ran over to see if there was anything I could do but he was dead before I reached him. While I was there another sergeant came to have a word with ours. He had just reached the very spot I had left when the next mortar struck, killing them both. I was half way back to them and behind one of the large trees when there came a burst from a machine-gun. I threw myself close in behind the tree, hearing a hail of bullets striking the trunk and fizzing past on either side.

During a lull a messenger came with orders for us all to retire as quickly as we could to the farmhouse where the company command post was. The distance was not far, with the last bit on open road. I saw three men in front of me and two behind on this little bit of road. Suddenly, two Messerschmitts fired on us from behind, striking sparks from the road. Two bullets drew blood from my arm and my thigh without harming me too much, but not one of the other five survived. You wonder why one man's life should be spared in desperate situations that cause the deaths of most of his comrades. Of all the men I had seen in those few hectic moments of action, I was the only one out of ten to reach the farmhouse alive.

The last order was that we should make for the shore about half a mile away with, 'Every man for himself!' The tanks were now like sheepdogs herding us to the edge of cliffs, which stood grim and steep, over two hundred feet high. On the bare tops there was no rock or outcrop that you could crouch behind to defend yourself. When it was clear there was no way out they closed in and ordered us to throw down our arms and surrender. Our war was over.

The Journey to Thorn

They took us into the town – a pretty little place, now in chaos. Most of the buildings were reduced to empty shells, sad reminders of the grief, ruin and sorrow which the accursed conflict of war brings upon innocent civilians.

We passed General Fortune, the commander of the Division. He was seated on a low wall and next to him the German commander had his arm about his shoulders. This was Rommel, who was to go on to earn such fame as a general in North Africa, earning his nickname of 'The Desert Fox'. Fortune looked especially sad and little wonder. At that moment his name seemed particularly inappropriate.

Before nightfall they took us an hour's walk out into the country to a farmer's field where they had gathered about 12,000 prisoners. Of those, nearly half were French, including Algerians, Senegalese and a group from the Foreign Legion. Here we spent two days and nights confined without food, drink or freedom of movement. The only thing in our favour was that the weather was warm and dry. After the fatigue and agonising exhaustion of the period we had just come through, sleep at least was sweet.

When I awoke on the third morning, I was surrounded by French soldiers who had been brought in during the night. I noticed that the nearest one had the end of a loaf of bread sticking out of his haversack. He saw me looking longingly at it with the greedy eyes of hunger so he cut off a handsome piece and offered it to me. It was so old and stale that it was full of green holes but hunger cares little for foul flavour or rotten meat. We were parched with thirst but our captors offered us not a drop of water.

They made ready to take us away. Every bridge had been destroyed and there was no transport other than Shanks' Pony. We marched in line three abreast and I was up near the front. As we passed through one little village, there were German soldiers standing along the side of the road. They may have been triumphant at seeing the fruits of victory before their eyes but they also had the spirit of compassion. When we pleaded with them for water, they soon found buckets and brought them to us. At times like these, manners and restraint forsake a man and I filled my mess-tin and emptied it in one draught.

But, oh! That drink was dearly bought! Before I had gone a hundred yards I was struck by the most agonising pain I have ever felt. I was not a complaining sort of person but this pain was so unbearable that I was rolling on the ground crying out aloud and totally unable to control myself. One of the Gordons stepped out to help me and suffered many heavy blows from the passing guards before he had to leave me. I myself received many kicks from heavy boots and blows from rifle-butts but cared nothing except that I should be put out of my agony. At the end of the column there was one who showed authority and a spirit of mercy. He sent a soldier running to a farmhouse for straw. I was placed on the straw in a little truck and taken into Rouen.

A large building, once a poorhouse, had been cleared and turned into a hospital for the wounded of St Valery. The house was so full that there was hardly enough space for the staff to move about. The nurses were Catholic nuns and great was their diligence, compassion and patience in the face of such a nightmare situation. A doctor gave me a morphine injection to alleviate the pain, but when I looked around to see and hear the injuries and agony and cries of suffering there, I felt ashamed that I had been complaining when of sound body.

By my side was a sergeant of the Gordons who had lost both his legs from the lower thighs. He told me that he felt the pain where his toes once had been. I was given an enema and was none the worse. The doctor had diagnosed food poisoning and when I told him of the stale bread that had turned green and the great draught of water when thirsty he told me it could have killed me.

In the three days I was there I witnessed twenty-three deaths – and that only in the small corner of the house that I could see. When you ponder the brutality, cruelty, hardship and grief caused by war, anyone in his right mind would place the blame squarely on those that allow manliness to be sacrificed for national pride and men's freedom to be put in chains of slavery to satisfy the aggressive arrogance that goes with power.

With two others I was taken away in a car and returned to join the prisoners, who had meantime walked more than eighty miles on very little food. There was only one question asked of me – did I get fed in hospital? You assume your higher talents and gifts will be important to you at all times but when suffering great pain, hunger and thirst, all other thoughts are banished to the back of the mind.

On the route, both sides of the road bore witness to the savage destruction that had passed that way. Scattered around were weapons of all kinds, abandoned by the dead, wounded and captured; towns bore the ugly scars of war. Passing through the odd place that had survived the conflict, women waited for us with slices of bread with butter or jam. But the offerings were small and the hungry so many that only rarely could you grab a little portion.

One day a big fair-haired lout of a guard demonstrated not a little spite and malice. He rode up and down on a bicycle with a wooden club striking out here and there – especially at women who were trying to offer us food. In the afternoon, as we were passing through the little town of Seclin, he saw four large formidable ladies coming to meet us, two of them with buckets of milk on yokes. He split the milk of the first one with a kick but, before he could do any more harm, revenge was taken on the scoundrel, which put an end to his arrogance. They knocked him over and beat him up with his own club! Not one of his own German colleagues went to his aid and we never saw him again.

The wearisome journey went on day after day. Certainly the weather was fine and the countryside pretty, but the anguish of hunger allied to the fatigue and filthiness of our bodies over-shadowed pleasure and beauty. We left France, passed through Belgium and entered Holland. We were in the area of that country where the mouth of the great river Rhine spreads out to the sea in bays and inlets.

It was while passing through a little town on the edge of one of those bays that a young woman standing inside her gate waved to us. It was obvious she was inviting some of us to run and hide. I looked all around and, with not a German in sight, I ducked through the gate and down the stone steps that descended to the front of the house. A man I took to be the girl's father stood in the doorway. He took me in to a place where there was a trap-door and let me into an under-floor cellar. When all the prisoners had passed by, the man, his wife and the girl came to me, bringing grilled fish and potatoes with bread and coffee to follow. I was in more need of that than ever a thief needed hanging!

They did not speak a word of English but I gathered that he was a fisherman and that they would try to put me on a boat that would carry me to safety. After I had eaten my fill – no small amount – a bed was made up for me in the cellar and I slept like a log. About eight o'clock next morning, having just had breakfast, I heard loud shouting and barking dogs above. In a few moments the trap-door opened and a large Alsatian leapt down, followed by two German soldiers. Fortunately for me they were not sadistic or brutish men. Like a lot of the Germans, they shouted loudly but did not beat or hit me.

They had found another three and, after searching the remaining houses, they took us away in a car. We did not have far to go. A large canvas camp had been erected at the end of the march. From there, barges would carry us up-river into Germany. We were released into the camp without punishment and that was the first and last attempt I made to escape.

There was every indication that thousands upon thousands of prisoners had occupied this camp before us. The straw that had been scattered on the bare floor at the beginning had grown wet and half-rotten with a putrid, sour, damp stink, as though the French before us had urinated where they slept. We had been infested with lice long before this but here they multiplied so that we were now alive with them.

On the second day we were taken out to listen to a long propaganda speech from a fawning disciple of Goebbels. The war was nearly over and Hitler was assured of victory so it was in our own interest to do our utmost to curry favour. They called the Irish out separately and then the Scots. When they saw how many there were of us, they tried to seduce us with flattering promises. He asked that all of us dissatisfied with the rule of England should stand out. One fool who did not understand the drift responded. The angry shout that came from the rest of us reproaching him was so threatening and uncompromising that they realised without further ado that we were not to be swayed by shallow flattery.

We spent three days on barges going upriver through Holland into the borders of Germany. After that, there was a further three days on a train, crammed so tightly into cattle trucks that we could not even turn round. It travelled so slowly that it was more often at a standstill. During the three days they gave us nothing to eat and only let us out twice.

Our destination was the little town of Thorn on the river Vistula in Poland – about halfway between Danzig* and Warsaw. This was the birthplace of the famous astronomer Copernicus. Having once been a fortress town it was surrounded by great stout fortifications – much of them underground. They were capable of accommodating between three and five thousand men in a degree of comfort. This was the POW camp called Stalag XXa.

Stalag XXa – Bromberg

We spent the first month in a balloon hangar. There were three thousand of us in a huge canvas marquee. Your allocated resting space was a bag of straw on the bare floor. The food ration was a loaf of bread with a little scrap of margarine, to be shared between five or between seven on alternate days. Once a day we had something they called soup. Very often the only flavour of the thin dishwater was from a horse's head. You counted yourself lucky if there was a scrap of potato or carrot floating in the small portion you received. It was depressing to finish the last spoonful or last crumbs of bread. There was so little that it served only to sharpen the disappointment and pangs of hunger.

We reached a point where we had nothing on our minds that was not in some way connected with food. If I pictured my home, I would be sitting at a meal or Mary would be lifting a pot of black puddings from the stove. The spirit of friendship or love can never compete with personal deprivation.

* Thorn, the Vistula and Danzig are now Torun, the Wista and Gdansk respectively.

Our masters were puffed up with pride for they were winning the war on all fronts. They made every effort to reduce us in body and soul to a wretched state without esteem or self-respect. They even took our clothes away and replaced them with rags they had collected from the countries they had conquered. Each outfit was different and mine consisted of: Czechoslovakian beret, French jacket, Dutch trousers and clogs and a Polish overcoat! I don't know where the shirt was from but it was a tattered rag. Gaunt, dishevelled and bearded with shaven heads, we would have cut a sorry figure even in smarter attire. They took photographs of us in this shameful state but we never saw them. No doubt that was just as well. Only a girl who had lost all hope could have made a pin-up of one of those!

If I had to get up during the night it sometimes took two attempts to remain upright. There was a little hill to climb to the latrine and often I needed to rest halfway up. We had a walkway round the boundary of the camp and our main pastime was dawdling around it like scruffy skeletons. With my good friend Roderick Morrison from Shader I sat one day beside the track listening to the conversation of each passing group. There was no escape or distraction from the one obsession – food. We thought one man had conquered the fixation, for he was praising his mother – but at the end of the eulogy the peak of her skills and virtues was that he had never seen anyone who could match her suet pudding!

But the school of suffering and pain has its own lessons for one who can learn from the experience. We were brought up to judge men differently according to their occupation, their success and their wealth; giving them respect and honour in relation to the degree they had risen above the level of the common herd. Here were men the war had brought together from all corners. Men unequal in terms of property, occupation, responsibility, opinions, religion, intelligence and education were now united by hunger and danger in a common kinship without division or dissension. Their only concern was when they might have their next meal. This acid test revealed the true qualities of man stripped of worldly privilege and honours. The gold or the dross, the worth or nastiness came to light in the furnace of suffering. Virtues or failings were determined not by your rank in the world but by the natural good or evil deep within us all.

Some days we were taken out to work. We had neither the strength nor energy to do very much but most days there were hidden angels waiting with some comfort for us. If there were trees nearby we learned to slip in amongst them while the guard's back was turned. Very often it would not be long before some food or tobacco was thrown to us – usually by Polish women. The Germans had the power and freedom to kill Poles out of hand for the slenderest of reasons. In view of the risk they ran we often wondered if we would have put ourselves in mortal danger for their sakes.

There was one man amongst us from a very wealthy family. I was one of two witnesses who countersigned his IOU promising one thousand pounds to any man who could bring him in a loaf of bread. I often wondered if he honoured the bargain after the war!

At the beginning of winter I was one of the first prisoners to be sent to work in the town of Bromberg. The balloon hangar was a great improvement for we had dry billets with beds. The food was a little better but, without that, it would have been impossible for us to work at all. Large factories for war supplies were being erected here and we had to dig the foundations. The weather was bitterly cold and we had only our rags to alleviate the suffering without warmth or charity. In terms of rights and reward our status was little better than that of slaves. The majority of those assisting the tradesmen were Polish women, some of them working through the night. It behoves us to remember the loss and misery these poor people endured as a result of the war. You understand a little of it when you realise that a third more were killed in Warsaw alone than the total lost by Britain and America together throughout the war.

One day a group of us were sent to unload a trainload of clay stones and that was where I had my first inkling of the atrocity unbeknown to most at that time, though much has been heard of it since. A train came in fully laden with people of all ages. Soldiers of the SS let those in each truck out in turn for water, but their treatment was wicked and brutal. The poor wretches were thrashed, kicked and beaten here and there to the accompaniment of savage shouts and curses. It was only afterwards that I realised that these were Jews on their way to one of the concentration camps.

It was in Bromberg, after seven months of gnawing hunger never satisfied, that we received the first food from the Red Cross – a cause of much joy and gratitude. One old boy from Harris got a tin of oatmeal in his parcel and immediately started to make porridge in an empty bean tin. Roddy and I were with him. He made seven servings of porridge without taking the tin off the fire. He had a stick to stir the porridge but he was so driven by hunger that he licked all seven from the stick.

Donald had been a shepherd at home and the lack of tobacco made him very unhappy. One day at work Roddy asked him, 'Donald, if you had your wish, where would you like to be now?' Donald replied that he dreamed of being out on the moor with dog and crook and a large haversack of food by his side. He would sit to wolf it down and then light his pipe. It was not a bad picture!

A Bad Master

At the end of winter we were brought back to the Stalag at Thorn. This particular camp, known as Fort 13, was commanded by an officer with only one arm and an empty sleeve hanging down. We called him 'Wingie' and, though he was full of threats, his bark was worse than his bite. That was proved to us one day when a young lad of seventeen was to be punished. The boy had found some skates before he escaped. The river Vistula was frozen over in winter and he reached Danzig in three nights, skating on the ice. He had been recaptured after boarding a Swedish ship.

When we were turned out to watch his public punishment the omens were weighted against mercy. Six armed soldiers stood in front of the lad and Wingie told us that the penalty for this offence was death by firing squad. But, in the end, he said that if his own son had done so brave a deed as a prisoner of the British he would have been full of pride for him.

It was here that I saw an English RSM called Letts turn Nazi because his needs were met with food and other favours. The Germans made him a supervisor of those of our lads who were convicted by them. The men reported that he was more brutal to them than the guards. I can tell you the end of this pathetic figure. Word of his misdeeds preceded him, so he would have been sentenced after the war, but nemesis overtook him on the way home.

After a month we were moved again to another camp, Fort 17, where about 5,000 men were confined. Here we were sorted out in accordance with our trade or occupation before the war. This was so we could be spread out in groups across the country according to our work experience. It came as something of a surprise to the Germans to discover that apparently two thirds of us were workers on the land. They didn't realise that hunger was the reason for this, as we hoped that farmers at least would have access to food!

I was sent out in a group of twenty-eight men, allocated two at a time to farmers. Two guards delivered us in the morning and returned us after the day's work to our sleeping place in the middle of an open space. There were five lads from Lewis and a Gaelic speaker from Oban in the group, together with five from Wales, who spoke their own national language. We pretended to the others that we could all understand each other and many a grumble they made to us about listening to sounds which they likened to the cackling of hens!

Your treatment while working for the farmers was a bit of a lottery. Most of the older ones had been in the Great War.* Not only had adversity squeezed poisonous hatred out of them but, secretly, they also had a fellow feeling for us. Those of the lads who ended up with them were often fortunate. On the other

* Many Polish farms had been allocated to Germans.

hand, many of the younger ones were puffed up with Hitler's
loathsome creed. As luck would have it, the lad from Birmingham and I ended up with one of those. We had the first
demonstration of his bad temper when he learnt that neither
of us was a worker on the land but rather barber and shopkeeper
respectively. Through time, he saw that I did not have too much
to learn – especially on the day that the cattleman was taken ill
and I did the milking morning and evening. That made him
moderate his behaviour towards me somewhat, but the
Birmingham lad was completely clueless and victimised accordingly. The five Polish workers on the farm were also treated
appallingly.

The work was arduous and the hours long – from seven till
seven, so long as light allowed. Our billet was mean and narrow,
with hay and pigeons above our heads and cattle on each side.
We were tormented by so many fleas that, despite fatigue, sleep
was broken by the restlessness of bodily suffering. We called
them the 'Black Watch' and any man they did not drive to
cursing would have been worthy of a place among the saints. I
composed a bardic satire but that did not weaken their vigour or
the irritation of their bites.*

Every farmer in the area under the age of fifty was in a
position of authority to keep the Poles in subjugation. Most of
them belonged to the Brown Shirts† and a few had close
connections with those spiteful bullies, the SS. My master
was one of those.

Today it is difficult for us to comprehend the state of malice
and hatred that developed in men like this under the influence
of the warped, corrupt propaganda that they were continually
subjected to via every possible medium. The picture painted
was so seductive. Hitler was the new Messiah who had brought
a conquered people out of the depths of the abyss. From a
despised state he had raised them to glory and to a point close to

---

* It was a common Gaelic bardic practice to compose a satire about any unwelcome
visitation (such as rats) in the belief that this would drive the pests away. Unfortunately, the bard found that these particular vermin did not understand Gaelic!
† The SA or Storm Troops – the military wing of the Nazi party, used to intimidate
or eliminate opposition.

their ambition to conquer those parts of the world not already on their side.

In this year of 1941 all was going so well for them that pride and arrogance had almost wholly supplanted virtue and reason. Every Thursday the Führer broadcast on the radio, glorifying the feats and victories of the armed forces. On that day our small farmers had to get into their suits and were marched in military order to a different house each week. They had to parade in two ranks and, as soon as the speech started, they were called to attention and remained like that till it was over. They had then, with one voice, to raise the roof with a great shout of '*Heil Hitler!*' before singing the national anthem, *Deutschland Uber Alles*. This brief exercise in triumphalism was reminiscent of the bloodlust of hounds in the fury of the chase.

In addition, on Thursday evenings, they set out on an odious mission. They were given a list of names of Jewish families to be rounded up secretly through the night, and taken to a certain place where they were loaded onto trains. This was the road of death and extermination on which six million were transported like cattle to slaughter. An armed busload would snatch these poor souls from their beds. Young and old, large and small were given but twenty minutes to leave their homes.

One Friday morning, having returned from one of these outings, my master loomed over me as I cleaned out the cattle gutter with a barrow. He was drunk, with a look of evil and hatred on his face. He shouted 'Heil Hitler!' three times at me but when I did not respond he threw me head first into the manure. The clothes I had on were all that I had at the time and they were now filthy from top to bottom with wet, stinking dung. I sought out the two soldiers guarding us. On seeing my state they understood my grievance and gave me the rest of the day off to clean up.

That was the only occasion he was violent towards me. Before the year was out, he himself was called up into the army. He came back on leave from the Russian front with the stupidity knocked out of him by the hardship and terror of battle. He was killed shortly after this – another lesson to those who would put their faith in evil until the day of reckoning shows them its fallibility. Who amongst us would not be arrogant when we are borne on fortune's wings through sunny and cloudless skies?

From our time with the farmers until towards the end of the war we received parcels from the Red Cross every week with food and tobacco. Bare bones put on flesh and gradually we changed from looking like scarecrows to the normal appearance of man. In the same way we received new uniforms, coats and army boots. If clothes maketh the man, certainly we were transformed. In a way we had an advantage for we now had three things unobtainable to them – tea, coffee and chocolate. The poor Poles who laboured with us were very appreciative when we shared these small luxuries with them.

It was an unexpected shock to the Germans when Hitler declared war on Russia. The thought that the two great powers of the United States and Russia were now opposed to them made them a little more humble – although that did not last for long. They had had so much success at the beginning that they expected Russia to be conquered by Christmas of that year. They had a particular hatred of the Russians. I think '*Schweinerei*' and 'Bolshevik'* were the two most offensive words on their lips. Out of the great number of Russian prisoners they captured, fewer than half survived to the end of the war and their treatment was brutal and inhumane beyond measure.

For a while I was laid low by sciatica in my back and was taken to see a doctor in a little town. We could hear the doctor in a rage giving his views to someone on the dreadful state into which civilisation and morals had declined in a country that had once taken pride in education and standards. The outburst ended when a guard emerged from the door with five Russian prisoners. From the look of them you would have thought that it was not possible for men to survive in their state. Some of the women and children present even started to cry in horror. When

* *Bolshevik* – a member of the ruling Russian socialist party but often used, as here, pejoratively. *Schweinerei* – disgusting. There is evidence that Hitler considered the Russians to be *untermenschen* – a sub-human species. He decreed that Russian POWs had no rights to treatment as honourable soldiers according to the Geneva Convention.

it was time for me to be examined, I heard the doctor telling my guard the reason for his anger. The Russians were working in the town and most nights some of them died from hunger and ill-treatment. The five we had seen had been caught cannibalising the dead and this was not the first such occurrence brought to his notice.

The lads we left in Fort 17 told me they had been moved out of that camp into wooden huts outside the prison. In their place went six thousand Russian POWs. After a couple of months they noticed a large army lorry with a six-wheeler trailer behind it coming to the main gate every morning. There it was filled with dead bodies – they reckoned about forty most days. After a while, however, their brutality backfired on the oppressors. A plague of typhus broke out among the poor wretches and there was great fear that it would spread. Through the Red Cross, supplies of plasma were brought from Switzerland to try and halt the spread of the deadly disease. Some of our doctors and a number of RAMC lads who were prisoners volunteered to go in amongst them to give transfusions and any other assistance or relief in their power. Our men made a collection among themselves of Red Cross food and tobacco to send to them.

It was heart-rending to hear the story our men had to report. There were only about six hundred Russians left alive and they in such a dreadful state that it could not be put in words. As each man received the transfusion he was given a share of the gifts of tobacco and food, which made them plead for a second transfusion, thinking they might get more. The disease was eventually confined to the infected area but few of the Russians survived it.

Three of our own lads were preparing for an escape bid. We were far from the border of any friendly country, with all sorts of obstacles, so that the chances of success were virtually nil. Despite that, thousands made the attempt for the spark of hope is difficult to extinguish. One of them decided to go it alone and the other two went together. They were soon missed and did not get far before they were recaptured. A soldier brought the pair back but it was armed farmers who caught the other and they killed him. His body was riddled with bullets.

After nearly two years of work on the land my health failed as the result of a stomach ulcer and I came back to a Stalag where a sort of hospital had been established for prisoners. It was run by three doctors, two of them Highland Scots, Mackay and Macmillan. A German doctor attended regularly. My condition was critical for some time and it was three months before I was deemed fit for work.

It was here that I made the acquaintance of one of the most pleasant and intelligent men I had ever met. Harvey from Sydney, Australia, was one of three hundred ambulance men captured in Greece. They were volunteers and many of a goodly age. He himself had been in France in the Great War and took a wife home with him from Peebles. One of his sons played test cricket against England in the years after the war.

Fortunately for me, I was placed beside him. When he learned I was a Scot his first question was whether I was from Dundee. A young lad from that city had been in the bed before me and in Harvey's opinion his mind and thoughts were solely taken up with football and other trivialities. He himself was a philosophical and argumentative man, fond of debate and opinions and many a field we traversed. It may be that we were not often of the same mind for differences in thinking, upbringing, education and way of life meant that the two of us would often approach the subject in different ways. However, rowing with one oar will not bring a boat to port and the one-tune piper is a pretty dull musician.

He was one of the top men in the workers' union in Australia and appeared in court cases all over the country. Since then I found out that his name was known throughout the country in his day and he was much respected.

He made every effort to persuade me to emigrate to Australia with my family after the war. The picture he painted and the promises he made me were very alluring and I was certain he was sincere and well-meaning in the proposition he put to me. He was repatriated through ill-health six months before the war ended and immediately sent letters to me and also to my home offering help with the fare for the voyage and finding suitable employment at the other end. I did not take the good man's advice. Doubtless I would have been much better off and more successful, but the man torn by the roots from his native land loses blooms which will not flourish through transplanting.

I spent three weeks in a camp for non-combatant soldiers, most of them RAMC. Among them were the three hundred Australians already mentioned and very fine men they were too. The German commandant had been a prisoner in Scotland during the Great War, most of the time in the Keiller Jam factory in Dundee. He was fluent in English and particularly in the swear words of that city! As far as his duty and powers permitted, he lightened the yoke and loosened the rein on men such as the ones I came across. Many a one still alive will testify that 'Scarface' was a fine man.

A general was due to visit the camp, Fort 15, while I was there. The prison was fortified in the usual way by a moat with drawbridge. We had two buglers and when the great man was near, Scarface sent them up to a tower on the wall with orders to play the appropriate British army salute for a general as the top brass came over the drawbridge. The great man entered followed by a long retinue and they stood ramrod straight on the bridge while the boys were playing. If they had had the slightest idea that the tune the rascals had used was 'Here Comes the Bride' their bearing would have not been so erect or their conduct so restrained!*

Groudenz – a Better Life

After this I was sent to work in Groudenz,† a little town on the Vistula to the north. Nearly a thousand of our lads working in various factories throughout the town were all billeted in one huge building, which had once been a poorhouse. In part of the factory to which I had been sent they were manufacturing the

* The tune known as 'Here comes the Bride' (and often parodied) is the grand wedding march from Wagner's opera *Lohengrin*. As such it would be well-known in Germany and not inappropriate as a processional!
† Now Grudziadz.

missile which Hitler hoped and expected would win the war for him – the V2. When we discovered this, we refused point-blank to take any part in the work. Though they threatened us with dire penalties unless we changed our minds, we stood our ground and it was they who had to give way.

The work was not so strenuous nor the accommodation so poor as on the farms. Among the many ways of passing the time we had plays and concerts almost as good as the entertainment in theatres at home. Most Sundays the Gestapo would arrive, ransacking and turning the place upside down. They suspected we had a radio – which indeed we did – but they never found it. Every night someone would go round with news of the war and from the times of the Normandy landings we were agog each night to hear what progress was being made day by day.

The lads had sorted themselves out in fours, with a little table and stools for each group. I did not know any of them but I was introduced to the three others I was to join. You only had to be with two of them for a short while to realise that they were men of intelligence and education. The third was a talkative little chap full of stories about nothing very much, with whom I soon became friendly. He was a salesman from Birmingham and knew every nook and cranny throughout the country. If he had a fault it was that there was no end to his stories nor anything thought-provoking in their substance. The other two I found through time to be very congenial company. One was a Londoner, a philosophy lecturer at London University and, interestingly, a communist. The other was the hero Plunkett – a little, slim, red-haired chap.

Where else could you have brought together four so completely different in background, education, rank and up-bringing? You would think that there was no possible way they could get on together but that was not the case at all. Each of us held views both rational and controversial, on which we could reach neither agreement or compromise to the satisfaction of all four. Yet we got on very well amongst ourselves. In terms of humility, benevolence and goodwill I would say that Plunkett was a step ahead. His unassuming manner concealed a wide-ranging, knowledgeable mind, cultured in arts such as music, art and theatre. Another lesson which brought home to me that merit, pleasantness and character cannot be gauged from outward appearance. After the war I saw his name mentioned as a house-guest of the king at Balmoral.

In this place I had a bit more spare time on my hands so it became my pastime to compose poetry, much of it humorous. If talent and imagination can bring a picture to mind this would be my choice of vocation or service to the world. The final result might be neither significant nor profound but in a life as strenuous as mine it was all too seldom that I allowed myself the time – and even more rarely that the soothing dew of poetry refreshed the meadows of the mind.

1944 was drawing to a close, a year full of incident and excitement. The all-conquering Reich, which had spread its boundaries from the west coast of Europe to Moscow, from the North Cape of Norway to the north of Africa and which was going to last a thousand years, had withered in strength and shrunk in size. It was being hard-pressed from all sides by such powerful forces that the inevitable hour of surrender was drawing near. The victorious heroes who had been close to bursting with pride and arrogance in their days of success were now to suffer infamy and retribution for brutality and injustice on a scale which had never been seen since the world began.

We expected that the next Russian assault would bring those of us on the east of the Vistula within their control so that we would be free to leave the camp. Alas, how little did those of us who nursed these hopes suspect that the last period of our captivity would surpass in suffering all that had gone before. It is just as well that future events are hidden from us. Who, otherwise, could preserve his sanity?

The Long March

On the eighth day of the year everything was normal. We came back from work at dusk and spent the evening in groups reflecting on the war situation and our hopes of imminent release. Suddenly we heard unusual shouts and commotion from men close at hand and a distant rumble like the sound of guns. As the night wore on, the noise grew ever louder and we anticipated that things were about to change for the better. Few of us lay down and sleep was impossible.

About three in the morning the guards appeared in a frenzy of rage and fury. Germans are naturally raucous and stentorian and, at a time of stress and haste like this, their bellowing would reverberate throughout creation. It was, '*Raus menge!*' '*Schnell, Schnell*!' and '*Schweinerei*!' here and there as they drove us out of the doors in a clamour of shouting and screaming panic.

We were told that the Russian army was advancing and closing fast so they were taking us away without delay. Apart from the clothes we stood in, we were allowed to take nothing other than a greatcoat, one blanket and a mess-tin. Dawn was breaking before we moved off and we had not gone far before we understood the reason for the disorder and chaos. We crossed a large bridge to the other side of the river – and what a scene of confusion and fear. The German army was there with tanks, artillery, anti-aircraft guns and trucks carrying infantry and wounded. Their pallor, bearing and manner spoke of suffering and their wretched situation.

To complete the chaos, half of the road as far as the eye could see in both directions was jammed with cart after cart of families fleeing from the Russians. For three years they had been taught that this was a savage, brutal and merciless enemy, capable of any atrocity and evil. The result of this propaganda was now evident: old people, women and children fleeing they knew not where without any protection from the cold and elements other than sheets stretched on sticks over their carts.

I had seen refugees in France escaping in the same way but this scene bore no comparison. The warmth of summer in a country not yet ruined by deprivation had favoured the French. Here, however, the temperature was below zero, want and misery were widespread and confusion and chaos precluded discipline.

Because of this unexpected chaos, during that first week it

was impossible for us find space to walk on the road. Things were tough enough for starving men in poor condition without having to drag step after step though snowdrifts. This was only the beginning of the cruel ordeal and we must still have had some reserves of stamina or we could not have stood up to it.

On the first two nights our only resting-place was the bare ground, without tree or shelter. Sleep was completely impossible in such cold. In any case, it was necessary to keep on the move, clapping our hands together to maintain circulation. The little food we had was soon gone and we knew for certain that we could not stand another night like that. Fatigue and sleep would take their inevitable course and there would be no awaking from that slumber.

Our group was particularly unfortunate. The officer in charge of us was a surly, spiteful scoundrel, without an ounce of compassion or kindness. He was a young lieutenant whose only ambition seemed to be to eliminate us all one by one. His revolver was hardly ever out of his hand and there was so much animosity in his face when he bawled at us that he frothed at the mouth. My tale will later prove how this upstart did everything in his power to abuse what little authority he had.

In the morning we asked the interpreter to inform this villain of an officer that he had the choice of finding us a place for the night or turning the guns on us to put us out of our misery. He said neither yes nor no, but that night we found shelter in a farmer's barns. Filthy dirty though they were, no noble's palace was more prized or welcome.

On the fourth day we met up with a similar number of Russian prisoners on the same weary trek as ourselves. Day by day we alternated between being in the lead or bringing up the rear. On the days that they were ahead of us we witnessed their sorry state. They had been weak and needy before this happened to them, so they did not have the stamina to resist for long the agony and torment of further suffering. When one of us reached the end of his strength and his legs gave up on him, he would just be left where he fell. Not even that small measure of compassion was shown to the Russians. When they were in the lead, not a day went by without us passing some of them as corpses despatched by a bullet.

Initially we were being taken to the city of Stettin* which, like Glasgow on the Clyde, stands near the mouth of the Oder. One day, when we were within two days of the city, I felt very ill and it was only stubbornness born of fear and despair that kept me going. That night, they found a large hay barn for us and it was with grateful relief that I made a bed for myself. We had barely settled when there came dreadful shouts to turn out again – the Russian army was close at hand.

This was the only time my courage and hope failed me. I knew for sure I could go no further and was unable to stop bursting into tears. I made no attempt to move; it was beyond me. Fortunately, this was a sort of false alarm. The Russians had cut through ahead of us to the south so that, although we now had to be taken north towards the Baltic, we were left till morning to enjoy the sleep of the exhausted. By then I had recovered sufficiently that I was never forced to give up.

As far as food was concerned, it was only very rarely that any arrangements were made to keep us alive. Sometimes we happened to pass the night in a farmer's barn and the potato boilers for the pigs would be loaded up for two-footed swine. The price of your consequent small share was the loss of vital sleeping time while waiting for it to be ready.

We grew devious and cunning. It is said that want is the mother of invention and we took any advantage of the guards to steal raw potatoes, corn, turnips or anything else that could stand between us and death by starvation. There was no bread or substantial energy-building fare in that meagre diet, but it is a truly disagreeable food that is not made palatable by hunger.

I also learned that a small man, though lacking in size and strength, can withstand a long period of hardship and suffering better than a bigger fellow. The strong man needs more food to keep him in good shape, so very few of them survived this

* Now Szczecin

dreadful journey. This is one of the ways in which nature balances its regime.

We were taken as far north as Rostock on the Baltic and crossed the Oder estuary by two ferries between the islands in the bay to the town of Schweenamunde. From there they took us to the north-west. We crossed the Elbe and reached so far west that we were close to Hamburg. In that length of journey there is much I could tell you but too long-drawn an account of such an unpleasant experience would soon bore the reader. After two weeks the Russians left us – that is, those of them who were still mobile. We slept one night in a camp which had been vacated by the Russians, except for those unable to walk. You would have thought it was impossible for men to survive in the condition they had been reduced to by the brutality of the guards and every kind of ill-treatment.

Near Schwerin the blackguard who was in charge of us fell ill. An older man with the rank of captain took over and the first thing he did was to gather us round so that he could talk to us. He saw that we were so emaciated and thin as to be close to giving up. He told us matters did not have to be thus, as the one who had been in charge had had the authority to requisition food in the name of the Army Command.

This fine man himself soon proved to us that this was indeed the case. He asked if there were any bakers amongst us and there were – more than enough. He took them into the little town nearby and they spent the night baking large loaves of rye bread. Every mother's son of us was given one each in the morning with enough left over to provide another half each. Not only that but he gave us a full day's rest. The next day he took us out of our way to a camp full of Americans. They had a store of Red Cross parcels and he asked them to part with some of them. When they saw what poor, ragged shape we were in they readily agreed and we were given a parcel between two.

This compassionate man was only with us for three days but he made a great improvement in our lot as well as raising our morale. On the fourth day the other surly oaf returned to take charge again and it was clear that all he had in mind for us was more oppression and suffering.

There is another day and night I remember about this time. As a harbinger of approaching spring we had a heavy downpour all day. The road which up to now had been covered in snow turned into a skating rink, which gave no footing or support to anyone on it. Apart from that, the rain drenched us to the skin. At dusk the rain stopped and the cold returned with a hard frost. Ice formed on most of our clothing and, what with shivering, chattering teeth and the slipperiness underfoot, the situation was grim. About midnight we came to a large farm which was to give us shelter till the morning – comfort and relief we were in desperate need of. But what disappointment was in store for us! Some other prisoners on the march had taken over every nook and cranny of it and we were left out in the open to struggle against the piercing agony of the icy cold. Some men died that night from the suffering.

I saw the glow of a cigarette a little way off and went to see what lucky man had such a luxury. Who should this be but Plunkett. An American we had passed the day before had given him a pack of ten and he gave me the only one he had left. He told me he had made himself a vow that if he was still alive in the morning and survived till the end of the war he would never come closer to a cold country than the Mediterranean!

Day after day as we moved further west we became more aware of the numbers, power and superiority of the British and American air forces and the enormous destruction they were wreaking. Squadrons of bombers flew over day and night but it was the fighters, sniffing and searching for anything on the move, that posed the greatest threat to us. It was understandable that they would see us as infantry, so we often had to hide in the woods till they disappeared.

Between Hamburg and Bremen we were diverted to the south. Those of us who were left had little strength or energy remaining but the one thing in our favour now was that the warmth of spring made life a little easier. They skirted around Bremen with us but we passed through part of Hanover on a moonlit night. That was an awful sight, for the bombers had raided it that very day and fires were still burning throughout. But the most horrific and disgusting sight was the number of people hanging by the neck from the lampposts. This was the punishment the police meted out to anyone caught looting in the chaos – a harsh warning to anyone contemplating doing likewise.

They promised us that when we reached Hildesheim on the river Weser our journey would be over. A man in dire straits will clutch at the tiniest straw and, though they had often deceived us with promises that turned out to be false, that spark of hope still lit our path.

At last we reached the place which we so longed for – our final destination. But what had yesterday been a town had now been demolished by the awful power of the bombers. It was night, but there was not a place or a dwelling in the shattered town where we could rest or lay our heads. Our guards were in a quandary as to where they could find secure accommodation for us. It was obvious to us that they themselves were fearful and lacking in confidence after witnessing so much to make them uneasy. They found a railway track going out into the country and they followed it to its end about three miles further on. There were four old trucks for cattle or freight at the end of the line and, with menacing threats that we would be shot if we did not obey orders, they crammed us into them so tightly that we could not move or turn. Then they locked the doors and left us.

In terms of torment and bodily exhaustion, the two days and nights we spent in this grim prison surpassed every other hardship and suffering we had experienced. I cannot believe that the Black Hole of Calcutta could have been any worse. The slightest sudden movement added to the discomfort of your fellow creatures. Relief of the calls of nature could only be achieved where you stood. If you passed out and fell below the feet of the others you could never have got up again alive. This happened to many. There were so many curses, cries of pain and moans among us – getting worse as the torture went on – that you could only compare it to the depths of hell.

Thirst, hunger, lack of sleep or fatigue – each separately is an ordeal. But when these afflictions all act together to exhaust the last ounce of your will and destroy your spirit you are on the brink of the precipice that drops sheer into the ocean of eternity. When they came for us after two days they brought horse-carts with them. They knew full well that many of us would have been trampled underfoot. After stretching our limbs, most of us were able to walk back into town. They denied that any had died, but we knew differently.

They took us to an area of the town where there had been a sugar factory. A landmine had dropped on it and you would scarcely credit the configuration the explosion had left. The hole it had made was big enough to bury a church in – and half full of black treacle from melted sugar. Two thirds of the way round the crater were tall rocks of sugar solidified like toffee. They allowed us to eat and drink as much as we wanted and it is a wonder we did not burst. I do believe that there could have been nothing better for restoring strength and energy to needy bodies.

We spent three days in the ruins before the call came to prepare ourselves to move on again. The American Army had crossed the river to the north of us and the retreat was now forcing our guards to take us back the way we had come. The mildness of spring took some of the sting out of the barbs of suffering while the hope of imminent liberation revived courage and determination. As for our bodily state, we were so emaciated that you would have said we scarcely looked human. Instead of walking, we dragged our feet. We had hardly a shred of flesh on our bones. There were hollows where our buttocks should have been, our calves had but loose skin with knees hardly visible.

On the tenth day of April it was evident that we were nearing the end of our journey. We spent much of the day taking shelter as the air force came and went unceasingly. All around us the din of battle broke out now and again. That made us very much aware that we were in the middle of the fire and the fear was that we would be burnt in the flames.

Amongst us was a big sturdy lad, intelligent and pleasant as well, from Kyles Scalpay in Harris. He became too sick to go any further and we did what we could for him. We laid him down on a straw bed in a farmer's barn and they promised to look after him. That very night a bomb fell on the place and a fine man, Robert Duncan Macleod, was killed, mere moments from freedom, after surviving five years as a prisoner.

Our last night in enemy captivity was passed in a large barn with enough hay and straw to give us a comfortable night's sleep. A railway ran past about two hundred yards away and when darkness fell the Germans brought a train equipped with heavy artillery within a quarter of a mile of us. I buried myself in the hay and, despite bangs and explosions, finally fell asleep. When they woke us in the morning I had great difficulty surfacing because of a heavy weight pressing down on me. The noise and vibration had caused the red tiles in the roof to fall in. The train pulled back at daybreak.

They lined us up in the usual order to continue our journey but, just as we were ready to move off, we heard the sound of a volley of bullets close by. There were four houses above us and, within moments, white flags of surrender appeared from the top windows of each house. The next thing that happened was that our guards fled, leaving us looking at each other, unable to believe that we were free. But we were not – just yet. Two tanks passed by without noticing us but the one in charge of us was so obdurate that he did not want to give in. He gathered his colleagues back and they marched us off again. When they halted us in a place of concealment at the bottom of a valley, a muttering spread amongst us that we should free ourselves by overpowering and disarming them. But they were alert and watchful, with weapons at the ready, and the more sensible amongst us cautioned against anyone risking his life after waiting so long for this moment.

They took us to another farmhouse and, realising that the end was near, began to show us much more care and attention. We had been three days without a bite to eat and there was a great heap of potatoes on the floor of the barn. Instead of guarding them and forbidding us access as usual, they told us to cook as much as we liked for ourselves. At the same time they found a horse-drawn water-cart and brought it so that we could slake our thirst. The tables had now been turned and swiftly their scowls changed to the fawning of those who had lost their authority.

This forced magnanimity was very nearly the death of us. Very soon there were fires all over the field, with potatoes being roasted in the embers of all of them. Some American tanks noticed the smoke, gave the range to the artillery behind them and in the blink of an eye all hell broke out. The shells went over the top of us but a hail of machine-gun bullets penetrated the wooden walls of the barn, reducing part of it to splinters. With no shelter on the level field, we could do nothing but fling ourselves flat where we were.

As so often happens, there was one in our midst who was brave and quick-thinking – a man Stevenson from Aberdeen. In a flash he found a long wooden pole. His shirt had once been white before grime obscured it. At any rate there was nothing better, so he tied it to the pole and leapt outside waving it without thought for his own safety. Fortunately, he was seen and the firing ceased immediately. Within ten minutes, two large Sherman tanks were amongst us. It was the finest sight I had ever seen – or ever will see so long as I draw breath.

Two of the guards panicked with fear. They ran across a hayfield, seeking to hide behind a small haystack. A little dark-haired chap emerged from the turret of a tank, took aim, and they both fell. The same burst killed a young foal. All he said was, 'I don't care about killing those two bastards but I'm very sorry about the foal.' One of our lads shouted, 'Good old Yank!' He noticed the lad was wearing a balmoral and asked him where he was from. On hearing it was Glasgow he told us that he was from there too – he had only been a short time in America.

The Americans were horrified by our appearance and poor state. When we asked them about food they told us there were plenty of animals and cattle all around us and that we should help ourselves. This good advice we rapidly put into practice.

Although I did not see it happen, apparently the one who had made our journey so miserable was killed. That vengeance may have been barbarous beyond measure but his harsh treatment of us from beginning to end rendered him unworthy of fairer handling. As proof of that there were only 332 of us left out of nearly a thousand who had set out on the march. Doubtless many of those who fell by the wayside were picked up and made it through to the end. But a man who is as sadistic as his brief moment of power allows him does not deserve good will or forgiveness.

Before the Yanks took the prisoners away, we asked if we could identify the ones who had been good to us. Those were in the majority, if they had been given the chance. A letter 'G' was written in chalk on their backs and the Americans promised to treat them well. One of them had been a great help to me on the trek. He had recognised the *Cabar-Fèidh** badge on my beret and told me that two of our regiment had been billeted with them after the First World War. The food they had shared had helped to alleviate the pangs of hunger for his family. He often managed to smuggle part of his own rations to me. Even in the darkness of suffering there is often a little ray of light.

There was a pen full of fat sheep ready for market in the farmer's byre and eight of them were killed immediately. We prepared three large boilers, normally used for potatoes for the pigs. The meat was cut up and mixed with everything else we could find: potatoes, carrots, turnips, cabbage, peas, beans and Lord knows what else. There was no shortage of butchers, cooks or pilferers and the sternest test of patience was curbing our anticipation till the feast was ready. Who has not seen a picture of Oliver Twist, bowl in hand, asking for more? Our state was similarly ravenous. It did not seem possible that your gluttony could be sated and though reason warned one ear that it was not wise to eat too much at first, the other was beguiled by pain and greed offering convenient deafness as justification.

* The stag's antlers badge of the Seaforth Highlanders.

The result was inevitable. We passed the night as men suffering from sea-sickness.

The next day three pigs were killed and prepared in the same way. In addition, some of us went out through the countryside in search of more. I myself made a trip and returned with great armfuls of bread, eggs and butter. The German people certainly changed their attitude; they would have you believe that they could not do enough for us.

On the third day, the Americans took us off to a little town – to a canvas marquee as long as a row of houses. As we entered at one end we handed over our clothes in a bundle with our names. Then, twenty by twenty, we were washed twice – first in showers and then in baths. Those filthy bodies were in dire need of such treatment. At the same time our clothing was going through hot ovens to eliminate the countless accursed parasites that infested every seam. At the far end of the tent each man was sprayed with a covering of DDT, which they told us to leave on. Our clothing was returned and they issued us with a day's food ration and packets of tobacco.

We wondered greatly at the facilities, efficiency and power of the United States army. When compared with the deficiencies and inadequacies of our own time in France you could only conclude that those who left us so poorly equipped should themselves have been punished.

The Americans obliged the people of the town to accept us into their homes for a few days. With three others I was taken in by a married couple whose sons were in the war. They lent us clothes and took our vile shabby garments to a public laundry in the town, from whence they were returned to us clean and neatly pressed.

They rejoiced in an unexpected windfall. A store of flour, sugar, clothing and footwear had been found in the town. By order of the American quartermaster, this was issued to the people. After such a long period of deprivation and destitution, plenty returned like a flood. Results were soon to be seen as flesh returned to bare bones. It will give you some idea of how wasted we were if I mention in passing that on the day we gained our freedom my weight on the farmer's scales was only six stones and a few pounds.*

There was fierce fighting at Magdeburg not far to the east of us and the main road there passed close by. Often it brought to our notice the many novel pieces of equipment which had appeared since the start of the war. There were machines for excavating, moving, transporting and spreading earth, floating bridges and self-propelled guns. How now, St Valery!

Freedom

There was a level field close by suitable for aircraft and, load by load, they started to carry us away. They took us only as far as Brussels, where a great reception camp had been set up to handle the transit of soldiers between the battlefield and Blighty. What a welcome we had from all sorts of bodies, especially the Red Cross and the churches. Man after man was de-briefed; particularly with regard to any mistreatment we might have suffered which was not in accordance with the Geneva Convention. One question which I did not give too much thought to was whether I had any money saved up in Germany. I had no idea whether I had or not. The rules said that a prisoner who worked was entitled to a little pay. As we were not allowed to buy anything, they told us that they were allowing it to accrue till the end of the war. Anyway, as a shot in the dark, I said I had eight hundred and fifty marks. I was soon to rue that I hadn't trebled the figure! Soon after I came home a cheque arrived in the post with the sum I had nominated – nearly sixty pounds. Reflection does not reduce regret!

We sailed from Ostend to the Albert Dock in London, where there was another happy reception for us. Ministers, priests, members of the Salvation Army, WRNS and many other hospitable and good people seemed to vie with one another to see who could do the most for us. We had really fallen on our feet!

Our next stop was a camp hidden in deep forest. We were

* i.e. about 40 kilos

issued with new uniforms and, in further cosseting, some wives living close by came to help out where the new garments required any sewing or alteration. All in all, we were nearly spoiled by extreme kindness but they were happy days for us. Then leave was granted until a time and place could be decided for our demobilisation.

The only member of my father's family to welcome me in Glasgow was Murdo, who was in charge of the Gaelic Free Church in Partick. At the same time I had a happy meeting with two daughters of my sister Mary who were completing a course at teachers' college. My brother Norman, who has lived for twenty years in South America, came across from Edinburgh. On the way home to Lewis I had the company of my cousin Roderick going on holiday with his family. One could not have wished for a better travelling companion.

My younger brother, the 'Boxer', had for health reasons made his home in South Dell, where he ran a shop. My younger sister, Peggy, had gone as a nurse first to India and then Burma. She had spent the last two years of the war following the army here and there at first-aid stations for sick and wounded. She was nearly captured by the Japanese when they invaded the boundaries of India. So that part of her life had its own share of hardship and danger.

My father was waiting for me at Kyle of Lochalsh. He was nearly eighty years of age but free from any bodily infirmity or illness. He was still a missionary in Waternish without any thought of retirement. He accompanied me home.

Who amongst us, even in happier circumstances, would not feel a warm glow as his journey drew near to the place of home and family? The time of hardship is now behind you. You are re-united with everything that is precious to you. You are in a situation so happy and joyous that your foolish heart could lead you to believe that this would be the end of all hard knocks, evil and ill-health for the rest of your life. A man's life is lacking if he has never experienced that feeling. Though short-lived, it is delightful while it lasts.

Mary, along with my eldest son and my brother, the Boxer, were on the pier at Stornoway to meet me. As we came near to the house, we saw that the boys had lit a huge bonfire in welcome. There was a large crowd of all sorts of people waiting. I have never had so much attention since! As for kisses, I was nearly overwhelmed with them. They are very enjoyable in moderation but excess should be avoided! Anyhow those days have gone for me.

In passing, let me tell you that five others from the same village were also prisoners of war. Three of them were sailors on the *Miamoa*, along with many others from Ness. The remaining two were with the Argyll and Sutherland Highlanders in France and among the few who escaped before St Valery. At the time I thought them extremely lucky, but consider the next turn the wheel of fortune had for them. They were ordered out to Malaya, where they were captured by the Japanese. My grievances may have been many as I have recorded – but they were but episodic compared to their continuous suffering without any comfort, help or relief to soften the impact. They were both involved in the construction of that dreadful project that became known as the Death Railway. Of those that survived there were many who came back as cripples or invalids as a result of endemic diseases and the oppressive climate of the country. Quite a few never made a complete recovery.

After his liberation on 11 April 1945, Angus Campbell returned to shopkeeping in Swainbost until mobile van competition proved too much. Retirement in the 1960s gave him more time to devote to his poetry and his collected verse, Moll is Cruithneachd, *was published in Glasgow in 1972.*

The autobiographical Suathadh ri Iomadh Rubha, *from which this extract is translated, was published the following year to great acclaim, winning a prize awarded by the Gaelic Books Council. The other chapters give a wonderfully vivid and often humorous picture of a vanished way of life in Lewis. Ronald Black of Edinburgh University described it as 'the twentieth century's leading work of Gaelic non-fictional prose'.*

Angus Campbell died in Stornoway on 28 January 1982 at the age of seventy-nine.

Appendix 1

51st Highland Division on the Maginot Line

MAJOR-GENERAL V.M. FORTUNE

Infantry

152 Brigade	Brigadier H.W.V. Stewart

  2nd Bn. Seaforth Highlanders
  4th Bn. Seaforth Highlanders
  4th Bn. Queen's Own Cameron Highlanders

153 Brigade	Brigadier G.T. Burney

  4th Bn. Black Watch
  1st Bn. Gordon Highlanders
  5th Bn. Gordon Highlanders

154 Brigade	Brigadier A.C.L. Stanley-Clarke

  1st Bn. Black Watch
  7th Bn. Argyll and Sutherland Highlanders
  8th Bn. Argyll and Sutherland Highlanders

Artillery	Brigadier H.C.H. Eden

  17th Field Regiment
  23rd Field Regiment
  75th Field Regiment
  51st Anti-Tank Regiment

Armour	Lt.Col M.P. Ansell

  1st Lothians and Border Horse (Yeomanry)

Engineers   Lt.Col. H.M. Smail
    26th Field Company.
    236th Field Company
    237th Field Company
    239th Field Park Company

Signals   Lt.Col. T.P.E.. Murray
    51st Divisional Signals Company

Medical Corps   Lt.Col. D.P. Levack.
    152nd Field Ambulance
    153rd Field Ambulance
    154th Field Ambulance

Royal Army Service Corps Lt.Col. T. Harris-Hunter
    525th Ammunition Company
    526th Petrol Company
    527th Supply Company

Attached Troops

Machine-Gunners
    1st Bn. Princess Louise's Kensington Regiment
    7th Bn. Royal Northumberland Fusiliers

Artillery
    51st Medium Regiment, RA
    1st Royal Horse Artillery (less one Battery)
    97th Field Regiment RA (one Battery)

plus
    213th Army Field Company, RE
    6th Bn. The Royal Scots Fusiliers (Pioneers)
    7th Bn. The Norfolk Regiment (Pioneers)
    Sections of the RAOC and the RASC

Total strength: about 22,000 men

Appendix 2

The Salt Mines

This account of conditions in the salt mines near Bad Salzungen in Thuringia is taken from a privately published memoir by Douglas Ledingham from Aberdeen, who was in the 51st HQ unit at St Valery.

We reached the mine head and, never having seen a pithead before, my state of nervousness reached a new height. Each man was given a metal disc with a number stamped on it. Thereupon about eight men got into each cage for descent to the mine itself. I was told the mine shaft was 150m deep. The descent was rapid and when I reached the bottom and emerged from the cage I was completely disorientated and had to be assisted by fellow prisoners.

My first reactions to my surroundings were, I later realised, claustrophobic but I was quickly jolted out of this condition and pushed into a seat on a miniature train. The train proceeded to the various work teams where men were dropped off to commence drilling into the rock-salt faces. The ceilings in the main thoroughfare of the mine were about nine feet high. The widths varied and were perhaps twenty feet wide. This allowed for conveyor belts and machinery to transport the mined salt to the pit bottom, where it was transported to the top of the mine for further transportation throughout Germany.

The gallery to which I was directed was about 75m from the main gallery. Here I found a German civilian boring into the rock salt face with a huge drilling machine which was fixed vertically between the floor and ceiling of the gallery. The ceiling height was about five feet.

My German workmate-to-be stopped boring on my arrival and greeted me with, '*Englander?*' '*Nein* – Scottish,' I replied, whereupon he ignored the subtlety and greeted me with '*Heil Hitler*'. I later found out that he was not very happy with his lot as a salt-miner, having been directed to the salt mine. Having benevolently given him the benefit of the doubt I came to the conclusion that the '*Heil Hitler*' welcome was a one-off performance because a rapport developed between us as time went on.

Experience in later years of miners' strikes and the solidarity of the mining fraternity during industrial disputes has made me realise with hindsight that there is a bond of comradeship among miners second to none. Here we were – so called enemies – both involuntarily working hundreds of feet below the earth, yet each dependent on the other with an unspoken bond existing between us. It was a bond which existed between all civilian miners and their prisoner assistants in the bowels of the earth.

My job as assistant to the rock face miner was to feed the drilling machine with drills. Each drill was one metre in length and had to be clipped into the machine drill as it bored one metre into the salt. The holes bored were stuffed with dynamite charges as we went along, the holes being about a metre apart along the vertical face. At the end of each shift the charges were linked together and it was between shifts that the charges were ignited bringing down tons of salt into the gallery. It was the work of the oncoming shift to shovel the salt into small bogies and to push the bogies down to the main railway which transported the bogies to the lift shaft and thence to the surface. The job was dangerous both from the point of view of drills striking gas, which was a regular occurrence, and transportation accidents, which were numerous and were usually of a serious nature.

At the end of each shift the miners, including ourselves, were provided with hot showers. This was essential if everyone was not to suffer salt rash. We were unfortunate to the extent that we had no dedicated underground clothing. Consequently, to avoid having our only battle dress encrusted with salt we fashioned towels into all sorts of alternative cover. The mine itself was extremely warm, so working three-quarters naked was not an insoluble problem.

Despite the showering after each shift down the mine, I began to show signs of salt rash on my crotch. This spread down my legs and was intensely irritating, made more so by the fact that my uniform was not of the cleanest. Unfortunately, there was no medication available, and the only relief was the inflamed skin being offered to the sun, which seemed to be efficacious. It was by this time July 1943, mid summer. Consequently, I used every opportunity to expose my legs to the sunshine. Two months of this regime brought a great improvement in my condition.

Selected Bibliography

Baxter, Ian *Western Front – SS Secret Archives* (Spellmount, Staplehurst 2003)

Bishop, Patrick *Fighter Boys* (HarperCollins 2003)

Bryant, Arthur *The Turn of the Tide 1939–43* (Collins, London 1957)

Caimbeul, Aonghas *A' Suathadh ri Iomadh Rubha* (Gairm, 1973)

Caskie, Dr Donald *The Tartan Pimpernel* (Oldbourne Book Co. Ltd 1957)

Churchill, Winston *The Second World War: Vol. ii – Their Finest Hour* (Cassel 1959)

Crankshaw, Edward *Gestapo: Instrument of Tyranny* (Puttnam & Co. Ltd 1956)

David, Saul, *Churchill's Sacrifice of the Highland Division* (Brassey's 1994)

Deighton, Len *Blitzkrieg* (Jonathan Cape Ltd 1979)

Deighton, Len *Fighter* (Triad/Panther books Ltd. 1979)

Ellis, Major L.F. (editor), *The War In France and Flanders 1939–40* (HMSO London, 1953)

Fergusson, Bernard *The Black Watch – A Short History* (printed by Woods of Perth 1955)

Forty, George & Duncan, John, *The Fall of France – Disaster in the West 1939–40* (Guild Publishing London, 1990)

Fowler, Will *France, Holland & Belgium 1940–41* (Ian Allan Publishing 2002)

Fuller, Major General J.F.C. *The Conduct of War 1789–1961* (Eyre & Spottiswoode 1961)

Galland, Adolf *The First and the Last* (Methuen & Co. 1955)

Gilbert, Adrian *Germany's Lightning War* (Amber Books Ltd 2000)

Grant, Roderick *The 51st Highland Division at War* (Ian Allan 1977)

Historical records of the Queen's Own Cameron Highlanders 1932–48 (William Blackwood & Sons 1952)

Guderian, General Heinz, *Panzer Leader* (Michael Joseph Ltd 1952)

Harman, Nicholas, *Dunkirk – The Necessary Myth* (Hodder & Stoughton 1980)

Keegan, John (editor) *Churchill's Generals* (Abacus 1999)

Lake, John *Blenheim Squadrons of WW2* (Osprey Publishing 1998)

Lang, Sir Derek *Return to St Valery* (Leo Cooper 1974)

Liddell Hart, Sir Basil H. *The Other Side of the Hill* (Cassell & Co. Ltd 1951)

Lord, Walter, *The Miracle of Dunkirk* (Allen Lane 1882)

Lukacs, John *Five Days in London, May 1940* (Yale Nota Bene 2001)

MacDonald, Donald John, *Chì Mi – I see – The Gaelic Poetry of Donald John MacDonald* (Birlinn 2001)

MacDonald, Donald John *Fo Sgàil a' Swastika* (Acair 2000)

MacDonald, Gregor *A Cameron Never Can Yield* (The Queen's Own Cameron Highlanders Regimental Association 1999)

Macmillan, James F. *Dreyfus to De Gaulle; Politics and Society in France 1898–1969* (Edward Arnold 1985)

Masters, David *With Pennants Flying* (Eyre & Spottiswoode 1943)

Miles, Wilfrid *The Gordon Highlanders 1919–45* (Frederick Warne 1980)

Moore, William *The Long Way Round* (Leo Cooper in association with Secker & Walburg 1986)

Nichol, John & Rennell, Tony *The Last Escape* (Penguin Books 2003)

Perrett, Brian *Knights of the Black Cross* (Robert Hale Ltd 1986)

Regan, Geoffrey *Someone Had Blundered* (B.T. Batsford Ltd London, 1987)

Pimlott, Dr John (editor) *Rommel and his Art of War* (Brown Packaging Ltd 1994)

Richey, Paul *Fighter Pilot* (BT Batsford Ltd 1941)

Robertson, Seona & Wilson, Les *Scotland's War* (Mainstream Publishing 1995)

Terraine, John *The Right of the Line* (Hodder & Stoughton 1985)

Veranov, Michael (editor) *The Third Reich at War* (Robinson Publishing 1997)

Warner, Philip *The Battle for France, 1940* (Simon & Schuster 1990)

Young, Desmond *Rommel* (Collins, London 1950)

Wilson, Patrick *The War Behind the Wire* (Leo Cooper 2000)

Privately published:

Ledingham, Douglas *Memoirs of a POW 1939–46*

McCallum, James *Captivity 1940–45*